THE
ULTIMATE
Hollywood
ACTOR TRIVIA BOOK

Thousands of
tidbits of trivia
on the earliest
Hollywood
actors and actresses

KEN WARREN

ISBN: 978-1-6847-1363-9 (sc)
ISBN: 978-1-6847-1362-2 (e)

Lulu Publishing Services rev. date: 11/22/2019

Dedication

This book is dedicated my wife Olga,
without whom it would have been published two years ago.
And to her daughter Linda Blecher,
without whom its publication date would still
be an unknown date in the future.
I love you both.

Contents

Bud Abbott (William Alexander Abbott) 1
Got 60% of the Abbot & Costello Income

George Abbott (George Francis Abbott) 2
Lived to be 107

Art Acord (Arthemus Ward Acord) 3
The Mormon Cowboy

Renee Adoree (Jeanne de la Fonte)...3
Talkies Killed Her Career

Fred Allen (John Florence Sullivan) 3
"A gentleman never hits a lady with his hat on."

Gracie Allen (Grace Ethel Cecile Rosalie Allen) 4
Had one blue eye and one green eye.

Gilbert Anderson (Gilbert Maxwell Henry Anderson)....................6
First big name, successful Western star.

Marian Anderson (Same) 7
Due to be on the back of the $20 bill in 2020.

Fatty Arbuckle (Roscoe Conkling Arbuckle) 7
First victim of the first movie pie in the face.

Richard Arlen (Sylvanus Richard Mattimore)................................9
First male actor to kiss another man on the lips.

George Arliss (Augustus George Andrews)......................................9
Earliest-born Oscar winner.

Edward Arnold (Gunther Edward Arnold Schneider) 10
First actor to play Nero Wolfe in the movies.

Fred Astaire (Frederick Austerlitz) 10
Said his favorite dancing partner was...Gene Kelly.

Agnes Ayers (Agnes Eyre Henkel) 13
Played the female lead opposite Valentino in The Sheik.

Fay Bainter (Fay Okell Bainter) 14
Buried in Arlington National Cemetery.

Theda Bara (Theodosia Burr Goodman) 14
Fist sex symbol of the movies.

Ethel Barrymore (Ethel Mae Blythe) 15
Cancelled her trip on the Lusitania at the last minute.

John Barrymore (John Sidney Blythe)................................... 16
Never nominated nor ever won an Oscar.

Lionel Barrymore (Lionel Herbert Blythe) 18
"I'll make pictures as long as I can wiggle."

Warner Baxter (Warner Leroy Baxter).................................20
Top Western star, deathly afraid of horses.

Wallace Beery (Wallace Fitzgerald Beery) 20
Star of the first ever in-flight movie ever shown.

Jack Benny (Benjamin Kubelsky).......................................21
His hometown high school team is called The 39'ers.

Charles Bickford (Charles Ambrose Bickford)......................24
Tried for murder at age 9.

Clara Blandick (Clara Blanchard Dickey)...........................25
Born in a ship off the coast of Hong Kong.

Monte Blue (Gerard Monte Blue) 25
Star of the first film featuring Leo the Lion mascott.

Humphrey Bogart (Humphrey DeForest Bogart)..........................26
Became a father for the first time at age 49.

John Boles (Same)..30
Starred in Frankenstein, 1931.

Beulah Bondi (Beulah Bondy)..31
Played Ma Bailey in It's a Wonderful Life, 1946.

Alice Brady (Mary Rose Brady)..31
Unknown man accepted and stole her Best Actress Oscar.

Walter Brennan (Walter Andrew Brennan)................................32
First actor to win 3 Oscars for acting.

Fanny Brice (Fania Borach) 33
"I'm a bad woman but I'm damn good company."

Joe E. Brown (Joseph Evans Brown) 33
One of two civilians to win the Bronze
Star for heroism during WW2.

John Bunny (Same) 34
Film's First King of Comedy.

Billie Burke (Mary William Etherlbert Appleton Burke) 34
Glinda the Witch in The Wizard of Oz.

George Burns (Nathan Birnbaum) 35
Quit driving because he was too short to
see over the steering wheel.

Francis X. Bushman (Francis Xavier Bushman)..........................38
The first screen matinee idol.

James Cagney (James Francis Cagney, Jr.) 39
Never said, "You dirty rat," in any of his movies.

Eddie Cantor (Edward Israel Iskowitz) 41
Creator of The March of Dimes.

Yakima Canutt (Enos Edward Canutt) 42
Broke a wild bronco at age 11.

Frank Capra (Francesco Rosario Capra)...43
WW1 US Army Mathematics instructor.

Harry Carey, Sr. (Harry Christopher Carabina) 44
Turned down an appointment to West Point.

Lon Chaney, Sr. (Leonidas Frank Chaney) 44
Son of deaf-mute parents.

Charlie Chaplin (Charles Spencer Chaplin)......................................45
Never a US citizen, never won an Oscar.

Ruth Chatterton (Same) 48
Licensed pilot, friend of Amelia Earhart.

Maurice Chevalier (Maurice Auguste Chevalier) 49
"Old age isn't so bad when you consider the alternative."

Charles Coburn (Charles Douville Coburn) 50
Didn't make a movie until age 60.

George Cohan (George Michael Cohan)...50
Awarded the first Congressional Gold Medal during WW1.

Ronald Colman (Ronald Charles Colman)..51
The Greatest Gentleman Hero in the History of Cinema.

Gladys Cooper (Gladys Constance Cooper) 52
England's favorite pin-up girl of WW1.

Noel Coward (Noel Peirce Coward) 52
First British 'tax exile' to be knighted.

Jane Darwell (Pattie Woodard) 53
Played Ma Joad in The Grapes of Wrath.

Marion Davies (Marion Cecelia Douras)..53
Lifelong stutterer but not when filming a movie.

Cecil B. De Mille (Cecil Blount De Mille)..54
Designed the US Air Force Academy cadet uniforms.

Richard Dix (Ernst Carlton Brimmer) 55
Ancestors came to America on the Mayflower.

Marie Dressler (Leila Marie Koerber)...56
Earliest-born female Oscar winner.

Margaret Dumont (Daisy Juliette Baker)...56
Bald as a billiard ball.

Irene Dunne (Irene Marie Dunn) 57
Shot a hole-in-one at golf.

Jimmy Durante (James Francis Durante) 58
Donated millions of dollars of his personal money to charity.

Jeanne Eagles (Eugenia Eagles)...59
First actress posthumously nominated for Best Actress.

Douglas Fairbanks, Sr. (Douglas Elton Thomas Ullman) 60
First movie star to live in Beverly Hills.

William Farnum (Same)...61
Star of If I Were King, 1921.

W. C. Fields (William Claude Dukenfield).....................................62
Put $50,000 in a German bank during WW2.

Barry Fitzgerald (William Joseph Shields).....................................65
Lived with his parents until age 38.

John Ford (John Martin Feeney) 66
Directed John Wayne in 24 movies.

William Frawley (William Clement Frawley) 67
Lived in the same bachelor apartment for 40 years.

Joe Frisco (Louis Wilson Joseph) 68
Used stuttering to his comedic advantage.

Mary Fuller (Mary Claire Fuller) 68
Wrote 8 screenplays that were made into movies.

Hoot Gibson (Edmund Richard Gibson) 69
"World's All Around Champion Cowboy" at age 20.

John Gilbert (John Cecil Pringle)......................................70
Drafted into the US Army the day WW1 ended.

Lillian Gish (Lillian Diana Gish) 70
Had longest career of any actress--75 years.

Samuel Goldwyn (Szmuel Gelbfisz)..................................71
"I may not always be right, but I am never wrong."

Ruth Gordon (Ruth Gordon Jones)..................................73
Nominated for three Academy Awards for being a writer.

Sydney Greenstreet (Sydney Hughes Greenstreet).........................74
He was the model for Jabba the Hut in the Star Wars movies.

D. W. Griffith (David Llewelyn Wark Griffith) 75
First director to say, "Lights, camera, action!"

Edmund Gwenn (Edmund John Kellaway) 76
His London home was destroyed by the German Luftwaffe.

Alan Hale, Sr. (Rufus Edward MacKahan)......................................76
Invented a greaseless potato chip.

Jack Haley (John Joseph Haley, Jr.) 77
The Tin Man's son married Dorothy's daughter.

Juanita Hansen (Juanita C. Hansen).....................................77
The Original Mack Sennett Girl.

Cedric Hardwicke (Cedric Webster Hardwicke) 78
"Actors and burglars work better at night."

Oliver Hardy (Norvell Hardy) 79
First actor to play The Tin Man in The Wizard of Oz.

Bobby Harron (Robert Emmett Harron) 80
Died at age 27.

William S. Hart (William Surrey Hart) 80
Model for Uncle Sam recruiting posters.

Henry Hathaway (Marquis Henri Leopold de Fiennes)..................81
"I'm a bastard and I know it."

Sessue Hawakaya (Kintaro Hayakawa) 81
First Asian actor to become a leading man in Hollywood.

Hays, Will H..82
"Things in the following list shall not appear..."

George "Gabby" Hayes (George Francis Hayes)...........................84
Couldn't ride a horse, hated making Westerns.

Jean Hersholt (Jean Pierre Hersholt)..................................85
Uncle of actor Leslie Neilsen.

Hitchcock, Alfred (Alfred Joseph Hitchcock) 85
Did not have a navel.

Jack Holt (Charles John Holt, Jr.)....................................90
Star of the first completely Western-themed serial.

Hedda Hopper (Elda Furry)..91
Called her Beverly Hills home The House That Fear Built.

Leslie Howard (Leslie Howard Stainer)..................................92
Died because his agent resembled Winston Churchill in the dark.

Moe Howard (Moses Harry Horwitz) 93
Sold real estate in retirement.

Shemp Howard (Samuel Horwitz) 94
In four episodes of The Three Stooges after he died.

Walter Huston (Walter Scott Huston) 94
"You need about $20,000,000 to live properly."

Thomas Ince (Thomas Harper Ince) 95
Killed because he looked like Charlie Chaplin.

Rex Ingram (Same)..95
Born on a Mississippi riverboat.

Emil Jannings (Theodor Fredrich Emil)..............................96
Winner of the first Best Actor Academy Award,
worked for Hitler during WW2.

Al Jolson (Asa Yoelson) 97
Paid his lookalike brother to stay out of show business.

Buck Jones (Charles Fredrick Gebhart) 98
Most popular cowboy of the silent era.

Boris Karloff (William Henry Pratt) 99
Did not get a name credit in Frankenstein.

Buster Keaton (Joseph Frank Keaton) 101
Never attended any school.

Guy Kibbee (Guy Bridges Kibbee) 102
Made 20 movies in one year.

Rod La Rocque (Roderick LaRocque de la Rou) 102
Talkies killed his career.

Carl Laemmle (Karl Lammle) 102
Founder of Universal Studios.

Bert Lahr (Irving Larheim)..................................... 103
Sang two songs in The Wizard of Oz to Judy Garland's one.

Charles Laughton (Same) 103
First actor to play Agatha Christie's detective Hercule Poirot.

Stan Laurel (Arthur Stanley Jefferson) 105
Filmed all of his movies shoeless.

Florence Lawrence (Florence Annie Bridgwood) 106
She is, literally, the first movie star.

Gertrude Lawrence (Gertrude Alice Dagmar Klasen).......... 107
First actor Broadway dimmed its lights for.

Beatrice Lillie (Beatrice Gladys Lillie) 107
NN: Funniest Woman in the World.

Elmo Lincoln (Otto Elmo Linkenhelt) 108
Not the first, but the second, actor to portray Tarzan.

Harold Lloyd (Harold Clayton Lloyd) 108
Created movies previews.

Bela Lugosi (Bella Ferenc Deszo Blasko) 109
Buried in his Dracula costume.

Paul Lukas (Pal Lukacs).. 111
Born on a train.

Moms Mabley (Loretta Mary Aitken) 111
First openly gay comedian, coming out in 1921.

Marjorie Main (Mary Tomlinson Krebbs)................................ 112
Play Ma of the Ma and Pa Kettle movies.

Frederic March (Ernst Frederick McIntyre Bickel) 112
Suggested his epitaph be "This is just my lot."

Chico Marx (Leonard Marx) 113
Raised in a brothel.

Groucho Marx (Julius Henry Marx).. 114
Absolutely unrecognizable without his fake eyebrows and glasses.

Harpo Marx (Adolph, later changed to Arthur, Marx)............ 117
Failed the 2nd grade twice and then quit school.

Zeppo Marx (Herbert Manfred Marx)..................................... 118
Multimillionaire from his engineering inventions.

Raymond Massey (Raymond Hart Massey) 119
His ancestors arrived in America in 1629.

Louis B. Mayer (Lazar Meir, later Louis Burt Mayer).................... 120
First American ever to receive a $1,000,000 annual salary.

Tim McCoy (Timothy John Fitzgerald McCoy)................................120
Star of the first movie filmed in Hollywood.

Hattie McDaniel (Same) AKA: Joanna Rose 121
First black woman to sing on the radio, 1930.

Victor McLaglen (Victor Andrew de Bier Everleigh McLaglen)...123
Fought heavyweight champ Jack Johnson to a draw.

Adolphe Menjou (Adolphe Jean Menjou)......................................124
Star of the first film shown in a drive-in theatre.

Tom Mix (Thomas Hezikiah Mix)...125
US Army deserter for 38 years.

Colleen Moore (Kathleen Morrison) 127
The Screen's first flapper.

Frank Morgan (Francis Phillip Wuppermann)..............................127
Played five different characters on The Wizard of Oz.

Ralph Morgan (Raphael Kuhner Wuppermann) 128
His ancestors came over on the Mayflower.

Alan Mowbray (Alfred Ernest Allen) 129
Screen Actors Guild first Vice President.

Carmel Myers (Same)..129
Ashes scattered in the Pickfair rose garden.

Nita Naldi (Mary Nonna Dooley) 130
Rudolph Valentino's most frequent co-star.

Alla Nazimova (Marem-Ides Adelaida Yakovlevna Leventon) 130
Owned the first known pool to have underwater lighting.

Pola Negri (Barbara Apolonia Chalupiec) 131
First-ever European actor to have a Hollywood contract.

Mable Normand (Mabel Ethelreid Normand) 132
She's the girl 'tied up on the railroad tracks.'

George O'Brien (Same) 133
Served on a submarine during WW1.

Pat O'Brien (William Joseph Patrick O'Brien) 133
Last screen appearance was on Happy Days, 1982.

Warner Oland (Johan Verner Ohlund) 134
This Charlie Chan was Swedish!

Maria Ouspenskaya (Maria Alekseyevna Ouspenskaya) 135
Best Supporting Actress nomination for four minutes on screen.

Louella Parsons (Louella Rose Oettinger) 136
Godmother to actress Mia Farrow.

Jack Pickford (John Charles Smith) 137
Kicked out of the US Navy.

Mary Pickford (Gladys Louise Smith) 137
"America's Sweetheart" was born in Canada.

Walter Pidgeon (Walter Davis Pidgeon) 140
"My face is my credit card."

ZaSu Pitts (Eliza Susan Pitts) 141
Switchboard operator in It's a Mad, Mad, Mad, Mad World.

William Powell (William Horatio Powell) 141
Married to Carole Lombard before Clark Gable was.

Claude Rains (William Claude Rains) 142
Paid more for making Casablanca than Bogart was.

Virginia Rappe (Virginia Caroline Rappe) 144
NN: The Best Dressed Girl in PIcutes.

Basil Rathbone (Philip St. John Basil Rathbone) 144
Won British Military Cross for Valor in WW1.

Wallace Reid (William Wallace Halleck Reid) 145
Owned the first underground swimming pool in Hollywood.

Paul Robeson (Paul Leroy Bustill Robeson) 146
Phi Beta Kappa and Class Valedictorian.

Bill "Bojangles" Robinson (Luther Robinson) 147
Held world records for running backwards.

Edward G. Robinson (Emmanuel Goldenberg) 149
First entertainer to land on Normandy Beach during WW2.

Will Rogers (William Penn Adair Rogers) 151
"Always drink upstream from the heard."

Randolph Scott (George Randolph Crane Scott) 153
Worth $100,000,000 at the time of his death.

Mack Sennett (Mikall Sinnott) 155
First American actor to play Sherlock Holmes in a movie.

C. Aubrey Smith (Charles Aubrey Smith) 156
Founder of the Hollywood Cricket Club.

Gale Sondergaard (Edith Holm Sondergaard) 156
First Best Supporting Actress Oscar winner.

Gloria Swanson (Gloria May Josephine Svensson) 157
Lifelong vegetarian.

Blanche Sweet (Sarah Blanche Sweet) 160
Made 150 silent films and only three talkies.

Norma Talmadge (Same) 161
Made 300 silent films but only three talkies.

Irving Thalberg (Irving Grant Thalberg) 161
"No Civil War Picture ever made a nickel."

Sophie Tucker (Sophie Kalish) 162
I've been rich and I've been poor. Rich is better."

Ben Turpin (Bernard Turpin) 162
First movie star mentioned by name in a magazine.

Rudolf Valentino (Rodolpho Alfonso Raffaello Pierre Filibert Guglielmi de Valentina D'Antongoulla)..163
Spent his honeymoon in jail.

Conrad Veidt (Hans Walter Conrad Veidt) 166
Sergeant in the German Army during WW1.

Erich Von Stroheim (Erich Oswald Hans Carl Maria von Stroheim) 167
Loved to play Nazis in the movies.

Raoul Walsh (Albert Edward Walsh) 167
First director to get a Hollywood Walk of Fame Star.

Jack Warner (Jacob Lebzelter Walter, Jr.) 168
WW2 US Army Lt. Colonel.

Ethel Waters (Same) 169
Born to a 12-year-old mother.

Clifton Webb (Webb Parmelee Hollenbeck) 169
Orphaned at age 71.

Mae West (Mary Jane West) 170
Q: Is sex dirty? A: "If you do it right, it is."

Pearl White (Pearl Fay White)..174
Biggest Hollywood actress before Mary Pickford.

Dame May Whitty (Mary Louise Webster) 174
First woman to be 'knighted' by the King.

Monty Woolley (Edgar Montillion Wooley)........................174
Born in a hotel.

Adolph Zukor (Same)..175
"The public is never wrong."

Acknowledgments

In the beginning, I was lost. I had decided to collect 100,000 bits of trivia on as many as 10,000 movie stars. My first thought was, "That's one hell of a lot of index cards." At least I knew I needed help, so I went to my local St. Charles, Missouri Adult Education Center where I met receptionist Deborah Evans. I asked her to introduce to me to one of their instructors who I would try to persuade to teach me more about Microsoft Word and get a grip on this giant project I was contemplating. Angel that she is, she said, "My husband Jack can help you with that." So we set up a meeting at my apartment for next Saturday. I met them as they were coming from the parking lot, he carrying his computer and she looking for numbers on apartment doors. I asked, "Are you Jack Evans?" and I knew instantly that he was no impostor because, without missing a beat, he said, "I better be. I'm sleeping with his wife." Instant bonding. Over the next few years he donated a hundred hours to teaching me how to better use my computer, how to organize data using Word and best of all, how to use an Excel program. After dozens of home-cooked meals and even more bottles of Cabernet, Jack got me into a position where I could run with this on my own and turn out the quality product you are about to read. I've heard that if you're lucky in life, you might have three, maybe four, real friends you can count on. This book could not have been written without the incalculable help of two of mine--Deb and Jack Evans.

I also owe a debt of gratitude to Dusty Nichols, owner of the Ms. Fixit Computer Repair shop in Ottawa, Kansas. Thanks to Doris Siemen, Manager of the El Dorado Cantina in Las Vegas for the best Mexican food in town and for your insightful editorial advice. Helpful hints always go down better with a margarita or two. Thanks to Heather Blecher for your proofreading. And lastly, but really always first, thanks to Ralph Wetterhahn of Long Beach, California for believing in me and always being there when needed.

Introduction

They're not stars for no reason. They're stars
because they're interesting people.

Gregory Peck
First native Californian to win a Best Acting Oscar.

Home is where the books are.

Richard Burton
Nominated seven times for a Best Acting Oscar, never won.

Trivia. It's an old Latin word that means 'where the three roads meet.'
I know--I don't get it, either. But I like it. I also like history and I used
to teach US Government and US History at Arizona State University.
I also like old movies and the movie stars who made them. So it
seems that it was inevitable that these three interests, history, movies
and actors (Hey! three roads) would eventually merge in my mind
to become an interest in trivia about old movie actors. My wife just
told me that I have to write more than this. It's a treat when I'm
reading a trivia book, a history book or a review for an old movie
and the author throws in a tidbit about one of the actors. It's not
trivia to know that any particular actor won a Best Acting Oscar.
However; knowing that he then took that Oscar home that night
and accidentally destroyed it by practicing with his 4-iron golf club,
is. It's not trivia knowing that the 20th century's premiere singer won
a Best Supporting Oscar for his role in a movie. However, knowing
that after he left the award ceremony and was walking home with his

Oscar in hand, he was arrested for stealing it by a policeman who did not recognize him, is. It's not trivia knowing one of the sweetest and most beloved comediennes of the last century made dozens of movies and appeared in 291 episodes of a popular television show, without a single one of these appearances ever being filmed in color. However, it is trivia to know that the reason was that she had one green eye and one blue eye and refused to be filmed in color. But the problem with trivia like this is that it seems to appear randomly in other sources, mixed in with dozens of other subjects and there just doesn't seem to be any one trivia book that is solely about movie stars. Hence, this book. This is not a collection of biographies, or a list of awards, or movie reviews; those types of books already exist in abundance. This is pure trivia.

When I first got the idea to collect this trivia and write this book, I was overwhelmed by the fact that I could possibly be writing about 10,000 actors. That would take me ten years or more. Or, knowing my work ethic, twenty years or more. So I narrowed the list down to Hollywood actors. Now I'm down to about 4,000 actors, but I am resolved to do the research on all of them. Now I'm reminded of a lesson from my college personnel management class, Q: How do you eat an elephant? A: One bite at a time. So I decided to start at the beginning but then I had to come up with a definition for "what is the beginning?" I decided to list all the actors I had trivia on by their date of birth, beginning with, well...the beginning. Turns out that the earliest-born actor (movie star) for which there is interesting trivia was born in 1868. Didn't know that, did you? Neither did I, and that's an example of what has made researching this book one of the most interesting projects I have ever done. I then decided to further break down this list of actors by decade of birth. That's what this book is. It's full of thousands of bits of trivia about well-known actors who were born before 1900. To be in this book, an actor had to be born in 1800-something. Those dates turned out to be April 10, 1868 through December 31, 1899. For the last few years, I've been telling my interested friends, "You have to be dead to be in this book." That makes this book Volume 1. Many of these actors were in their teens and twenties when they started making movies around 1910 and they were in their height of their careers in the 1930's, 1940's and beyond. You know these people. Actors born between January 1, 1900 through December 31, 1909 will be covered in Volume 2. Volume 3 will start with dates of birth January 1, 1910 and so on.

To write this book, I did the hard work for you. It has taken me about four years to view over 5,000 web sites, read more than 400 actors' biographies and autobiographies, collect almost every trivia book ever written in the English language, spend more than 2,000 hours at the libraries, take hand-written notes until my hand wouldn't work for six months, attend several library book sales in various large cities (excellent source of OLD free and very inexpensive books!), purchase more than 600 books on Hollywood, actors, movies and entertainment, and view hundreds of hours of television shows to mine them for a trivial morsel here and there.

WHAT THIS BOOK WILL DO FOR YOU: Trivia is all about knowing something interesting that the average person doesn't. Knowing what's in this book can make you the expert on something in your social circle. You'll be able to have something interesting to say about one or more of the actors when you're watching an old movie. You will actually learn a little about US and World History. You'll know of a dozen ways that Adolph Hitler had an impact on what happened (or didn't happen) in Hollywood. You'll be able to win bets by being able to contradict accepted common knowledge that is just plain wrong, thereby recouping the cost of this book. You'll have a list of "That actor never said...." facts. You'll have a list of "bets you can't lose." I've included thousands of quotes about the actors and quotes from actors on every subject. You'll be able to converse about any subject and appear to be very witty. I dare you to not use the quote, "Why is there always so much month left at the end of my money?" in the next month. And I'll go ahead and tell you now what the greatest quote of all time is that's in this book: A reporter asked Mae West, "Is sex dirty?" She said, "If you do it right, it is." You will be able to win trivia contests. People will come to you to settle bets. (There's no shame in saying, "I'll get back to you on that." It makes you look very intelligent.) And lastly, but not least, (and most hilariously to me) you'll be able to converse easily with old people. All you have to do is lead with, "Did you know that George Burns....?" or "Did you know that Walter Brennan.....?"

When President John Kennedy was holding a press conference in 1962, an irate female reporter asked him, "What have you done for women's rights?" and he jokingly replied, "I'm sure I haven't done enough." With that in mind, I'm sure I haven't captured all the good, interesting trivia on this subject during my research. If you know something that's not in this book, something that's not generally publicly known and it's worthy of being called good trivia, please send it to me. I am also particularly interested in hearing about your personal stories about contacts and conversations you've had with movie stars. Send me your personal stories. For example, I was lucky enough to spend an hour alone with singer Lou Rawls at 2am in the Las Vegas airport. I asked what was the motivation behind his writing and performing his Grammy-winning hit You'll Never Find Another Love Like Mine. He said, "Hell, that's easy. I was just trying to get laid." Hey, maybe that's one more thing this book can help you with.

Ken Warren, Wellsville, Kansas, September 2019
Kennolga@yahoo.com

How To Read This Book

The facts and trivia for each actor is presented in the following chronological order:

1. STAGE NAME. This is the name that the actors are best known for as a performer. This is the name that the general public knows them by and would use to 'look them up.'
2. (BIRTH NAME). This is their legal given name at birth. About three-fourths of all actors have changed their name, some by adding or subtracting only one or two letters. A stage name and a birth name that differ by only one or two letters in this work is not a typo. AKA, also known as, when it applies.
3. DOB: This is the date of birth deemed to be the most correct as of 2019. Many actors, especially those born in the 1800's and in countries other than the United States, often have unknown, disputed, or deliberately altered dates of birth. Sometimes the actor would lie about his or her age to make themselves older to get an acting job, and sometimes they would make themselves younger for the same reason. Sometimes it would be their studio who did the lying for them. I've pointed this out where it is interesting trivia. The release of one hundred-year-old US Census records are helping with this when they are released every ten years.
4. DOD: Actor's dates of death are in not so much dispute since the majority of them lived into the 1940's and later, when it became almost impossible to fake a date of death. There are a few cases where a deceased actor's body was not immediately discovered upon death, but the approximate dates of death

given by coroners are almost always accepted in the absence of any evidence to the contrary.

5. LONGEVITY. This is the number of years, months and days the actor lived. Good to know. A list of all of the actor's names by longevity are an appendix in this book so you can compare their relative lengths of lifespan. It's interesting trivia to see who lived longer than who and who's first and last on this list.

6. # FILMS. This is the author's best informed, researched opinion of how many movies the actor made during their career. In many cases, such as early silent films, lost films and films that have disintegrated and self-destructed before they could be catalogued, causing a definitive count to be impossible to make.

7. # MARRIED. This is the number of marriages for each actor than can be reasonably attributed through credible means. Some actors are known to have been married many more times than their publicity states, but professional biographers and researchers have been unable to find acceptable documentation.

8. NN: NICKNAME. Nicknames provide a little bit of a look into the actor's persona or reputation, whether it is correct or deserved or not. Some nicknames were given to several different actors over the years. For example, more than one actor was known as The King of Hollywood or The Most Beautiful Woman in the World because they worked in different decades.

9. BKF: BEST KNOWN FOR: I included this at the beginning of the entry to help you more quickly get a picture in your mind's eye of the actor in question. For example, you may not be very much interested in reading the trivia about a guy named Frank Morgan unless I first remind you that he was The Wizard of Oz.

10. BEFORE ACTING. Most actors started out life in an obscure, nondescript existence with the prospect of an ordinary, unremarkable life ahead of them. They held all kinds of

jobs and some, no job at all. Some of these pre-acting jobs will surprise you and in some cases, they were able to draw on their previous work experience for motivation in future movies made. For example, one actor spent years as a prisoner in Alcatraz Prison and later in life played the Warden of Alcatraz in a movie. Some actors retired from acting to go back into their pre-acting line of work.

11. WAR SERVICE. Whether it's the Boer War, Spanish-American War, World War 1, World War 2 or the Korean War, everyone did something during the war. Even the women, those who served, tried to serve, avoided serving and those who served with particular distinction, everyone did something, including those who hid out in the military in Hollywood. I made a special, concerted effort to learn what everyone did during the war. What I found will surprise you.

12. TRIVIA. This section is the actual reason for the book. This book in not a collection of mini-biographies of movie stars of the past. There's no lists of Academy Awards, their best-known movies, their major accomplishments and the like. This book is about the other stuff--tidbits of interesting trivia. It's the ultimate "bet you didn't know ...." book. It's chock full of "Who was the first, or only, or last actor to ...?" The purpose of this book, besides hopefully being the most interesting trivia book you've ever read, is to help you win trivia contests regarding Hollywood actors.

13. 13. QUOTES FROM THE STAR and 14. QUOTES ABOUT THE STAR. What way to better to get to know someone's personality than to see what they've had to say about their lives? Sometimes, the difference between their professional reputation and what they say in private is quite shocking. Not to mention what other actors have to say about them.

14. POST ACTING. Many actors have famously died young but for those who lived long enough to voluntarily retire and pursue other interests, it's here in this book.

15. LAST WORDS. From, "This is no way to live," to "Surprise me," when asked if he wanted to be buried in his black or blue suit, these actors revealed some interesting last thoughts.

16. COD: Cause of Death. They're all here: natural causes, suicide, murder, heart attack, stroke, cancer, emphysema, and of course, drugs and alcoholism. With all the trivial, interesting details added.

17. EPITAPH/BURIED. Many actors suggested one or more epitaphs for themselves when they were alive but actually got another one when it was all done. Some epitaphs are as touching as "Together Again" and one actor's epitaph actually reads "#$%&@%#?!@^#!*@*$!&%?."

18. AUTOBIOGRAPHY. I've done my best to find each actor's autobiography, when one was written. One actor wrote nine autobiographies.

19. WHAT HAPPENED TO THEM AFTER THEY DIED. When I started work on researching this book, I had no idea at all that I would be adding this section, but it has turned out to be one of the most interesting parts of the book. Just look up the trivia on Charlie Chaplin.

THE ULTIMATE HOLLYWOOD ACTOR TRIVIA BOOK

Thousands of bits of trivia about the
earliest actors and actresses

Bud Abbott (William Alexander Abbott)

b. 2 Oct 1895, d. 24 Apr 1974 = 78 yrs, 6 mos, 22 days. Made 38 movies. Married 1 time.

BKF: Straight man of the Abbott & Costello Comedy Team, "Who's On First?" Born in a circus tent. Dropped out of school at age 10. Coney Island Animal Park employee--lion tamer. Box office treasurer for the Casino Burlesque in NYC. Bud Abbott, Groucho Marx and George "Spanky" McFarland were born on the same day, 2 Oct 1895. Eleven of his 38 films have his name in the title. An abbreviated version of "Who's On First?" first appeared in One Night in the Tropics, 1940. {Just so you know: Who is on first, What is on second, I Don't Know is on third, Today is watching and Tomorrow is pitching.} The first movie containing their entire Who's On First routine was The Naughty Nineties, 1945. Because of the popularity of this routine, they were inducted into the Baseball Hall of Fame. They performed their Who's On First routine more than 15,000 times during their career. Abbot & Costello's income was divided 60%-40% in favor of Abbott, the straight man. Their studio had separate contracts with each of them that expired at different times so they could control their income. They made 37 movies together from 1940 to 1956. They played poker for serious money while between takes on the set of their movies. Whenever either one of them would run out of money they would send a runner to the bank to get $10,000 or more in cash. They would not go back to work until they couldn't get any more cash. They had an insurance policy for $100,000 against anyone laughing themselves to death in their audience and a $250,000 policy against having a career ending argument. He was an epileptic and at the start of a seizure, his partner Lou Costello would punch him in the stomach to stop it. The audience thought it was part of the act. They were Honorary Colonels in the Wisconsin State Militia. He owned one of Adolph Hitler's shotguns. After paying the IRS $750,000 in back taxes, he and his wife then lived on monthly Social Security checks of about $180 per month. After the death of Lou Costello in the 1960's, he teamed up with comedian Candy Candido. He was so forgetful that he greeted everyone with, "Hi ya, neighbor." He had a twin sister who died at age 101 on 8 August 1997. COD: A broken hip in 1972, followed by a series of strokes aggravated by epilepsy. Cremated, ashes scattered over the Pacific Ocean.

George Abbott (George Francis Abbott)

b. 25 Jun 1887, d. 31 Jan 1995, = 107 yrs, 7 mos, 6 days. Made 40 movies. Married 3 times.

NN: Mr. Broadway. BKF: Damn Yankees, 1955. When he went to a performance of Damn Yankees at age 106, he received a standing ovation. He said, "There must be somebody important here." "Many great minds have made a botch of matters because their emotions fettered their thinking." "It's because I love the theater so much that I thought I'd stick around." 1982 Kennedy Center Honoree. COD: A stroke at age 107. Autobiography: Mister Abbott, 1963.

Art Acord (Arthemus Ward Acord)

b. 17 Apr 1890, d. 4 Jan 1931, = 40 yrs, 8 mos, 18 days. Made 100+ movies. Married 3 times. AKA Buck Parvin.

NN: The Mormon Cowboy. He was one-half Ute Indian. 1912 World Champion Steer Bulldogging Champion, defeating fellow actor Hoot Gibson for the title. He was a miner in Mexico. Served a prison term for rum running. WW1 hero, awarded the French Croix de Guerre for bravery for killing numerous German soldiers with his bare hands. Rodeo road shows. Liked to have fistfights on the set with rival cowboy star Hoot Gibson. Their fights were legendary. Actor Tim McCoy said, "They'd beat the hell out of each other. And then they'd come to the bar and have a drink. They loved it." COD: Suicide by cyanide poison, aggravated by acute alcoholism. Told his doctor that he had deliberately taken poison because he wanted to die. His body lay in a Chihuahua, Mexico hotel for a week before his family came to claim it. Buried with full military honors in Glendale, California.

Renee Adoree (Jeanne de la Fonte)

b. 30 Sep 1898, d. 5 Oct 1939, = 35 yrs, 5 days. Made 45 movies. Married 2 times.

BKF: Playing opposite John Gilbert in The Big Parade (1925). Circus performer. Talkies killed her career. COD: Tuberculosis. Her estate at the time of her death was valued at $2,429.

Fred Allen (John Florence Sullivan)

b. 31 May 1894, d. 17 Mar 1956, = 61 yrs, 1 mo, 15 days. Made 13 movies, Married 1 time.

BKF: 135 TV and 179 radio episodes of the Fred Allen Show. Vaudeville, boxed as Fred St. James, Boston Public Library clerk, piano mover. Herman Wouk began his career writing for Fred Allen. "A celebrity is a person who works hard all his life to become well known, and then wears dark glasses to avoid being recognized." "Cocktail party: A gathering held to enable forty people to talk about themselves at the same time. The man who remains after the liquor is gone is the host." "Television is a new medium. It's called medium because it's rare when anything is well-done." "Television is a device that permits people who haven't anything to do to watch people who can't do anything." "Ed Sullivan will be around as long as other people have talent. He's a pointer. A dog could do that show." "I'm going to Boston to see my doctor. He's a very sick man." "What's on your mind, if you'll allow the overstatement?" "A gentleman never strikes a lady with his hat on." "California happens to be a wonderful place--if you happen to be an orange." "All I know about humor is that I don't know anything about it." COD: Heart attack. While he did die while out on a stroll, he was not walking a dog as is often reported. Epitaph: John F. Sullivan - Fred Allen 1894 - 1956. Autobiography: Much Ado About Me, 1956.

Gracie Allen (Grace Ethel Cecile Rosalie Allen)

b. 26 July 1895, d. 27 Aug 1964, = 69 yrs, 1 mo, 1 day. Made 32 movies. Married 1 time.

NN: The Smartest Dumbbell in the History of Show Business. BKF: Lambchops (1929) and 291 television episodes of The Burns & Allen Show. Her birth certificate was destroyed during the California earthquake of 1906, and as a result, she was able to lie about her age for the rest of her life. She and George even incorporated this fact into their act. George would say, "But Gracie, you were born *after* the earthquake." And she would say, "It was a big earthquake." When she died, he family guessed she was born about 1902 for the death certificate. Her true date of birth was not known until the 1900 Census became public in the year 2000. Turns out that she was six months older than George Burns. Danced with her 3 sisters as

"The Four Colleens." Vaudeville, stenographer, student. She was 5' 0" and weighed barely 100 lbs. Her and George Burns' two children, Ronnie and Sandra were adopted. They had no children of their own. Gracie always wore a dress with long sleeves to hide a severe burn on her left arm. She had one green eye and one blue eye, a condition called heterochromia iridum, that affects about one in five hundred people. Because of that, she refused to be filmed in color. She ran for President of the United States in 1940 on the Surprise Party ticket. Why the Surprise Party? Because "My father was a Democrat, my mother was a Republican and I was born a Surprise." Her campaign slogan was, "My girdle is killing me." Asked about the Neutrality Bill currently in Congress, she said, "If we owe it, we should pay it." She said during the campaign, "Everybody knows a woman is better than a man when it comes to introducing bills into the house." The Surprise Party mascot was a kangaroo because, "...after all, it is a leap year." She proposed the idea of promoting sew-on campaign buttons in favor of pin-on buttons "...to make it harder for voters to change their mind in mid-campaign." A friend wrote a campaign song for her that contained the line, "If the country's going Gracie, so can you." During a campaign stop in Monominee, Michigan she was elected mayor but was prevented from assuming office because she wasn't a resident of the city. She said, "A person can't live everywhere." One of her campaign promises was to "put Congress on commission: If the country did well, then Congress would get a cut, If the country did not do well, then Congress would not get so much." Harvard University endorsed her candidacy, which must have hurt President Roosevelt--he was a Harvard graduate. She was unanimously nominated by thousands of student delegates at Omaha's Creighton University. She did not allow for a vice-presidential nominee because she said, "I won't allow any vice in my administration." When asked about her party platform she said, "It's redwood trimmed with 'nutty' pine." President Roosevelt got 27 million votes in the general election, Wendell Willkie got 22 million votes and Gracie got about 2,000 write-in votes. Gracie Allen never said, "Goodnight, Gracie" on her television show. She missed one, and only one, performance during her 35-year career with George Burns. Jane Wyman filled in for her. "A nonentity can be just as famous as anybody else if enough people know about him." "My husband will never chase another woman. He's too fine, too decent, too old." "When I was born I was so surprised that I couldn't talk for a year and a half." "All I had to say was, "Gracie, how's your brother?' and she talked for 38 years." George Burns. "The first time I saw George Burns on stage, I could see that he had what it takes to be a big star: Gracie." Bob Hope. Retired in 1958 due to ill health. COD: Heart attack after ten years of heart disease. Last words: "I'm sorry boys. I'm all wet." Epitaph: Gracie Allen (1902-1964) and George Burns (1896-1996) Together Again. The Gracie Allen rose is named for her. The scientific name is Rosa WEKuyreg. She was on the US Postal Service 44-cent stamp in 2009. There are crossroads named for her and George Burns near Cedars Sinai Hospital in Beverly Hills.

Gilbert Anderson (Gilbert Maxwell Henry Anderson)

b. 21 May 1880, d. 20 Jan 1971, = 90 yrs, 7 mos, 30 days. Made 300+ movies. Married 1 time.

NN: Bronco Billy and The Jewish Cowboy. First Star of the Western Film Genre. Vaudeville, photographer's model, newspaper vendor, produced NY plays. Got his first acting gig by lying about his ability to ride a horse. When filming began, he mounted the horse from the wrong side, was thrown off, and the rest of his scenes were of him on foot. He was the first successful Western star. He had several roles in 1903's The Great Train Robbery, including the passenger shot by the bad guys as he was trying to escape. The James Boys in Illinois and The Night Riders, two films that he directed, were the subjects of the first movie censorship court case in America. They were banned in Chicago in 1909. His horse's name was Old Fooler. Retired in 1920 but had a cameo at age 85 in The Bounty Killer in 1965. He was the first actor to receive an Oscar for cowboy roles, an Honorary Oscar in

1957 for "his contributions to the development of the motion pictures entertainment." COD: Natural causes. Cremated, ashes scattered.

Marian Anderson (Same)

b. 27 Feb 1897, d. 8 Apr 1993, = 90 yrs, 10 mos, 1 day. Made 3 movies. Married 1 time.

WW1 Entertained troops in Europe. Was the first African-American to perform for Japan's Imperial Court, 1953. Was on a US postage stamp on 17 Jan 2006. Due to be on the back of the US $5 bill in 2020. US Delegate to the UN, 1958, 1978 Kennedy Center Honoree. "I suppose I might insist on making issues of things. But that is not my nature, and I always bear in mind that my mission is to leave behind me the kind of impression that will make it easier for those to follow." COD: Stroke one month after a heart attack. Buried in Philadelphia, Pennsylvania. Autobiography: My Lord, What a Morning, 1956.

Fatty Arbuckle (Roscoe Conkling Arbuckle)

b. 24 Mar 1887, d. 29 Jun 1933, = 46 yrs, 3 mos, 5 days. Made 300+ movies. Married 3 times.

NN: The Prince of Whales, King of the Custard Pies and Hercules of the Winged Dessert. BKF: Hollywood's first scandal, the death of actress Virginia Rappe. Weighed 16 lbs. at birth. Child stage performer, and at 300 lbs, he could do a perfect, graceful backwards somersault. "Discovered" when he was working on Mack Sennett's home kitchen drain. Made $3 a day in 1913 as a Keystone Kop. He was the victim of the first custard pie thrown in a film, thrown by Mabel Normand. He hated the nickname Fatty and insisted that his friends call him Roscoe, which they did. "I got a name, you know." His 1920-23 annual movie contract for $1,000,000 per year is worth $13,000,000 per year in today's money. He was the first actor to endorse a cigarette--Murads. He owned a $25,000 custom-built

Pierce Arrow. He was also the first actor to direct himself in his movies. He was addicted to morphine due to a leg injury. His part in the death of Virginia Rappe is the reason that studios started putting morality clauses in their contracts. When the jury took all of five minutes to find him not guilty in a third trial, they also made this statement: "We the jury find Roscoe Arbuckle not guilty of manslaughter. Acquittal is not enough for Roscoe Arbuckle. We feel a great injustice has been done to him. We feel also that it was only our plain duty to give him this exoneration, under the evidence, for there was not the slightest proof adduced to connect him in any way with the commission of a crime. He was manly throughout the case, and told a straightforward story on the witness stand, which we all believed. The happening at the hotel was an unfortunate affair for which Arbuckle, so the evidence shows, was in no way responsible. We wish him success...Roscoe Arbuckle is entirely innocent and free from all blame." During these legal troubles, his studio impounded and refused to release more than one million dollars worth of his movies to the public, which led to loss of income, popularity and his ability to get hired anywhere to work. Before that, he was second only to Charlie Chaplin in popularity and critical acclaim. He used the alias William B. Good (Will Be Good) after the trial. He was eventually allowed to work behind the camera until his death in 1933. "I don't weigh a pound over one hundred and eighty, and what's more, I never did." After hearing him sing, Enrico Caruso told him, "Give up this nonsense you do for a living, with training you could become the second-greatest singer in the world." "I don't believe there is any finer mission on earth than just make people laugh." "How did I become a star? I don't know how it happened. When I look at my old pictures, I can't tell how it happened." "I read what they printed about me in the newspapers. Reporters used words because they made their stories sound better, without stopping to think what they would do to a man. After things are once printed, whether they are true or not, you can't change people's ideas. But it didn't seem as if they were talking about me." COD: Heart attack. Died in his sleep with less than $2,000 to his name. Cremated. He did not get a star on the Hollywood Walk of Fame until 1960.

Richard Arlen (Sylvanus Richard Mattimore)

b. 1 Sep 1899, d. 28 Mar 1976, = 76 yrs, 6 mos, 27 days. Made 153 movies. Married 3 times.

BKF: Playing a pilot in Wings (1927). Messenger, newspaper sports editor, film lab delivery boy. When he was making a delivery to Paramount Pictures, he was 'discovered' when they gave attention to his broken leg. WW1 Canadian AF pilot, WW2 US Army Air Force flight instructor. Being unable to cry on cue, even with a raw onion in hand, he gave the rolling camera the finger. He was the first male actor to kiss another man (actor Jack Powell) on the lips--in Wings. He lost his hearing in the 1950's and learned to read lips to keep working. COD: Emphysema.

George Arliss (Augustus George Andrews)

b. 10 Apr 1868, d. 5 Feb 1946, = 77 yrs, 9 mos, 26 days. Made 28 movies. Married 1 time.

NN: First Gentleman of the Talking Screen. BKF: Being the earliest-born Best Actor Oscar winner, for Disraeli (1929). He won that Oscar on 5 November 1939. Three days before that, he posed, with Oscar in hand, for publicity photos. The results had been leaked beforehand. Discovered and promoted by Bette Davis. Voluntarily stayed in London during WW2. He was the first British actor to win an Oscar and the first actor to win an Academy Award for playing a living person--British Prime Minister Benjamin Disraeli, who was in office the day he was born. He is also the first actor to win an Academy Award for playing a role he previously played on stage, that of Disraeli. Played a millionaire posing as a poor man in three films and a millionaire in one film. Appearing in court to testify, he described himself as "The World's Greatest Living Actor," and then added, "You see, I am on oath." COD: Bronchitis. Buried in London. His epitaph mentions only his MA Degree from Columbia University in 1919, the one highlight of his life he was most proud of.

Edward Arnold (Gunther Edward Arnold Schneider)

b. 18 Feb 1890, d. 26 Apr 1956, = 66 yrs, 2 mos, 8 days. Made 150+ movies. Married 3 times.

BKF: First actor to play Nero Wolfe, in 1936, and playing Diamond Jim Brady. Born on the same day as Adolphe Menjou. SAG President 1940-42. Portrayed a different president on the weekly radio show Mr. President," from 1947 to 1953. He was so good at character acting, he often worked on two movies at once. COD: Cerebral hemorrhage. Autobiography: Lorenzo Goes to Hollywood, 1940.

Fred Astaire (Frederick Austerlitz)

b. 10 May 1899, d. 22 June 1987, = 88 yrs, 1 mo, 12 days. Made 42 movies. Married 2 times.

NN: Daddy Long Legs and The Ultimate Dancer. BKF: Dancing musicals with Ginger Rogers. Vaudeville dancer with his sister Adele. Started dancing professionally at age four. Began his career calling himself "The World's Worst Juggler." The results of his first screen test in 1930 were, "Can't act. Slightly bald. Can dance a little." A later screen test review by Producer/Director David O. Selznick was, "I am still a little uncertain about the man, but I feel, in spite of his enormous ears and bad chin line, that his charm is so tremendous that it comes through even in this wretched test." Fred and Ginger Rogers made 10 movies together: 1. Flying Down to Rio, (After making this first movie with her, he told his agent, "I don't mind working with her but, as far as this team thing goes, it's out!") 2. The Gay Divorcee, 3. Roberta, 4. Top Hat, 5. Follow the Fleet, 6. Swing Time (his only film appearance in blackface, as a tribute to Bill "Bojangles" Robinson), 7. Shall We Dance, 8. Carefree, 9. The Story of Vernon and Irene Castle, and 10. The Barkleys of Broadway (the only one filmed in Technicolor). Fred Astaire's first screen dancing partner was Joan Crawford, in the 1933 movie Dancing Lady. He wore size 8 1/2 shoes and his feet were insured for $650,000. His legs were insured for $1,000,000. He entertained the troops on the front lines during WW1 and WW2. His draft number during WW2 was 156 but he was never called up for service. He said his favorite dancing partner was... Gene Kelly. The only film they made together was Ziegfeld Follies in 1943. He later added that his favorite female dance partner was Rita Hayworth. "You know, that Kelly, he's just terrific. That's all there is to it. He dances like crazy, he directs like crazy. I adore the guy. I really am crazy about his work." Because he had very large hands, he curled his fingers inward when dancing. His dancing partner Cyd Charisse was taller than he was so she bent her knees to slump down to make him look taller when they were dancing. He said of her, "When you dance with Cyd Charisse, you stay danced." "What's all this talk about me being teamed up with Ginger Rogers? I will not have it, Leland--I did not get into pictures to be teamed up with her or anyone else...I don't mind making another picture with her, but as for this team idea, it's out! I've just managed to live down one partnership, and I don't want to be bothered with any more." To his agent. His contract said he had final approval over his dance partners' costumes. His dance scene with Ginger Rogers in Continental lasted 17 minutes and 15 seconds. His nickname for Ginger Rogers was Feathers. He made only one movie in which he was neither a dancer or a musician. It was Carefree, in 1938. Fred Astaire didn't kiss Ginger Rogers until their 8th film, which was Carefree. This was also the first Astaire/Rogers film that lost money in its original release. When making Holiday Inn in 1942, he lost 14 pounds and his weight dropped down to 126 lbs. He wore a necktie around his waist instead of a belt, a habit he learned from his friend Douglas Fairbanks, Sr. The first Fred Astaire Dance Studio opened in NYC on 7 March 1947. When accepting his Honorary Oscar from Ginger Rogers in 1949, he said, "Remember, I had a partner," to which Ginger Rogers replied, "That's not what it says on the citation." He always had his lines memorized and was insulted that anyone would think that he needed what he called 'idiot cards' to help him with his lines. He bought race horses throughout his adult life. One night he went out and painted his racing colors on the mailboxes of his Beverly Hills neighbors. His horse Triplicate won the 1946 Hollywood Gold Cup. He was the 1960 Cecil B. De Mille Award winner. Of all the comedy and dancing movies he made, the only one he was ever nominated for an Oscar for was a disaster film, The Towering Inferno, in 1974. His likeness is on the cover of the Beatles' Lonely Hearts Club Band album cover, 1967. Tried extremely hard to get the lead role in Willy Wonka & the Chocolate Factory, but at age 70, was deemed too old. The role went to Gene Wilder on condition that he be allowed to perform a somersault in the opening scene. At age 80, in 1980, he married 36-year-old jockey Robyn Smith. His will prevents any movie ever being made about him: "It is there because I have no particular desire to have my life misinterpreted, which it will be." "I didn't want to leave this world without knowing who my descendant was, thank you, Michael," referring to Michael Jackson." "Get it 'til it's perfect, then cut two minutes." "Old age is like everything else. To make a success of it, you've got to start young." On dancing: "I have no desire to prove anything by it. I have never used it as an outlet or as a means of expressing myself. I just dance." "I'm just a hoofer with a spare set of tails." "I am not sending messages with my feet. All I ever wanted was to not come up empty. I did it for the dough, and for the old applause." On modern films: "They tend to overdue the vulgarity. I'm not embarrassed by the language itself, but it's embarrassing to be listening to it, sitting next to perfect strangers." "The history of dance on film begins with Fred Astaire." Gene Kelly. "He knew the value of a song and his feet were in it before his heart took over." Gene Kelly. "He gives her class and she gives him sex." Katharine Hepburn on Fred & Ginger. On Ginger Rogers,

"Ginger was brilliantly effective. She made everything work for her. Actually, she made everything work very fine for both of us and she deserves most of the credit for our success." "He is the nearest we are ever going to get to a human Mickey Mouse." Graham Greene. "No dancer can watch Fred Astaire and not know that we all should have been in another business." Mikhail Baryshnikov. "The hardest job kids face today is learning good manners without seeing any." "I don't want to be the oldest performer in captivity...I don't want to look like a little old man dancing out there." He died eighteen years to the day after Judy Garland, his co-star in 1948's Christmas Parade. He signed his will about seventeen months before he died and left an estimated $10,000,000 in trust for his entire estate. His will stated that "I direct that my funeral be private and that there be no memorial service." In 1996 his widow allowed the use of film showing him dancing to be used in a commercial for the Dirt Devil Vacuum Cleaner. His daughter said she was "saddened that after his wonderful career he was sold to the devil." Horse racing, 1978 Kennedy Center Honoree, last movie was Ghost Story, 1981. COD: Pneumonia. Buried in Oakwood Memorial Park, Epitaph says: FRED ASTAIRE/I WILL ALWAYS LOVE YOU MY DARLING/ THANK YOU. By pure coincidence, Ginger Rogers is buried only a few feet from his grave. Autobiography: Steps in Time. (5'9")

Agnes Ayers (Agnes Eyre Henkel)

b. 4 Apr 1898, d. 25 Dec 1940, = 42 yrs, 8 mos, 21 days. Made 55 movies. Married 2 times.

BKF: Playing the female lead opposite Rudolph Valentino in The Sheik (1921). She was hired by Virtagraph Pictures solely based on her strong resemblance to movie star Alice Joyce. Lost her entire fortune in the 1929 stock market crash. Talkies killed her career. Committed to a sanatorium in 1938. COD: Cerebral hemorrhage. Buried in Hollywood Forever Cemetery.

Fay Bainter (Fay Okell Bainter)

b. 7 Dec 1893, d. 16 Apr 1968, = 74 yrs, 4 mos, 9 days. Made 39 movies. Married 1 time.

Started acting at age six. First actress to be nominated for an Academy Award in two different categories in the same year; Best Actress for White Banners and Best Supporting Actress for Jezebel (1938), winning for Jezebel. She was the first native Californian to win the Best Actress Oscar. She was the presenter who handed Hattie McDaniel her Best Supporting Actress for Gone With the Wind in 1940. Aunt of actress Dorothy Burgess. Guest appearance on The Donna Reed Show, 1962. COD: Pneumonia. Buried at Arlington National Cemetery due to her husband being a career US Naval officer.

Theda Bara (Theodosia Burr Goodman)

b. 29 July 1985, d. 7 Apr 1955, = 69 yrs, 8 mos, 9 days. Made 45 movies. Married 1 time.

NN: Theo, The Vamp and The First Sex Queen. BKF: Her femme fatale roles and her famous line, "Kiss me, my fool." She is named after the daughter of Vice President Aaron Burr. Graduate of the University of Cincinnati, 1907. She is known as the first sex symbol of the movies. Her Fox Studio contract from 1916 stipulated: 1. You cannot marry within three years, 2. You must be heavily veiled while in public, 3. You cannot take public transportation, 4. You cannot appear in the theater, 5. You cannot attend Turkish baths, 6. You cannot pose for snapshots, 7. You must close the curtains on the windows of your limousine, 8. You can only go out at night. She made all 39 of her films for Fox in only five years. She was the first actress to play Cleopatra, in 1917. Most of her films were destroyed in a Fox Studios fire in 1937. Only six of her films survive. The only known recordings of her voice are from a guest spot on the radio show Texas

Star Theater, in 1939. A reporter: "Miss Bara, we all know that you were born on the banks of the Nile. But *where?*" In her most serious sounding voice, she replied, "On the left bank." When she died, she was survived by her mother. "I started out as a star and remained a star." "I will continue doing vampires as long as people sin." "I have the face of a vampire but the heart of a feminist." "It is good to be forgotten. I'm going to be so bad, I'll always be remembered." "There's a little bit of vampire instinct in every woman." "She was hysterically, insanely malevolent." Bette Davis. "She is pretty bad, but not bad enough to be remembered always." Alexander Wolcott. She was on a US postage stamp in 1994. Voluntarily retired in 1926, never having made a talking film. COD: Stomach cancer. She was worth $400,000 at the time of her death and left half of it to local children's hospitals. Buried in Glendale, California. Autobiography: What Women Never Tell. (5'6")

Ethel Barrymore (Ethel Mae Blythe)

b. 15 Aug 1879, d. 18 Jun 1959, = 79 yrs, 10 mos, 3 days. Made 44 movies. Married 1 time.

NN: First Lady of the American Theater. BKF: Being a member of the Barrymore acting family. In the 1920's Winston Churchill proposed marriage to her. She turned him down because she thought he didn't have much of a future. The woman Churchill eventually did marry bears a striking resemblance to Ethel. She and her brother Lionel were the first Oscar-winning brother-sister. She was supposed to have been a passenger on the Lusitania, but cancelled at the last minute. She was the first American actress to have a theater named after her. It opened in New York City in 1928. The only all-Barrymore movies were National Red Cross Pageant (1917) and Rasputin and the Empress (1932), now considered to be a lost film. Appeared on What's My Line in 1952. Awarded an Honorary Doctorate by New York University in 1952. Her last movie was Johnny Trouble in 1957. "You grow up the day you have your first real laugh--at yourself." "For an actress to be a success, she must have the face of a Venus, the brains of a Minerva, the grace of Terpsichore, the memory of a Macaulay, the figure of Juno and the hide of a rhinoceros." "Half the people in Hollywood are dying to be discovered and the other half are afraid they will be." "The best time to make friends is before you need them." "Wrinkles should only indicate where smiles have been." She was a serious fan of prize fighting. She never missed a Joe Louis or Henry Armstrong fight. Collected boxing prints. Last words: "Is everybody happy? I want everyone to be happy. I know I'm happy." COD: Cardiovascular disease. Epitaph: Ethel Barrymore Colt 1879 - 1959.

John Barrymore (John Sidney Blythe).

b. 14 Feb 1882, d. 29 May 1942, = 60 yrs, 3 mos, 15 days. Made 66 movies. Married 4 times.

NN: The Great Profile, The Great Lover, The American Stage's Greatest Hamlet. BKF: Being the most revered and influential actor of his time. He was never nominated for nor won an Oscar, but he is considered to the best Barrymore actor. On never even being nominated for an Oscar he said, "I think they were afraid I'd show up at the banquet drunk, embarrassing both myself and them. But I wouldn't have, you know." Studied art in England in an attempt to separate himself from his acting family. Artist, painter, commercial illustrator for New York's Evening Journal. When that didn't pan out he reluctantly went into acting on stage. Born on Valentine's Day (as was Thelma Ritter). He was in San Francisco during the Great Earthquake of 1906. It knocked him into the bathtub. Rejected by the US Army during WW1 due to varicose veins. He played the first Don Juan in Don Juan in 1926. It was the first movie to synchronize sound effects on to a sound track. He kissed 191 different women during the 167-minute movie. He had a pet vulture named Maloney, which would sit on his lap and hiss. He fed it by scavenging the garbage cans of is his neighbors. His 1925 studio contract gave him $76,250 per picture, plus a percentage of the profit for seven weeks' work. It also paid for his transportation, a four-rrom suite at a posh Los Angeles hotel and a limousine and chauffeur. His affair with Dolores Costello in 1926 (whom he later married) caused her parents to divorce. Had it in his contract, that due to his heavy drinking, he did not have to start work before 10:30am. His movie, Don Juan, 1926 was the first film made with a synchronized score. Declared bankruptcy in 1937. His daughter committed suicide. In 1938 he was labeled 'Box Office Poison' due to his heavy drinking. His second wife was a poetess who wrote under the name Michael Strange. He once rented an entire brothel in India for a week just for himself. Said the left side of his face was the moneymaking side. Wrote a novel called Mr. Cantonwine: A Moral Tale. When he died, his friend director Raoul Walsh retreived his body from the morgue and propped him up, with a drink in his hand, in a chair in Errol Flynn's home. Flynn tells of it in his autobiography: "As I opened the door I pressed the button. The lights went on and - I stared in the face of Barrymore... They hadn't embalmed him yet. I let out a delirious scream... I went back in, still shaking. I returned to my room upstairs shaken and sober. My heart pounded. I couldn't sleep the rest of the night." It was a joke among friends and Flynn said he couldn't go to sleep that night. "It takes an earthquake to get Jack out of bed, a flood to make him wash and the United States Army to put him to work." His brother Lionel. "Thank goodness I don't have to act with you anymore." Katharine Hepburn. "The way to fight a woman is with your hat. Grab it and run." "A man is not old until his regrets take the place of his dreams." "In Hollywood I can loaf and earn ten times what I do on the stage." "Brides aren't happy. They are just triumphant." "Why is there so much month left at the end of my money?" "Sex: The thing that takes of the least amount of time and causes most of the trouble." "You never realize how short a month is until you pay alimony." "When archaeologists discover the missing arms of the Venus de Milo they will find she was wearing boxing gloves." "The good die young--because they see it's no use living if you've got to be good." "Method acting? Mine involves a lot of talent, a glass and some cracked ice." "My only regret in the theater is that I could never sit out front and watch me." "I like to be introduced as America's foremost actor. It saves the necessity of further effort." "There isn't any romance about how I went on stage. I needed the money." "It will be impossible for me to accept because of a previous engagement, which I shall make as soon as possible." "America is the country where you buy a lifetime supply of aspirin for one dollar, and use it up in two weeks." "So many beautiful women and so little time." "I simply cannot eat on an empty stomach." "Happiness sneaks in through a door you didn't know you left open." "I've done everything I've wanted to do. I've played Hamlet in London; I've had every woman I've ever wanted; I have a son to carry on my name...I'm bored and I'm tired." "When asked on his deathbed if he had anything to confess, he said, "Yes, father. Carnal thoughts about the lady standing behind you." He later said, "Die? I should say not dear fellow. No Barrymore would allow such a conventional thing to happen to him." COD: Cirrhosis of the liver and pneumonia. "He told me that he was not a good enough Catholic to go to Mass, but too good a Catholic to kill himself. So he drank himself to death. It took him ten years." John Carradine. He left specific instructions that he be cremated, but his brother and sister wouldn't allow it due to their Catholic beliefs. His pallbearers were W.C. Fields, David O. Selznick, Louis B. Mayer, and Herbert Marshall. When asked what he wanted on his tombstone, he said, "I've played everything but the harp." His actual epitaph says: "Good Night, Sweet Prince." His son exhumed his body in 1980 and had him cremated. Ashes buried in Philadelphia. He earned $3,000,000 in his lifetime but died broke. His likeness was on a US postage stamp in 2010.

Lionel Barrymore (Lionel Herbert Blythe)

b. 28 Apr 1878, d. 15 Nov 1954, = 76 yrs, 6 mos, 18 days. Made 221 movies. Married 2 times.

BKF: Playing the banker Mr. Potter in It's a Wonderful Life, 1946 and playing Dr. Leonard Gillespie in 9 Dr. Kildare movies. 5' 8" tall.

His two daughters did not survive infancy. Trained as an artist but still gravitated toward the family business of acting. Registered for the draft during WW2 despite being wheelchair-bound and 63 years old. He is credited with inventing the overhead boom microphone in 1929. Due to a hip that was broken twice and never healed, and the arthritis that it caused, he was addicted to morphine by 1929. He appeared in drag as a woman in The Devil Doll. He was the first actor to have a 30-year career while being confined to a wheelchair. Played himself in Free and Easy, 1930. He and Spring Byington played a married couple in Ah Wilderness in 1935. Three years later, in 1938, he played her father in You Can't Take It With You. In 1941 he composed a symphony titled "Tableau Russe." It was played in the film Dr. Kildare's Wedding Day. He was typecast as a grouchy, but sweet elderly man. He had so much trouble with the IRS in the last twenty years of his life, he would just send them all of his paychecks, and they would send back to him what they thought he needed to live on. "I didn't want to act. I wanted to paint or draw. Theater was not in my blood, I was related to the theater by marriage only; it was merely a kind of in-law of mine I had to live with." Later in life, he said, "I've got a lot of ham in me." "L.B. (Louis B. Meyer) gets me $400 worth of cocaine a day to ease my pain. I don't know where he gets it. And I don't care. But I bless him every time it puts me to sleep." "I choose to act because I choose to eat." On retiring: "I've never given it a thought. I'll make pictures as long as I can wiggle." In the 1930's President Roosevelt was asked if Lionel Barrymore was the best actor in America. He said, "I am the best actor in America." "I remember when nobody believed an actor and didn't care what he believed." When a reporter asked him what he wanted on his tombstone, he said, "Well, I've played everything but the harp." COD: Heart attack. His actual epitaph bears only his name. Autobiography: We Barrymores, 1951.

Warner Baxter (Warner Leroy Baxter)

b. 29 Mar 1889, d. 7 May 1951, = 61 yrs, 11 mos, 8 days. Made 111 movies. Married 2 times.

BKF: Winning the second Academy Award for Best Actor in 1925, for playing the Cisco Kid in In Old Arizona. (It was his 46th movie.) Also created the Crime Doctor Series. Lost everything in the 1906 San Francisco earthquake and was homeless. Went to Columbus, Ohio to become an insurance salesman. In Old Arizona was billed as the first all-talking drama filmed outdoors. He got the part only after the original star, Raoul Walsh, lost one eye in a bizarre auto accident. Famous for his many westerns, he had a serious fear of horses. He went to Polytechnic High School in San Francisco, the alma mater of Janet Gaynor and George O'Brien. He was an office boy, auto salesman, typewriter salesman, insurance agent and a partner in an auto garage before going to Hollywood. He invented a moving target that lights up for target practice and a remote device that changes street lights so police and emergency vehicles could go through. On how he got into show business: "I discovered a boy a block away who would eat worms and swallow flies for a penny. For one-third of the profits, I exhibited him in a tent." At $248,000 per year, he was the highest paid actor in Hollywood in 1936. His horse's name was Diablo. His last movie was Crime Doctor's Diary, 1949. COD: Pneumonia after a lobotomy to ease the pain of arthritis. When he died he was survived by his mother, who lived another ten years.

Wallace Beery (Wallace Fitzgerald Beery)

b. 1 Apr 1885, d. 15 Apr 1949, = 64 yrs, 14 days. Made 250+ movies. Married 2 times.

BKF: Playing Bill in Bill and Min, 1930. Engine wiper in a railroad roundhouse. In 1932 he came in 2nd place in the Best Actor voting to Fredric March by one vote. By the rules in place at the time, he also received a Best Actor Oscar for coming within three votes of the winner. Both he and Fredrick March had adopted children earlier in the year. At his acceptance speech, March said, "It seems a little odd that Wally and I were both given awards for the best male performance of the year." Elephant trainer for Ringling Bros. Circus. He described the job as "chambermaid to the elephants." He quit the job when a lion clawed his arm. WW1 Lt. Commander in the US Naval Reserve. His contract stipulated that his pay always be $1 more than the 2nd-highest paid actor. Married Gloria Swanson on 27 March 1916, her 17th birthday. He was 31. Held the record for the largest sea bass caught off Catalina Island, at 515 lbs. That record stood from 1916 to 1951. He and Betsy Love were the star of the first-ever in-flight movie ever shown. It was on a British Airways flight in 1925. He held a private pilot's license and accumulated 14,000 hours air time as a pilot from 1925 to 1941. He was generally rude, difficult to get along with, insulting, and lacked manners or any class. His ex-wife said that they had been invited to every fashionable home in Beverly Hills - "Once!" "He ignored everybody and everything. He never said 'hello.' He never said 'goodbye.' He never smiled." Jane Powell. "I was warned that he was an inveterate scene-stealer and woulde even get his face in the camera when it was a close-up on the other players." Ronald Reagan. His co-star Jackie Cooper said that he treated him "like an unwanted dog" the second the cameras stopped rolling. "No man is indispensible but some are irreplaceable." "My mug is my fortune." "I have no art in my soul, I don't try to be different. I'm just plain me in every picture, and the public continues to accept me." He was being sued for paternity when he died at age 64. Actress Gloria Schumm claimed he was the father of her 13-month old son. COD: Heart attack. Buried in Glendale, California.

Jack Benny (Benjamin Kubelsky)

14 Feb 1894, d. 26 Dec 1974, = 80 yrs, 10 mos, 12 days. Made 33 movies. Married 1 time.

BKF: Being cheap, always being 39 years old and 931 episodes of The Jack Benny Show, 1932-1955. NN: The Meanest Man in the World and The Aristocrat of Humor. His catchphrase was, "Now, cut that out!" Taught to play the violin by pro football player Otto Graham's father. Played his violin in vaudeville theaters for $7.50 per week. Expelled from high school for poor grades. Touring vaudevillian. In the US Navy during WW1, entertained the troops with his violin playing. His career began when he was almost booed off the stage and he saved the performance with a comedy routine. Chose the name Jack because it was a common sailor's nickname. Was on The $64,000 Question in 1957, the subject was violins. He won $64, but only because he insisted on quitting after only one question. Made his radio debut on The Ed Sullivan Show in 1932. Turned 39 for real in 1933. His home address in Beverly Hills was 1002 North Roxbury Drive. Lucille Ball and Desi Arnaz lived at 1000 North Roxbury Drive and Peter Falk lived at 1004 Roxbury Drive. His best friend for life was George Burns. Together, in 1939, they pleaded guilty to buying smuggled jewelry worth over $2,000. He was given a one year and one day (to make it a felony) suspended jail sentence and fined $10,000. Said his 1943 USO tour to North Africa was "the most thrilling and memorable trip I ever made in my life." During the war, he converted his Badminton court into a victory garden. He said To Be or Not To Be was "the best picture I ever made." In Charlie's Aunt, he appeared in drag as a woman. When he arrived at the White House to perform for President Harry Truman's inauguration in January, 1949, a guard asked what was in the violin case he was carrying. He replied, "It's a Thompson sub-machine gun," to which the guard replied, "Oh, that's a relief. I was afraid it was your violin." His decade-long over-the-radio feud with comedian Fred Allen in the 1950's was a scripted comic put-on. They were actually the best of friends. "People have often asked me if Fred Allen and I were really friends in real life. My answer is always the same. You couldn't have such a long-running and successful feud as we did, without having a deep and sincere friendship at the heart of it." Fred Allen wrote in his autobiography: "For years people have been asking me if Jack and I are friendly. I don't think that Jack Benny has an enemy in the world...He is my favourite (sic) comedian and I hope to be his friend until he is forty. That will be forever." "I don't care who gets the laughs on my show as long as the show is funny." The theme song of the Jack Benny Show was Love in Bloom. "I don't deserve this award but I have arthritis and I don't deserve that either." On playing the violin, he said, "You have to practice just to be bad." He was known as "Not one who says funny things, but one who say things funny." "My wife, Mary, and I have been married for forty-seven years and not once have we had an argument serious enough to consider divorce; murder, yes, but divorce, never." "Give me golf clubs, fresh air and a beautiful partner and you can keep the golf clubs and fresh air." "Modesty is my best quality." "Everything good that happened to me happened by accident. I was not filled by ambition or fired by a drive toward a clear-cut goal. I never knew where I was going." No children except one adopted daughter named Joan. On the occasion of forever-39 Jack Benny's 80th birthday, Frank Sinatra gave him two copies of the book "Life Begins at Forty." He was awarded the Procrastinator of the Year Award by the Procrastinators Club of America, for never getting around to turning forty. British comedian Alfred Hawthorne took the stage name Benny Hill as a tribute to him. The Texas Hold'em poker hand 3-9 is called a Jack Benny. When he appeared on the game show Password All-Stars in 1961, he got the word "miser." He then gave the clue "Me," which was the show-stopper. Had a cameo in It's a Mad, Mad, Mad, Mad World, 1963. He got the lead role in The Sunshine Boys in 1974 but due to failing health had to withdraw in favor is his best friend George Burns. Burns took the role and went on the win the Academy Award for Best Actor. "If he can't take it with him, he ain't gonna' go." Eddie 'Rochester' Anderson. "It's absolutely true. I won't tell you how much insurance I carry with Prudential, but I can say this--when I go, they go." "When Jack Benny has a party, you not only have to bring your own scotch, you have to bring your own rocks." George Burns. COD: Pancreatic cancer. Died in his sleep at home the day after Christmas. Buried in Los Angeles, California. Autobiography: (unpublished) I Always Had Shoes, and (published posthumously): Sunday Nights at Seven. His will provided that one red rose be delivered to his wife Mary every day for the rest of her life. She survived him by nine years and received more than 3,000 roses. Signed his will about six months before he died. He was worth $4,000,000 at the time of his death. Left $20,000 to his sister and the rest to his wife. He also left his Stradivarius violin to the Los Angeles Philharmonic Orchestra. He joked, "If it isn't a $30,000 Strad, I'm out $120. "Bob Hope said, "For a man who was the undisputed master of comedy timing, you would have to say that this is the only time when Jack Benny's timing was all wrong. He left us much too soon." You can still join The International Jack Benny Fan Club. There is a senior high school named for him in his hometown of Waukegan, Illinois. Their football team is called "The 39ers." He is on the US Postal Service's 2006 29-cent stamp, even though the public petitioned for the 39-cent stamp. He is buried in Culver City, California and tourists still leave pennies on his crypt. (5' 10")

Charles Bickford (Charles Ambrose Bickford)

b. 1 Jan 1891, d. 9 Nov 1967, = 76 yrs, 10 mos, 8 days. Made 113 movies. Married 1 time.

BKF: The Big Country (1958) and A Big Hand For the Little Lady (1966). The fifth of seven children. Lumberjack, ran a pest extermination business. WW1 US Navy fireman, then US Army 1st Lt. engineer. At age 9, he was tried and acquitted of the attempted murder of a trolley operator who purposefully ran over and killed his dog. Nearly killed by a lion while filming East of Eden in 1935. Never put all of his money in one place. At one time he simultaneously owned a gas station and a garage, a half-interest in a pearling schooner, a pair of whaling boats, a hog farm, a chicken ranch, a lingerie shop, and an island off the coast of the Indonesian island of Java where coconuts were harvested. He also owned a gold mine near San Bernardino, California. Never watched his own movies. He said, "Perhaps it's because I'm too critical that I don't usually see my own stuff. Very often it's a weird experience, and sometimes it's a little nauseating." COD: Blood infection. His close friend Jennifer Jones attempted suicide on the day he died. Autobiography: Bulls, Balls, Bicycles and Actors, 1965.

Clara Blandick (Clara Blanchard Dickey)

b. 4 June 1876, d. 15 Apr 1962, = 85 yrs, 10 mos, 11 days. Made 175 movies. Married 1 time.

BKF: Playing Auntie Em in The Wizard of Oz. Born on an American ship off the coast of Hong Kong. Stage performer. WW1 entertained the troops of the American Expeditionary Force in France. Did not make her second movie until age forty-eight, but would make more than 100 more movies in the next twenty years. Paid $750 for two weeks' work on The Wizard of Oz. Voluntarily retired at age 69. COD: After returning home from Sunday church services, suicide by overdose of sleeping pills and tying a plastic bag around her neck. Suicide note: "I am now about to make the great adventure. I cannot endure this agonizing pain any longer. It is all over my body. Neither can I face the impending blindness. I pray the Lord my soul to take. Amen." Cremated, ashes scattered in Glendale, California.

Monte Blue (Gerard Monte Blue)

b. 11 Jan 1887, d. 18 Feb 1963, = 76, yrs, 1 mo, 7 days. Made 110+ movies. Married 3 times.

BKF: Playing the sheriff in Key Largo. Put in an orphanage at age 8 when his father was killed in a railroad accident. His father was a scout for the iconic frontiersman Buffalo Bill Cody. 6'3" fireman, railroad worker, coal miner, cowpuncher, ranch hand, circus rider, lumberjack, day laborer, stuntman, movie extra. He was the star of White Shadows in the South Seas in 1928, the first film to feature MGM mascot Leo the Lion roaring at the beginning of the film. Lost

$750,000 in the 1929 stock market crash. Guest starred on The Lone Ranger television show five times as a sheriff and once as an Indian chief, from 1949 to 1953. COD: Heart attack and influenza. Buried in Glendale, California.

Humphrey Bogart (Humphrey DeForest Bogart)

b. 23 Jan 1899, d. 14 Jan 1957, = 57 yrs, 11 mos, 22 days. Made 75+ films. Married 4 times.

BKF: Playing Rick Blaine in Casablanca. 5' 5". For decades it was believed that he was born on Christmas Day, 1899, but that turned out to be Warner Bros. studio propaganda, "...because a guy born on Christmas can't be all bad." NN: Bogey and Whiskey Straight (to his friends only.) The Screen's #1 Bad Guy. He is The American Film Institute's #1 Greatest Movie Star of All Time. His ancestors on both his mother's and father's sides of the family have lived in the United States since the 1600's. He was the son of a wealthy New York surgeon and world-famous magazine illustrator Maud Humphrey, who were listed in New York's Blue Book. His mother was a commercial artist who used his likeness that was on millions of packages of Mellin's Baby Food. His childhood home address was 245 W. 103rd Street in the Upper West Side of New York City, which is now public housing. Expelled from Phillips Andover Academy for dunking a professor he didn't like. It is not known for sure how he got his lip scar and lisp. One story says it was a result of a childhood operation to remove a splinter. One false studio story says it happened when the ship he was on while in the US Navy during WW1 was attacked. On his WW1 experiences as a helmsman on the troop ship Leviathan, he said, "At 18, war was great stuff. Paris! Sexy French girls! Hot damn!" His son Stephen later said that his short time in the US Navy was characterized by "long stints in the brig" for fighting. Played a Japanese butler in a Broadway play in 1921. In the 1920's he supported himself by playing chess for $1 a game in a Manhattan arcade. He got married for the first time in 1924. This is also the year that his future wife Lauren

Bacall was born. He appeared with Bette Davis in eight films from 1931 to 1943. His only film with close friend Spencer Tracy was Up the River, 1930. Made eight pictures with Joan Crawford. Made only one horror film in his career--the Return of Dr. X, in 1939. He played a zombie. Co-founder of a drinking club called Rat Pack. In 1940 he was called to explain to the House Un-American Activities Committee why he donated a small amount of money to striking lettuce workers. Played chess by mail with American G.I.s during WW2. Entertained the troops in North Africa and Africa during a three-month USO tour in early 1944. Named his only son Steve after his character's name in To Have and Have Not, 1944. Met Lauren Bacall at a friend's farm in Ohio, while still married to his third wife. He once showed up at a posh New York nightclub with a friend and two stuffed pandas. He introduced the pandas as their dates and demanded a table for four. After a fist fight and being thrown out, he was asked, "Were you drunk?" His reply was, "Isn't everybody at three in the morning.?" He was paid $3,500 per week to make Casablanca. US Coast Guard Reserve during WW2. He was the star of The Maltese Falcon, 1941, which was the first film noir to be nominated for Best Picture. While filming Casablanca, his wife threatened to kill him if he got involved with Ingrid Bergman. She then convinced herself that he was in love with Bergman and almost succeeded at committing suicide. As a result, he took his wife with him on a lengthy worldwide WW2 USO tour. Being 5' 5", he had to wear platform shoes with 5" heels to stand next to Ingrid Bergman while filming and between filming scenes, taught her how to play poker. The line, "Here's looking at you Kid," was completely improvised and not in the script. It's what he said to her while they were playing poker between takes on the set. After Casablanca became a huge success, he signed a contract that made him the highest paid actor of all time. He had made 50 movies before he made his first movie with future wife Lauren Bacall. It was also her first movie, To Have and Have Not, 1945. Became a father for the first time at age 49. Their daughter is named Leslie Howard Bogart, after actor Leslie Howard, who was killed during WW2. While filming The African Queen in the Belgian Congo with Katherine

Hepburn, their caterer was arrested on suspicion of cannibalism. He would not let the makeup department fill in the wrinkles on his face. He said, "Leave in the lines, I'm proud of them." When you see him in the barber's chair in Treasure of the Sierra Madre, 1948, it was the last time his real hair appeared in a movie. After that, he always wore a full toupee. When nominated for Best Actor, he said, "Hell, I hope I'm never nominated again. It's meat and potatoes roles for me from now on." Accepting the Oscar for Best Actor in 1951, he said, "It's been a long way from the Belgian Congo to the Pantages Theater, but I'd rather be here than there. I'm not going to thank anybody; I'm just going to say I damn well deserve it." His concrete slab at Graumann's Chinese Theater is inscribed: "Sid, may you never die until I kill you." Couldn't stand working with Audrey Hepburn in Sabrina, 1954. He acted on television only once--when he played Duke Mantee in a version of The Petrified Forrest in 1955. His only other television credit was a guest appearance on Producer's Showcase on 30 May 1955. His personal yacht was called The Santana and his production company was called Santana Pictures. Santana Pictures made five movies in six years, the last being The Harder They Fall. Said he went into acting "so I could sleep late." "Next to being an actor, I'd rather be a sailor than anything. A sailor is in lots of ways better off than an actor. He is safer, he is freer from the restrictions of civilization...." On the Academy Award for best actor, he said, "Awards are meaningless, unless they all play the same part. The only honest way to find the best actor would be to let everybody play Hamlet and let the best man win. Of course, you'd get some pretty funny Hamlets that way." Bogart never said, "Play it again, Sam," in Casablanca. He did say, "What's that you're playing?" and "Play it." It was Ingrid Bergman who said, "Play it Sam. Play As Time Goes By." The piano that Sam played later sold for $81,000 at auction. The statuette from The Maltese Falcon sold for $398,500 at auction. "The trouble with the world is that it is always one drink behind." "Acting is like sex: You either do it and don't talk about it or you talk about it and don't do it." "A hot dog at the ballpark is better than a steak at the Ritz." "Things are never so bad that they can't be made worse." He never said, "Tennis, anyone?" even though it's erroneously attributed to him in Bartlett's Quotations. Director John Huston said, "The trouble with Bogart is that he thinks he's Bogart." He said the best movie he ever made--by far--was In A Lonely Place in 1950. Said he liked to go boating with men only because, "When there are women on board, you can't pee off the side." His only dramatic role on TV was in The Petrified Forrest, 1956. Called Gina Lollobrigida Frigidaire on the set of Beat the Devil, 1956, because he couldn't pronounce her name. His last film was The Harder They Fall, 1956. He said, "The only good reason to have money is this: So you can tell any SOB in the world to go to hell." "You're not a star until they can spell your name in Karachi." "Even when I was carrying a gun, she (Bette Davis) scared the be-Jesus out of me." His last words in public were, "I should have never switched from scotch to martinis." "Next to being an actor, I'd rather be a sailor than anything. A sailor in lots of ways is much better off than an actor. He is safer, he is freer of the restrictions of civilization..." "In my first thirty-four pictures, I was shot twelve times, electrocuted or hanged in eight, and I was a jailbird in nine...I played more scenes writhing around on the floor that I did standing up. I was the Little Lord Fauntleroy of the lot!" "Fame creates its own standard. A guy who twitches his lips is just another guy with a lip-twitch--unless he's Humphrey Bogart." Sammy Davis, Jr. "He was a real man--nothing feminine about him. He knew he was a natural aristocrat--better than anybody." Katharine Hepburn. "I hated that bastard." William Holden. "He has charm and he doesn't waste energy by pretending to act. He was an exciting personality and let's it do the work." "He was polite naturally, but I always felt there was a distance; he was behind a wall. I was intimidated by him." Ingrid Bergman. "He was a pro, but an affable, easy person, fond of gentle ribbing." Ronald Reagan. Writer James Agate. BOGART/Bacall movies: 1. To Have and Have Not, 1944, 2. The Big Sleep, 1946, 3. Two Guys From Milwaukee, 1946, 4. Dark Passage, 1947, 5. Key Largo, 1948. His last words in private were to his wife Lauren Bacall were, "Goodbye Kid. Hurry back," instead of his usual "Good night, Kid," as she left to pick up their children from school. Also said, "Goodnight,

Spence," to Spencer Tracy, who was his last private visitor the night before he died. When she returned, she found him comatose in his wheelchair. He died at 2am the next day. Weighed only 80 pounds when he died. COD: Esophageal cancer. His ashes are in an urn with a small, gold whistle with the inscription: "If you need anything, just whistle." Those were her words to him in To Have and Have Not, their first film together. His eulogy was delivered by John Huston, who said, "Himself, he never took too seriously--his work, most seriously. His life, though not a long one measured in years, was a rich, deep life. He got what he asked for out of life and more. He is quite irreplaceable." His address at the time of his death was 232 South Mapleton Drive, Los Angeles, California. He signed his will seven months before he died. His will begins, "I am married to Betty Bogart (also known as Lauren Bacall Bogart)..." He established a trust that left her everything for her lifetime with a portion for his son and daughter when they reached the age of forty-five years. He also instructed the trustees of his estate to make grants "...for the aid of medical research, with special reference to the field of cancer." A hat described as "his signature Fedora" sold for $6,325 at auction in 2003. He is distantly related to Princess Dianna through her American relatives.

John Boles (Same)

b. 28 Oct 1895, d. 27 Feb 1969, = 73 yrs, 3 mos, 3 days. Made 25 movies. Married 1 time.

BKF: Playing Victor Moritz in Frankenstein (1931). Graduate of the University of Texas, a pre-med student. Taught French and singing in a New York high school. Entertained the troops on a US spy ship during WW1, in the Mediterranean Sea. COD: Heart attack.

Beulah Bondi (Beulah Bondy)

b. 3 May 1889, d. 11 Jan 1981, = 91 yrs, 8 mos, 8 days. Made 77 movies. Never married.

BKF: Playing Jimmy Stewart's mother in four movies (and one television show) and an Emmy-winning guest appearance on The Walton's in 1976. Broadway actress. She did not make her first movie until age 43. She changed the spelling of her last name so all of the letters would fit on one line for top billing on movie marquees. Her most famous role was as "Ma Bailey" in It's a Wonderful Life (1946). Holds a Master's Degree in Oratory from Valparaiso University. She played a 70 -year-old when she was 33. She said her favorite role was, "It has always been the one I was playing at the moment that I liked best." She was the first choice to play the role that went to Jane Darwell in the Grapes of Wrath, 1940. Darwell won the Best Supporting Actress Oscar for that role. "I'm very cooperative, and if you'll tell me exactly what you want, I'll always try to do it." COD: Pulmonary complications caused by broken ribs when she tripped over her cat at home at age 91.

Alice Brady (Mary Rose Brady)

b. 2 Nov 1892, d. 28 Oct 1939, = 46 yrs, 11 mos, 26 days. Made 80+ movies. Married 1 time.

Made more than 50 silent movies and didn't make her first talkie until 1933. She won the Best Supporting Actress Oscar in 1937. She was not present at the ceremony due to a broken ankle and it was accepted by an unknown man who disappeared with it. It has never been found and she died before it could be replaced. She played Alla Nazimova's mother in 1947's Mourning Becomes Electra, even though she was only thirteen years older than her. She liked the color red. In her house the walls, furnishings, pictures frames, candelabra were all red and white. Her last movie was Young Mr. Lincoln in 1939. Her son died at age 19 only three years after her. COD: Cancer.

Walter Brennan (Walter Andrew Brennan)

b. 25 July 1894, d. 12 Sep 1974, 80 yrs, 1 mo, 18 days. Made 244 movies. Married 1 time.

BKF: Playing Judge Roy Bean in The Westerner and 244 episodes of The Real McCoys television show, 1957-1962. Left home at age 11. Served in the 101st Field artillery in France during WW1. His unique, high-pitched voice was a result of being attacked with poison gas during the war. After the war he was a ditch digger, lumberjack, bank messenger and real estate salesman and studied to be an engineer. He then went to Guatemala to raise pineapples. He was a handyman on a studio set and was 'discovered' when it was learned he could bray like a donkey on cue. Had a cameo role in The Three Stooges' Restless Knights, 1934. He was the first actor to win three Best Supporting Actor Oscars: 1. Come and Get It, 1936, 2. Kentucky, 1938, and 3. The Westerner, 1940, and be nominated for a fourth. He and Katharine Hepburn are the only two actors to win acting Oscars in three consecutive nominations. Lost his front teeth in a fall off a horse while performing a movie stunt. He said he "had two styles of acting: Teeth in and teeth out." He was having a conversation with director Howard Hawks, who could not quite remember the name of actor he was taking with. Brennan took his teeth out and said, "Do you recognize me now?" He did. Even though he is known for playing southerners, he had a distinct New England accent when not on film. In appreciation of his fans, he said, "I can't stand performers who snub the people they work for." Advice to young actors: "Go ahead and learn how to act, but don't get caught at it." "I never made a movie I would not take my family to see." Owner of a 12,000 acre ranch in Joseph, Oregon (that's 18.75 square miles). He had a Top 5 hit with Dutchman's Gold in 1960 and another Top 5 hit with Old Man

Rivers in 1962. Member of the Cowboy Hall of Fame, 1970. COD: Emphysema. Buried in San Fernando, California.

Fanny Brice (Fania Borach)

b. 29 Oct 1891, d. 29 May 1957, = 65 yrs, 7 mos, 0 days. Made 8 movies. Married 3 times.

BKF: 154 episodes of The Baby Snooks Show, on radio, 1937 to 1951. Dropped out of school to go into burlesque. Famous for singing My Man and Second Hand Rose as a Ziegfeld Follies girl in 1921. Barbara Streisand won the 1968 Best Actress Oscar for portraying her in Funny Girl. "I'm a bad woman, but I'm damn good company." COD: Cerebral hemorrhage. Cremated, ashes interred at Westwood Memorial Park Cemetery in Los Angeles.

Joe E. Brown (Joseph Evans Brown)

b. 28 July 1891, d. 6 July 1973, = 81 yrs, 11 mos, 8 days. Made 72 movies. Married 1 time.

Dropped out of school at the age of 10 to join the circus and quickly became the main attraction at the Ringling Bros. acrobatic show. He was a professional baseball player for the St. Paul, Minnesota team. Turned down an offer to sign with the New York Yankees so he could be an entertainer. He had a clause in his contract that required Warner Bros. to maintain a full team of baseball players among the staff who worked on his movies. Traveled more than 200,000 miles to entertain the troops during WW2. He did this mostly at his own expense and he visited Alaska and the Caribbean before the USO was created. He was only one of two civilians to be awarded the Bronze Star for heroism in WW2. This was in recognition of the fact that he was willing to risk his life to travel more than 200,000 miles to out-of-the-way, dangerous locations, in contrast to most other Hollywood entertainers, who became known as "the Bop Hopes of the

USO." The other civilian to be awarded the Bronze Star for heroism was Ernest Hemingway. Brown's son was killed during WW2. In Shut My Mouth, he appeared in drag as a woman. He said is only ambition was "to make people happy." Had a cameo in Around the World in 80 Days. COD: Arteriosclerosis after heart surgery. Buried at Forest Lawn in Glendale, California.

John Bunny (Same)

b. 21 Sep 1863, d. 26 Apr 1915, = 51 yrs, 5 mos, 5 days. Made 300+ movies. Married 1 time.

BKF: A Cure For Pokeritis, 1912, which can be viewed on Youtube. com. NN: Film's First King of Comedy. Stage actor and manager. Despite the fact that he was the screen's most popular comedian, his co-workers found him arrogant, ill-tempered and hard to work with. He did not drink or smoke. Weighed 300 pounds. Despite the fact that it is a popularly accepted trivia fact, he was not the first actor to play Santa Clause in a movie. It had been done about six times before he did it. His face was insured for $100,000. He had only a five year career in movies before he died. "Here's to our wives and sweethearts--may they never meet!" Went into comedy because, as he said, "How could I play Romeo with a figure like mine?" COD: Bright's disease. Buried in Brooklyn, NY.

Billie Burke (Mary William Etherlbert Appleton Burke)

b. 7 Aug 1884, d. 14 May 1970, = 85 yrs, 9 mos, 7 days. Made 65+ movies, Married 1 time.

BKF: Playing Glinda, the Good Witch, in The Wizard of Oz. She is named for her father, who was the internationally known English clown with the Barnum & Bailey circus. She was the first wife of Florenz Ziegfeld. She had retired a very wealthy person but the stock market crash of 1929 forced her to go back to work. Her singing in the

Wizard of Oz was dubbed by Lorraine Rogers. Made Topper in 1937 and sequels Topper Takes a Trip in 1939 and Topper Returns in 1941. She is the only actor in all three movies. On why she retired: "Acting just wasn't fun anymore." "Age is something that doesn't matter, unless you are a cheese." COD: Natural causes. Buried in Valhalla, NY. Autobiographies: With a Feather On My Nose, 1949, and With Powder On My Nose, 1959. In 2015, a crater near the north pole of the planet Mercury was named after her.

George Burns (Nathan Birnbaum)

b. 20 Jan 1896, d. 9 Mar 1996, = 100 yrs, 1 mo, 18 days. Made 50 movies. Married 2 times.

BKF: 291 Episodes of The George Burns and Gracie Allen Show, 1950-1958 and three Oh, God! movies. He was the 9th of 13 children. 5' 9". Dropped out of school in the fourth grade. At age thirteen, he was hustling immigrants coming from Ellis Island. He charged them $5 for dance lessons, telling them that it was a prerequisite to becoming an American citizen. Started smoking cigars at age 14. He had one gold tooth. He was drafted in the US Army during WW1 but was not accepted because he was nearsighted. Changed his name to hide his Jewish heritage. Started his career playing "lousy little theaters that played lousy little acts--and I was one of them." He often had to change his name to get a second booking at the same venue. He called his and Gracie's style of comedy 'illogical logic.' Their act was going nowhere until they decided to switch roles and he played the straight man and she played the ditzy airhead. Jack Benny was the best man at their wedding. They had two adopted children, Sandra and Ronnie, and none of their own. His theme song was Ain't Misbehavin'. In 1939, along with his friend Jack Benny, he was convicted of a felony in Federal Court and fined $8,000 and given a one year suspended sentence for buying smuggled jewelry from a known fence. He made thirteen films from 1932 to 1939, had a 36-year gap and then made 8 more films from 1975 to 1988. He is responsible for discovering and promoting Ann Margaret. After Gracie died in 1964, he kept the light on her side of the bed on for three years and visited her grave once a month. He was the voice of Mr. Ed in at least one episode. He was in show business for 89 of his 100 years. At age 80, he is the oldest Best Supporting Actor Oscar winner, for The Sunshine Boys in 1975. The role was supposed to go to Jack Benny but he had to drop out due to his end of life illness. Accepting his Oscar he said, "It couldn't have happened to on older guy." A few years later he added, "I was thrilled when I was nominated, but it was very, very exciting to win an Oscar. Imagine, winning an Oscar when you're eighty years old. I've been in show business all my life, and I've always played myself, George Burns. Here I make one movie, The Sunshine Boys, where for the first time I didn't play myself. I played a character, 'Al Lewis,' and I won an Oscar. I guess that could mean I've been doing the wrong thing for the last eighty years. It's a good thing I found out before it's too late." At age 97, he signed a 5-year contract with a Las Vegas Casino and said, "I limited it to five years because I can't be sure how long they'll be around." Booked himself to play the London Palladium on his 100th birthday, but couldn't make it due to ill health. He died 48 days later. Smoked ten cigars a day right up to the time of his death. "Someone who makes you laugh is a comedian. Someone who makes you think--and then laugh--is a humorist." "You know you're getting old when you stoop to tie your shoes and wonder what else you can do while you're down there." "I was married by a judge. I should have asked for a jury." "If it's a good script I'll do it. If it's a bad script and they pay me enough, I'll do it." "Smartness runs in my family. When I went to school I was so smart my teacher was in my class for five years." "Retirement at age sixty-five is ridiculous. When I was sixty-five I still had pimples." "There is no reason for me to die. I already died in Altoona." "In what other business can a guy my age drink martinis, smoke cigars and sing? I think all people who retire should go into show business. I've been retired all my life." "When I was young, the Dead Sea was still alive." "Do you know what it means to come home at night to a woman who'll give you a little love, a little affection, a little tenderness? It means you're in the wrong house." "Dress simply.

If you wear a dinner jacket don't wear anything else on it...like lunch or dinner." "Happiness is having a large, loving, caring, close-knit family in another city." "Happiness? A good cigar, a good woman--or a bad woman; it depends on how much happiness you can handle." "By the time you're eighty years old you've learned everything. You only have to remember it." "At my age, flowers scare me." "I should have been a country-western singer. After all, I'm older than most western countries." "I'd announce that I was going to sing, and all our guests would make a ring around the piano. But somehow I managed to fight my way through the ring and sing anyway." "It only takes one drink to get me drunk. The trouble is, I can't remember if it's the thirteenth or fourteenth." "Nice to be here? At my age it's nice to be anywhere." "People ask me what I'd most appreciate getting for my eighty-seventh birthday. I tell them: a paternity suit." "I'm at that age now where just putting my cigar in its holder is a thrill." "Sex after ninety is like trying to shoot pool with a rope." "Everything that goes up must come down. But there comes a time when not everything that's down can come up." "It's hard for me to get used to these changing times--I can remember when air was clean and sex was dirty." "If you want to live a long time, you have to smoke cigars, drink martinis and dance close." "If you live to be 100, you've got it made. Very few people die past that age." "The most important thing in acting is honesty. If you can fake that, you're got it made." "George reads Playboy for the same reason he reads National Geographic--to see places he'll never get to visit." Jackie Gleason. His star on the Walk of Fame also includes an imprint of his cigar. He has three stars, one each for live theater, motion pictures and television. "I'd rather be a failure at something I enjoy than a success at something I hate." When asked how he got the role in Oh, God!, he said, "I was the closest to him in age." He bought a new Cadillac every year until he was ninety-three. He had to quit driving because was too short to see over the steering wheel. "I'm going to stay in show business until I'm the only one left." At 100, he gave his secret for longevity: "Fall in love with what you do for a living." "The happiest people I know are the ones who are still working." "How can I get sick? I've already had everything." "There are many ways to die in bed, but the best way is not alone." "Critics are eunuchs at a gang-bang." "I was brought up to respect my elders and now I don't have to respect ANYBODY." "At my age, the only thing waiting for me in my dressing room is a bowl of soup." COD: Heart attack. He is buried in a dark blue suit, with a light blue shirt and red tie. Included in the casket are three cigars, his toupee, a watch given to him by Gracie, his wedding ring, keys and wallet with ten $100 bills, a $5 bill and three $1 dollar bills because, as Gracie said, "In case he wanted to play bridge." His epitaph says: "Gracie Allen (1902 -1964) & George Burns (1896 - 1996) - Together Again." Gracie's date of birth is incorrect on her epitaph but that was not known until the year 2000. While a great deal of his notoriety comes from reaching age 100, his wife Gracie was actually six months older than he was. He was the author of ten bestselling books: 1. I Love Her, That's Why, 1955, 2. Living It Up: or, They Still Love Me In Altoona, 1976, 3. The Third Time Around, 1980, 4. How to Live to Be 100--Or More--The Ultimate Diet, Sex and Exercise Book, 1983, 5. Dr. Burns Prescription for Happiness: Buy Two Books and Call Me in the Morning, 1984, 6. Dear George, 1985, 7. Gracie: A Love Story, 1988, 8. All My Best Friends, 1889, 9. Wisdom of the 90's, 1991, 10: 100 Years 100 Stories, 1996.

Francis X. Bushman (Francis Xavier Bushman)

b. 10 Jan 1883, d. 23 Aug 1966, = 83 yrs, 7 mos, 13 days. Made 400+ movies. Married 4 times.

BKF: Playing the lead role of Messala, the villain in the original Ben-Hur in 1925. NN: The King of the Movies, The King of Photoplay, The Handsomest Man in the World. He was a male model (sometimes nude) who modeled for the Statue of Nathan Hale at Harvard and of Lord Baltimore in Baltimore. Got into the movie business by way of winning a 'most handsome man' competition. He was the first screen matinee idol. He was the most popular leading man in American cinema from 1914 to 1917. He was the first male pin-up star when he wore Tarzan-type pants in one of his movies. He and Beverly Bayne were the screen's first love duo, in 1912's The House of Pride. When he divorced his wife to marry Beverly Bayne in 1918, theater owners refused to show his movies. He said he had received more than 17,000 marriage proposals from female fans. His son committed suicide in 1957. COD: Heart attack while in his kitchen, which caused him to be further injured. He was pronounced dead by the ambulance crew. Buried in Glendale, California. Died 40 years to the day after Rudolf Valentino.

James Cagney (James Francis Cagney, Jr.)

b. 17 July 1899, d. 30 Mar 1986, = 86 yrs, 8 mos, 13 days. Made 70+ movies. Married 1 time.

BKF: Playing tough-guy mobsters. He was born on 17 July 1899 but his studio changed it to 1904. 5' 5". Bellhop, ticket clerk, waiter, bellhop, doorkeeper, copy boy for The New York Sun, brokerage house runner. Amateur boxer, runner-up for the New York State Lightweight Title. He wanted to be a professional boxer but his mother objected, saying, "If you want to become a professional fighter, then your first fight will have to be against me." His two brothers were doctors. His Vaudeville job required him to dress as a chorus girl in a play called Every Sailor. He was not embarrassed at all, saying, "For there I am not myself. I am not that fellow, Jim Cagney, at all. I certainly lost all consciousness of him when I put on skirts, wig, paint, powder, feathers and spangles." Majored in Art at Columbia University but did not graduate. His father died in the worldwide Influenza Epidemic of 1918. Played semi-pro baseball for the Yorkville Nut Club. He was discovered by Al Jolson. Made $400 per week in his first contract with Warner Bros. in 1930. When he made the mob movie Little Caesar in 1930, the Chicago mob was so worried about how the movie was going to affect them they sent spies to Hollywood to find out how the movie was going. Many of them ended up working as extras on the movie. He was making $12,500 per week by 1939. Made only one film with

Edward G. Robinson, Smart Money in 1931. In Public Enemy, 1931, those bullets hitting the wall behind him are real bullets being fired by a professional sharpshooter. He was never paid for his roles in The Seven Little Foys. He sued Warner Bros. for breach of contract in 1935 and won. In Angels With Dirty Faces, 1938, he fired his gun more than 100 times without reloading it, which got him hundreds of write-in complaints from around the country. As a result, when he made The Oklahoma Kid in 1940, reloading his gun was made an obvious part of the movie. Made only one film with George Raft, Each Dawn I Die, 1939. He played a boxer in City For Conquest in 1940, losing weight from 185 to 135 pounds to get the role. He felt that the studio had butchered the film so badly that he wrote a letter of apology to the author of the novel the movie was based on. Had the 2nd-highest salary in Hollywood in 1941, earning only slightly less than MGM studio head Louis B. Meyer. He was the first actor to win the Best Actor Oscar for a musical role, Yankee Doodle Dandy, in 1942. He adamantly refused to made the movie at first, had to be talked into it personally by President Roosevelt, and the after he won the Oscar for it, he said it was his favorite role. Rosemary de Camp played his mother even though she was fourteen years younger than he was. Accepting his Oscar, he said, "I've always maintained that in this business, you're only as good as the other fellow thinks you are. It's nice to know that you people thought I did a good job." He never said, "You dirty rat!" in any of his movies. He did say, "You dirty, double-crossing rat," and "You dirty, yellow-bellied rat." He was SAG President from 1942-1944. He was the owner of the Santa Barbara Pier in the 1940's. Went to England with the USO in 1944. Said he was supposed "to dance a few jigs, sing a few songs, say hello to the boys and that's all." During the war, the Mafia threatened to kill him for resisting their move into Hollywood. Upon hearing this, his friend George Raft made a phone call and got the hit called off. He is the person who discovered and single-handedly convinced WW2 war hero Audie Murphy to go into acting. He earned a black belt in Judo. The only movie he directed was Shortcut to Hell, in 1957. He said, "We shot it in twenty days, and that was long enough for me. I find directing a bore, I have no desire to tell other people their business." "I'm just a song-and-dance man." His secret to acting was: Hated method acting, he said, "You just go out and do it." "You walk in, plant yourself squarely on both feet, look the other fella in the eye, and tell the truth." "When I drove through that studio gate and the thrill was gone, I knew it was time to quit." On deciding to retire in the 1960's. He turned down an offer to be in The Godfather II. He bred cattle and horses on a 500 acre ranch in New York. "He was maybe the greatest actor who ever appeared in front of a camera." Orson Welles. "He's a professional against-er." "I never said, 'you dirty rat.' What I said was 'Judy, Judy, Judy,' a joking reference to Cary Grant. "I came out here (to Hollywood) on a three week guarantee, and I stayed, to my absolute amazement, for thirty-one years." His #1 Rule for acting was: "Never Relax!" He tap danced for one hour every morning to stay in shape. His favorite activities in retirement were horseback riding, dancing and painting, until he had a stroke in 1977. His favorite flower was the morning glory. He signed and sold only one painting during his lifetime--to Johnny Carson. His last movie was Terrible Joe Moran in 1984. Unable to speak perfectly due to a series of strokes, his voice was dubbed by impressionist Rich Little. He was awarded the AFI Lifetime Achievement Award in 1974, which was likely the most-attended event of its kind. A columnist said that a bomb in the dining room would have ended the movie industry. He was a Kennedy Center Honoree in 1980. Hasty Pudding Man of the Year in 1982. He was awarded the US Medal of Freedom in 1984 by his former actor friend, President Ronald Reagan. COD: Heart attack at home, died on Easter Sunday. President Reagan also delivered his eulogy. Buried in Hawthorne, New York. Autobiography: Cagney by Cagney, 1976. His likeness was on a US Postal Service 33-cent stamp in 1999.

Eddie Cantor (Edward Israel Iskowitz)

b. 21 Sep 1892, d. 10 Oct 1964, = 72 yrs, 19 days. Made 27 movies. Married 1 time.

NN: Banjo Eyes, The Apostle of Pep. Orphaned at age two. One of the richest men in show business, he lost everything in the 1929 stock market crash. He then wrote a humorous account about it called Caught Short. He received 3,200 write-in votes for President in 1928. He turned down the role that went to Al Jolson in The Jazz Singer. Created the March of Dimes. In 1938 he asked his radio listeners to send a dime to the nation's most well known polio victim, President Franklin Roosevelt. The White House received 2,680,000 dimes. He is credited with being the first person to invent and create the concept of a live radio audience. His theme songs were If You Knew Susie and One Hour With You. He always ate corn flakes for dinner, even in high-class restaurants. SAG President 1933-1935. In Ali Baba Goes to Town, he appeared in drag as a woman. In 1944, he was the first victim of live television censorship. The studio cut out certain lines and blurred his face when he sang We're Havin' a Baby, My Baby and Me. Emcee of The $64,000 Question, 1949-1950. He was the only person who was ever told in advance that he was going to be the subject on This Is Your Life. He had just had a heart attack and they didn't want to kill him with the surprise. "It takes twenty years to make an overnight success." On The Eddie Cantor Story, which was about his life, he said, "If that's my life, I didn't live." "Marriage is an attempt to solve problems together which you didn't have when you were on your own." "A wedding is a funeral where you smell your own flowers." "All women are natural born espionage agents." Received the US Service Medal from President Johnson in 1964. He is the father-in-law of Hogan's Heroes actor Robert Clary, who played Corporal Louis LeBeau. COD: Heart attack. Buried in Culver City, California. Autobiography: My Life Is In Your Hands, 1928.

Yakima Canutt (Enos Edward Canutt)

b. 29 Nov 1895, d. 24 May 1986, = 90 yrs, 5 mos, 25 days. Acted in 185 movies, stuntman in 276 movies. Married 2 times.

BKF: He and Busby Berkeley were born on the same day. Stuntman for every major actor for forty years, directing the stunts in Ben-Hur, 1959. Dropped out of elementary school. Got his nickname from the Yakima River Valley in Washington. Broke a wild bronco at age eleven. Broke horses for the French government at the beginning of WW1. Enlisted in the US Navy in 1918, they gave him a 30 day leave to defend his rodeo title. Discovered by Tom Mix while visiting Hollywood. Member of the Stuntmen's Hall of Fame. First stuntman to be awarded an Oscar, he was awarded an Honorary Academy Award for "developing safety devices to protect all stunt men everywhere," in 1966. COD: Heart attack while a hospital patient. Cremated, ashes scattered at Valhalla Memorial Park in Hollywood.

Frank Capra (Francesco Rosario Capra)

b. 18 May 1897, d. 3 Sep 1991, = 94 yrs, 3 mos, 16 day. Directed 58 movies, acted in 2 movies. Married 2 times.

NN: America's Dream Personified. BKF: Directing It Happened One Night, Mr. Smith Goes to Washington and It's a Wonderful Life. Youngest of seven children born in Italy. Sold newspapers, waiter. Graduated from the California Institute of Technology with a degree in Chemical Engineering. WW1: US Army 2nd Lieutenant teaching mathematics to artillerymen at Fort Point, San Francisco. Became a naturalized citizen in 1920. Discharged due to contracting the Spanish Flu. Moved to Hollywood and became a prop master, film cutter and assistant director. He invented and got a patent for a for a guidance system to release bombs by radio control in 1939. WW2: Resigned as President of the Screen Actors Guild to accept a commission as a Major in the US Army Signal Corps at the beginning of the war. Promoted to Colonel and was awarded the Legion of Merit and the Distinguished Service Medal. He was the first person to win an Oscar for directing and for producing, It's a Wonderful Life in 1946. "A hunch is creativity trying to tell you something." "The only rule in filmmaking is that there are no rules." "There are no rules in filmmaking. Only sins. And the cardinal sin is dullness." "My advice to young filmmakers is this: Don't follow trends. Start them!" "I made some mistakes in drama. I thought drama was when the actors cried, but drama is when the audience cries." "My films must let every man, woman and child know that God loves them, that I love them, and that peace and salvation will become a reality only when they all learn to love each other." His hobby was writing songs, playing the guitar and collecting rare books. His book collection sold for $68,000 in 1949. May 12, 1962 was 'Frank Capra Day' in Los Angeles. 1982 AFI Lifetime Achievement Award. COD: Heart failure after a series of strokes. Buried in Coachella, California. Autobiography: The Name Above the Title, 1971. It is considered to be one of the greatest book ever written about Hollywood.

Harry Carey, Sr. (Harry Christopher Carabina)

b. 16 Jan 1878, d. 21 Sep 1947, = 69 yrs, 8 mos, 5 days. Made 267 movies. Married 2, possibly 3 times.

BKF: Being one of the first stars of the Western genre and playing the President of the Senate in Mr. Smith Goes to Washington, 1939. Son of New York judge. Studied law and wrote several plays. Cowboy, railway superintendent, author, lawyer, playwright. Screen debut at age 30 in several silent films. Owned a 1,000 acre ranch North of Los Angeles, which is now Tesoro Adobe Historic Park. Member of the Cowboy Hall of Fame, 1976. COD: Lung cancer, emphysema and coronary thrombosis from a lifetime of heavy cigar smoking.

Lon Chaney, Sr. (Leonidas Frank Chaney)

b. 1 Apr 1883, d. 26 Aug 1930, = 47 yrs, 4 mos, 25 days. Made 157 movies, 100 are considered to be lost. Married 2 times.

NN: The Master of Makeup, The Man of a Thousand Faces. BKF: Playing The Hunchback of Notre Dame, 1923, and The Phantom of the Opera, 1925. Son of deaf-mute parents, which made him an expert at pantomime. Grandson of a US Congressman from Ohio. It took over four hours to put on his makeup for The Hunchback of Notre Dame. He wrote the original article on theater makeup for the Encyclopedia Britannica. The United States Marine Corps made him their first honorary member from the film industry in 1926. He was an extremely private recluse, saying, "Between pictures, there is no Lon Chaney," and "My whole career has been devoted to keeping people from knowing me." A popular joke at the height of his popularity was, "Don't step on it; it might be Lon Chaney." "Find something no one else can or will do--the secret in movies lies in being different from anyone else." On why he would never do a talkie: "I have a thousand faces but only one voice." Did make one talkie, The Unholy Tree, 1930. In that movie he was the voice of the ventriloquist, the old woman, a parrot, the dummy and the girl. Joan Crawford said, "I learned more about acting from watching Lon Chaney work than from anyone else in my career. It was then I became aware for the first time of the difference between standing in front of a camera, and acting." "I wanted to remind people that the lowest types of humanity may have within them the capacity for supreme self-sacrifice." COD: While filming Thunder in 1929, he choked on a cornflake which was being used to simulate snow. This caused an infection which caused a throat hemorrhage, exacerbated by bronchial cancer. Buried in Glendale, California, his crypt is unmarked.

Charlie Chaplin (Charles Spencer Chaplin)

b. 16 Apr 1889, d. 25 Dec 1977, = 88 yrs, 8 mos, 9 days. Acted in 87 movies. Directed 88 movies. Married 4 times. Had 11 children, the last one at age 73.

BKF: Being the creator of The Tramp and being one of the founding fathers of the Hollywood motion picture industry. NN: The Tramp, The One Genius Created by the Cinema. 5' 4". Quit school to join a troupe of clog dancers. Left-handed. Played a woman in A Busy Life

(1914) and A Woman (1915). Made 35 films in 1915. Earned $1,250 per week in 1915 which jumped to $10,000 week in 1916. Debuted his 'tramp' look in 1914's Kid Auto Races at Venice. He believed that iodine prevented the spread of venereal disease. Accordingly, he painted his penis a bright orange before having sex. Early in his career the following saga occurred: He acted with Lolita Mac Murray when she was six years old. He began an affair with her when she was barely thirteen years old. Because of his wealth and celebrity status, her mother approved. She changed her name to Lolita Grey. When she got pregnant, he offered her $20,000 to marry someone else. Her mother threatened him with a paternity suit and statutory rape charges. He agreed to marry her in Mexico. On the train on the way to Mexico, he encouraged her to throw herself off the train. She refused and they got married in Mexico in 1924. Her mother Nana moved in with the newlyweds and--kept a secret diary of their sex life and pillow talk. She published the diary and it became a best-seller and the basis of several stag films. They got divorced in 1927. Adolph Hitler's mustache was a copy of Charlie Chaplin's mustache in The Little Tramp. Insured his feet for $250,000. The sole of the shoe that he ate in The Gold Rush was actually made of black licorice. His mustache was made of crepe paper. He referred to himself as "The Eighth Wonder of the World" due to the size of his johnson. When he and his girlfriend were seen having sex on the public beaches of Catalina Island, the locals started calling the goats on the Island 'Charlies,' as a tribute to the size of his equipment. When making City Lights, he demanded 342 retakes of the scene where the blind girl sells him a flower. Said the movie he most enjoyed making was The Gold Rush in 1925. He was the first actor to appear on the cover of Time Magazine on 6 July 1925. Played himself in Show People, 1928. Entered a Charlie Chaplin look-alike contest in Monte Carlo. He came in third. He was never an American citizen, although he refused an offer to become one in 1924. The name of his dog in A Dog's Life, 1926, is Scraps. When he Made Modern Times in 1936, it was banned by Mussolini in Italy and by Hitler in Germany as Communist propaganda. When he made The Great Dictator in 1940,

Hitler placed him on his execution list. He made Limelight in 1952 and it won an Oscar for Best Dramatic Score twenty years later in 1972. It was the only competitive Oscar any of his movies ever won. When he went to London in 1952, FBI Director J. Edgar Hoover ordered the INS to not allow him back into the country, alleging that he was a Communist and calling him a 'parlor Boschevik.' He was not; the real reason was that Hoover just didn't like him. He was not allowed back in the US until 1972, when he accepted an Honorary Oscar. He never won a competitive Oscar. He had a telescope in the bedroom of his Los Angeles mansion so he could spy into the bedroom of his neighbor John Barrymore. Hitler banned his movies in Germany because he thought Chaplin looked too much like him. A 1943 trial determined him to be the father of his lover Joan Barry's child, even though a blood test submitted as evidence in court proved he was not. He went on trial in 1944 on charges of sexual misconduct with a minor. He was acquitted because one of the jurors said of him, "As an artist, he could never have sex on his mind." "Hitler is the madman and I'm the comic. Just think--it could have been the other way around." His star on the Hollywood Walk of Fame was either removed or covered up in the early 1950's due to the intense public hostility generated toward him by Senator Joe McCarthy. In the 1950's Winston Churchill said that Chaplin had failed to answer a fan letter from him he had written to him in the 1920's. His reply was, "Think of Churchill even remembering that I had failed to answer him. Me!" He paid the IRS $425,000 in back taxes in 1958. Knighted by Queen Elizabeth in 1975. "All I need to make a comedy is a park, a policeman and a pretty girl." "Movies are a fad. Audiences really want to see live actors on a stage." "In the end, everything is a gag." "The most beautiful form of human life is a very young girl just starting to bloom." He married a 19-year old, an 18-year old and two 16-year old girls. His daughter Geraldine said that she and her other brothers and sisters could never figure out exactly how many wives he had. They never learned the truth until he published his autobiography in 1964. When she learned that all of his wives were young women, she said she was "certainly quite proud of it." He became a father at age 81. "I remain one thing and one thing only, and that is a clown. It places me on a far higher plane than any politician." "In the end, everything is a gag." His last wife was Oona, the daughter of playwright Eugene O'Neill. She became the wealthiest widow in the world when he died, leaving her a net worth of over $100,000,000. Mary Pickford said he was, "That obstinate, suspicious, maddening, and lovable genius of a problem child. His last words were, "Why not, it belongs to Him," after a priest said, "May the Lord have mercy on your soul." His little tramp character was portrayed on a US postage stamp in 1998. COD: Stroke while sleeping. Buried (and reburied) in Switzerland. His corpse was stolen after he was buried in a kidnap-ransom-extortion plot. His body was recovered and reburied under six feet of concrete. The two crooks who kidnapped his coffin were given 5 years hard labor and 18 months suspended sentence. His famous Bowler hat and cane were sold at auction for $151,800 in 1987. The two fake mustaches he wore in The Great Dictator sold for $24,000 and $34,300. The cane he used in Modern Times sold for $91,919. Autobiography: My Autobiography, 1964. His autobiography made no mention of his former wife Lita Gray. When asked about it, his reply was, "I didn't want to say anything unfavorable about the mother of my two sons."

Ruth Chatterton (Same)

b. 24 Dec 1892, d. 24 Nov 1961, = 68 yrs, 11 mos, 0 days. Made 26 movies. Married 3 times.

BKF: Playing Fran Dodsworth in Dodsworth, 1936. Dropped out of school to join the chorus of a stage show. She was so successful on Broadway that she turned down $300,000 to make silent movies. She was discovered by Emil Jannings. Did not make her first movie until age 35. She was a composer and licensed pilot, being a close friend of Amelia Earhart. She opened the National Air Races in Los Angeles in 1936. She was one of the finalists for the role of Scarlett O'Hara in Gone With the Wind. Wrote two novels, Homeward Bourne, which was a best seller in 1950, and the Southern Wild. COD: Cerebral hemorrhage while visiting with friends at home. Cremated, ashes interred in New Rochelle, New York.

Maurice Chevalier (Maurice Auguste Chevalier)

b. 12 Sep 1888, d. 1 Jan 1972, = 83 yrs, 3 mos, 19 days. Made 62 movies. Married 2 times.

NN: The French Lover. Acrobat until an accident forced him to turn to singing and dancing. 5' 10 1/2". He was in the French Army during WW1. He was captured by the Germans and spent 1914-1916 in a POW camp. He learned English from his fellow prisoners. He was released two years before the end of the war due to the secret request of King Alfonso XIII of Spain, the only king of a neutral country who was related to both the British and German Royal families. Entertained American and British soldiers in Paris for the rest of the war. In 1929 his studio ordered him to not take any English lessons so as to preserve his French accent. He entertained Allied troops in Nazi POW camps during WW2 with one show being at the same POW camp he was held in during WW1. In exchange for his performance there, the Nazis released ten French prisoners. For this, and for a meeting with Hermann Goering, he was sentenced to death by the Marquis for alleged collaboration with the enemy. He was later cleared of all charges. His theme song was Louise. 1958 Cecil B. De Mille Award winner. He said he "preferred a successful career to success with women." "If you wait for the perfect moment when all is safe and assured, it may never arrive. Mountains will not be climbed, races won, or lasting happiness achieved." "The cinema is rather like a beautiful woman whom you would court only by telephone." On the occasion of his 65th birthday: "Old age isn't so bad when you consider the alternative." "Many a man has fallen in love with a girl in a light so dim he would not have chosen a suit by it." On why he refused to do screen tests for movies later in his career: "Either people are interested in hiring me or not. I don't audition anymore." "I am too old for women, too old for that extra glass of wine, too old for sports.

All I have left is the audience, but I have found it quite enough." "He was a great artiste but a small human being." Josephine Baker. Last words: "There's fun in the air." COD: Kidney failure. Buried outside Paris, France. Autobiography: I Remember It Well.

Charles Coburn (Charles Douville Coburn)

b. 19 June 1877, d. 30 Aug 1961, = 84 yrs, 2 mos, 11 days. Made 99 movies. Married 2 times.

BKF: Playing the doctor who needlessly amputated Ronald Reagan's legs in Kings Row. Reagan used this as the inspiration for the title of his own autobiography, Where's the Rest of Me? At 18, he married a movie theater owner in Savannah, Georgia. Didn't start acting in movies until age 60. Always wore his trademark monocle, which he actually needed to see. He said, "No point having two window panes when one will do." He did not wear it while eating because, "I once lost one in a bowl of soup." Accepting his Best Supporting Actor Oscar in 1943 at age 76, he said, "Yes, I'll accept the prize. You don't have to urge me. I hope that at the end of another fifty years of service in the theater, your children and your children's children will have enough courage to vote for me again." Always carried pre-autographed cards to meet fan requests. Actress Piper Laurie said, "Charles Coburn loved pinching women's bottoms. It for him was like a tic. Every female under one hundred and five had to move fast around him." Has a cameo in Around the World in 80 Days. COD: Heart attack. His Best Supporting Oscar was sold at auction for $170,459 in 2012.

George Cohan (George Michael Cohan)

b. 3 Jul 1873, d. 5 Nov 1942, = 86 yrs, 2mos, 8 days. Acted in 5 movies, wrote the music for hundreds of other movies. Married 2 times.

Child vaudeville performer. Wrote more than 300 songs, including Over There and You're a Grand Old Flag. Won a lawsuit against the

Internal Revenue Service (IRS) in 1930 which allowed him to deduct business and travel expenses even though he didn't have exact, precise entries. This became known as the "Cohan Rule." He was awarded the Congressional Gold Medal for his work during WW1, by President Roosevelt, which made him the first entertainer to earn that medal. "My mother thanks you, my father thanks you, my sister thanks you and I thank you." To acknowledge applause at the end of every show. COD: Abdominal cancer. His funeral was attended by five governors of New York. Buried in the Bronx, New York. Autobiography: Twenty Years on Broadway and the Years It Took To Get There, 1925.

Ronald Colman (Ronald Charles Colman)

b. 9 Feb 1891, d. 19 May 1958, = 67 yrs, 3 mos, 10 days. Made 62 movies. Married 2 times.

BKF: What Encyclopedia Britannica called his "resonant, mellifluous speaking voice with a unique, pleasing timbre." NN: The Greatest Gentleman Hero in the History of Cinema. Born and raised in London, studied at Cambridge to become a barrister, but dropped out due to his father's death. Made several successful movies in England and then tried the stage in the US. When his agent sent his photo to a Hollywood studio, it was returned with the note, "This man will never photograph." #1 Box Office star in 1926, 1927 and 1928. Wounded in France during WW1 by poison gas but was too old for WW2. He appealed and was accepted into the London Scottish Regiment, where he suffered a severe hip injury which gave him a limp, which he tried to hide all of his life. "Fame robbed me of my freedom and shut me up in prison, and because the prison walls are gilded, and the key that locks me in is gold, does not make it any more tolerable." "A man usually falls in love with a women who asks the kinds of questions he is able to answer." Has a cameo in Around the World in 80 Days. COD: Emphysema. Buried in Santa Barbara California. His Best Actor Oscar for A Double Life sold at auction for $174,500 in 1972.

Gladys Cooper (Gladys Constance Cooper)

b. 18 Dec 1888, d. 17 Nov 1971, = 82 yrs, 10 mos, 30 days. Made 75 movies. Married 3 times.

Photographer's model at age 6. She was England's favorite pinup girl of WW1. She played Laurence Olivier's sister in Rebecca, 1940, and his wife in That Hamilton Woman, 1941. Her career spanned seven decades. Last words: If this is what viral pneumonia does to one, I really don't think I shall bother to have it again." She died later that night. COD: Pneumonia. Buried in Oxfordshire, England.

Noel Coward (Noel Peirce Coward)

b. 16 Dec 1899, d. 26 Mar 1973, = 73 yrs, 3 mos, 10 days. Made 30 movies, wrote 132 movie scripts. Never married.

NN: The Master. He explained, "Oh, you know, Jack of all trades, master of none." Wrote more than 300 songs. Named Noel because his birthday was so close to Christmas. He is credited with starting the turtleneck sweater fashion fad in the 1920's. He and Leslie Howard are the only two Hollywood actors that British Intelligence confirms worked for them during WW2. Later learned that his name was in The Black Book, the Nazi list of people to be executed if the Germans ever invaded England. When offered the title role of Dr. No in the 1962 James Bond film, he said, "No, no, no, a thousand times, no." "My advice about acting? Speak clearly, don't bump into people, and, if you must have motivation, think of your pay package on Friday." "I've sometimes thought about marrying and then I've thought again." "Do I believe in God? I can't say No and I can't say Yes. To me it's anybody's guess." "Having to read a footnote resembles having to go downstairs to answer the door while in the midst of making love." Has a cameo in Around the World in 80 Days. Knighted in 1970. He was the first 'tax exile,' a British subject living abroad to avoid the 90% British income tax, to be knighted. Last words: "Good night, my darlings. I'll see you in the morning." COD: Heart failure. Buried in Jamaica. He and Frances Dee died on the same day.

Jane Darwell (Pattie Woodard)

b. b. 15 Oct 1878, d. 13 Oct 1967, = 88 yrs, 11 mos, 28 days. Made 209 movies. Never married.

BKF: Playing Ma Joad in The Grapes of Wrath and the Bird Woman in Mary Poppins. Also played in numerous Shirley Temple films as the housekeeper or grandmother. "I've played Henry Fonda's mother so often that, whenever we run into each other, I call him "Son" and he calls me "Ma," just to save time. COD: Heart attack. Died on Friday the 13th. Buried in Glendale, California.

Marion Davies (Marion Cecelia Douras)

b. 3 Jan 1897, d. 22 Sep 1961, = 64 yrs, 8 mos, 19 days. Made 50 movies. Married 1 time.

BKF: Peg of My Heart, 1934, and being over-managed by William Randolph Hearst. She and actress Pola Negri were born on the same day. Educated in a convent. Lifelong stutterer but managed to not stutter while filming a movie. Captain of her high school championship basketball team. Broadway chorus girl, model and Ziegfeld Follies girl. She was the subject of the first photograph transmitted by wire (fax) in 1925. It was a photo of her receiving a makeup box from Louis B. Mayer The US Secretary of War stopped the granting of the honorary rank of Colonel after she got hers. She was voted the #1 female box office star by theater owners and named "Queen of the Screen" in 1924. She once was able to get President Calvin Coolidge drunk by telling him that the wine he was drinking was fruit juice. Hearst moved her to one of their three homes 250 miles north of San Francisco when Pearl Harbor was attacked. She hated it and called it the Palace Spittoon. It is generally believed that she was married to Hearst. That was not true. He would not divorce his current wife because he said her settlement demands were too high. She never married for the first time until after his death. She inherited 51% of his estate. The mansion she lived in with Hearst was so lavish that George Bernard Shaw said, "This is what God would have built if had had the money." It had a marble-lined swimming pool with lockers for one thousand visitors. Winston Churchill and his son visited in 1929. Hearst disapproved of her drinking habit so she hid her gin in many of the fifty-five bathroom toilet tanks in the mansion. Hearst died in a bedroom that was later occupied by John and Jackie Kennedy while on their honeymoon in 1953. She had an operation on her jawbone in 1956 and twelve days later fell and broke her leg while still in the hospital. Her last public appearance was when she was seated just a few feet away from President Kennedy at his inauguration on 20 January 1961. "With me, it's 5% talent and 95% publicity." "I had a really good time at MGM. I liked it there. I was very fond of Irving (Thalberg) and L.B. Mayer And we had no quarrels, much except that once in a while I'd go up to the front office and say I thought I should be doing something big...like washing elephants." "She has two expressions: joy and indigestion." Dorothy Parker. COD: Stomach cancer and cancer of the jaw. Her estate was worth $20,000,000 at the time of her death. Autobiography: The Times We Had, published posthumously in 1975. She is entombed just feet away from Tyrone Power.

Cecil B. De Mille (Cecil Blount De Mille)

b. 21 Oct 1881, d. 21 Jan 1959, = 77 yrs, 3 mos, 0 days. Produced 88 movies, directed 80 movies, acted in 22 movies. Married 1 time.

BKF: Being the most successful director of all time, including directing The Ten Commandments. It is still the 7th highest-grossing film of all time, when adjusted for inflation. NN: The Shark, The Killer. Wrote his first play at age 15. Stage actor, writer. Directed The Squaw Man in 1913, the first feature-length film and the first film to have credits.

He looked down on actors who would not perform their own stunts; once calling Victor Mature "100 percent yellow" for refusing to do a dangerous stunt. He narrated every film he made from 1940 on. At the personal request of the Secretary of the Air Force, he is the person who designed the cadet uniforms for the opening of the US Air Force Academy in 1954. "My ministry has been to make religious movies and to get more people to read the Bible than anyone else ever has." "Give me any two pages of the Bible and I'll give you a picture." "A picture is made a success not on the set but on the drawing board." "I make pictures for people, not for critics." "I didn't write the Bible and I didn't invent sin." Last words, when asked a week before his death what his future plans were: "Another picture, I imagine..or, perhaps, another world." Last words, in writing: Written at the end of a script of proposed remarks to be made at his funeral, he wrote: "After these words are spoken, what am I?" I am only what I have accomplished. How much good have I spread? For whatever I am after death--a spirit, a soul, a bodiless mind--I shall have to look back and forward, for I have to take with me both." He died later that night. "I learned an awful lot from him by doing the opposite." Howard Hawks. COD: Heart ailment. He and Carl "Alfafa" Switzer died on the same day. Buried in Hollywood, California. During the Apollo 11 moon mission in July 1969, astronaut Buzz Aldrin referred to himself as "Cecil B. De Aldrin," as a reference to DeMille.

Richard Dix (Ernst Carlton Brimmer)

b. 18 Jul 1893, d. 20 Sep 1949, = 56 yrs, 2 mos, 2 days. Made 100 movies. Married 2 times.

BKF: His lead role in Cimarron, 1931 and playing a different character in 7 of the Whistler series of films. His ancestors came to America on the Mayflower. Studied to be a surgeon. Bank clerk. His hobby was raising thousands of chickens and turkeys on his ranch. Earned $250,000 a year during the Depression. His horse's name was Dice.

His son was killed in a logging accident at age 18. COD: Heart attack due to alcoholism.

Marie Dressler (Leila Marie Koerber)

b. 9 Nov 1868, d. 28 July 1934, = 65 yrs, 8 mos, 19 days. Made 30 movies. Married 2 times.

BKF: Playing the Waterfront Hag in Anna Christie, 1930. NN: The Grand Lady of Hollywood and The World's Greatest Actress. She is the earliest-born female Oscar winner. Her father was the last surviving officer of the Crimean War. She was born in Canada. Stage and Vaudeville actress. Star of Tillie's Punctured Romance, which was the first comedy feature movie. WW1: Sold war bonds and entertained the doughboys overseas. She was so popular the soldiers named a cow after her. The cow was killed in action which led to the headline: Marie Dressler: Killed in the Line of Duty. Visited veteran's hospitals after the war. After learning she had cancer in 1931, she made six more movies. Highest-paid actress in Hollywood in 1932-1933. "You're only as good as your last picture." "To know what one has never really tried--that is the only death." "If ants are such busy workers, how come they find the time to go to all the picnics?" "I enjoy reading biographies because I want to know about the people who messed up the world." "Being in the same cast with her was a break for me. She's one trooper I'd never try to steal a scene from. It'd be like trying to carry Italy against Mussolini." Bette Davis. COD: Cancer. Buried in Glendale, California. Worth $310,000 at the time of her death. Autobiography: The Life Story of An Ugly Duckling, 1924, and My Story, 1933.

Margaret Dumont (Daisy Juliette Baker)

b. 20 Oct 1882, d. 6 Mar 1965, = 82 yrs, 4 mos, 14 days. Made 57 movies. Married 1 time.

BKF: 7 movies as the straight woman with the Marx Brothers. NN: The 5th Marx Brother. Born on the same day as Bela Lugosi. Married a millionaire at age 18. She was as bald as a billiard ball. Harpo Marx would steal her wigs while filming movies with her. She had everyone convinced that she never really understood the jokes in the Mars Brothers movies, but she was just staying in character, which she thought was a joke in itself. COD: Heart attack. Cremated, ashes interred in Los Angeles, California.

Irene Dunne (Irene Marie Dunn)

b. 20 Dec 1898, d. 4 Sep 1990, = 91 yrs, 8 mos, 15 days. Made 50 movies. Married 1 time.

BKF: I Remember Mama, 1948. NN: Lady Irene, The First Lady of Hollywood and The Female Cary Grant. Her father was a dentist. When he became ill later in life she turned down roles to stay home and take care of him. This led to an involuntary retirement. No children of her own, had one adopted child. Added the e to her surname. Earned a diploma to teach art. Wanted to be an opera singer but failed the audition. Made her first movie at age 32. Her contract stipulated that she did not have to work before 10am. She christened the Liberty Ship S.S. Carole Lombard in 1944. Bought the 5 millionth ticket at Radio City Music Hall in 1934. Shot a hole in one at golf. US Representative to the United Nations, she addressed the General Assembly on 4 October 1957. 5 Oscar nominations, no wins. Popularly recognized as "The Best Actress to Never Win an Oscar." Present at the opening of Disneyland in 1955, she christened the Mark Twain River Boat. She was the first female board member of Technicolor Corporation. Member of The Knights of Malta. 1985 Kennedy Center Honoree. "I lack the terrifying ambition of some other actresses. I drifted into acting and drifted out. Acting is not everything. Living is." "I don't know why the public took a liking to me so fast. Popularity is a curious thing. The public responds to a dimple, a smile, a giggle, a hairstyle, an attitude. Acting talent has less to do with it than personality." "You can really call Irene Dunne The First Lady of Hollywood, because he's the first real *lady* Hollywood has ever seen." Leo Carey. COD: Natural causes. Buried in East Los Angeles.

Jimmy Durante (James Francis Durante)

b. 10 Feb 1893, d. 29 Jan 1980, = 86 yrs, 11 mos, 19 days. Made 48 movies, sang the soundtrack in 72 movies. Married 2 times.

BKF: His gravelly voice. NN: Schnozzola. He and tennis champion Bill Tilden were born on the same day. His nose measured 2 5/8th inch from head to tip and was insured by Lloyds of London for $140,000. Dropped out of the 7th grade to become a ragtime pianist. He was the piano player at the Coney Island Saloon while Eddie Cantor was the singer and waiter during WW1. They were both unknown at the time. He made $25 a week playing the piano. His first singing partner was his cousin, who was also named Jimmy Durante. Once boxed as Kid Salerno, his record was 0-1. His theme song was Inka Dinka Doo. He was the first white bandleader to have black musicians in his live, touring band, as early as 1918. His first wife died on Valentine's Day, 1943. He didn't remarry until 1960, when he married the girl who had been the hatcheck girl at the Copacabana in 1943. She was 28 years younger than he. They adopted a baby girl and, years later, the adoption was challenged on the grounds that he was too old to care for a child. The judge dismissed the case, saying, "I've heard this man sing Young at Heart." Catchphrase was, "Everybody wants to get into the act!" His other catchphrase was, "Goodnight, Mrs. Calabash, wherever you are." After his death it was revealed that he was referring to a restaurant owner in Calabash, North Carolina. Jimmy and his party often ate there and one day early in his career he told her, "One day, I'm going to make you famous." His other catchphrases were, "Stop da music," and "Dese are de conditions that prevail." While on a war bond tour with Marlene Dietrich during WW2, they promised to "wash all the windows in your house free of charge" to anyone who bought a war bond. She later said, "We did exactly what Jimmy had promised. I've still got a sore back to prove it." In 1942, US soldiers voted June Allyson the person they would like most to live next door to. Jimmy came in in second place. His sidekick on his radio show from 1943 to 1948 was Gary Moore. He was present at the party where Marilyn Monroe famously sang "Happy Birthday To You, Mr. President" to President Kennedy in 1962. Performing with Bob Hope, who had a pretty big nose himself, he said, "When it comes to noses, you're a retailer. I'm a wholesaler!" "Be nice to people on your way up because you meet them on your way down." "I hate music--especially when it's played." "I like to make people laugh. Dey like me. What more could I want?" "There's a million good lookin' guys in the world, but I'm a novelty." "My wife has a slight impediment in her speech. Every now and then she stops to breath." "Why doesn't everybody leave everybody else the hell alone?" Did commercials for Kellogg's Frosted Flakes cereal and another commercial for the Volkswagen Beetle. His line was the new Beetle had "plenty of breathin' room...for de old schnozzola!" His last on screen appearance was in It's a Mad, Mad, Mad, Mad World, 1963. He gave away most of his multi-million dollar estate to charity. He also raised more than $20,000,000 for handicapped and abused children. Suffered a stroke in 1972. COD: Pneumonia. Buried in Culver City, California.

Jeanne Eagles (Eugenia Eagles)

b. 26 Jun 1890, d. 3 Oct 1929, = 39 yrs, 3 mos, 7 days. Made 12 movies. Married 2 times.

Dropped out of grade school at age 11. Department store clerk. Dancer, Broadway stage performer. Ziegfeld Girl. Had an affair with Arthur Fiedler, who was later the conductor of the Boston "Pops" concerts. He said she was the one great love of his life and kept an autographed picture of her on his desk until he died. Died right before the 1928-29 Academy Awards. She was the first person posthumously nominated for Best Actress or Best Supporting Actress, for The Letter, 1928-29. It was the first posthumous nomination for any actor, male or female. "Jeanne Eagles was the most beautiful person I ever saw and if you ever saw her, she was the most beautiful person YOU ever saw." Ruth Gordon. "I am the greatest actress in the world and the greatest failure. And nobody gives a damn." She went into convulsions while in a hospital waiting room and died shortly thereafter. COD: Alcoholic psychosis, heroin and an unintended accumulation of heroin and choral hydrate in her organs. Buried in Kansas City, Kansas. Worth $52,000 at the time of her death.

Douglas Fairbanks, Sr. (Douglas Elton Thomas Ullman)

b. 23 May 1883, d. 12 Dec 1939, = 56 yrs, 6 mos, 19 days. Made 51 movies. Married 3 times.

BKF: Swashbuckling roles such a Robin Hood and The Mark of Zorro. NN: The King of Hollywood, Everybody's Hero and Jumping Jack, due to his fondness for exercise while on the set. Attended Denver, Colorado East High School and was expelled for cutting the wires on the school's piano. Traveling stage actor. A review of a play he was in in 1900 said: "The supporting company was bad, but worst of all was Douglas Fairbanks as Laertes." First appeared on Broadway in 1902. His father was a founding member of the US Law Association, which later became the American Bar Association. Graduate of the Colorado School of Mines. Walked across Cuba in 1908. WW1: Toured the US by train with Charlie Chaplin, selling war bonds. Made $2,000 per week in 1915 which jumped to $10,000 per week in 1916. Had a peak in Yosemite National Park named for him in 1917. He was the first movie star to live in the newly incorporated town of Beverly Hills. He once seriously suggested that Hollywood be encircled by a wall to keep it exclusive. Co-founded United Artists in 1919 with Charlie Chaplin, D.W. Griffith, and Mary Pickford. The first time searchlights were used to advertise the premier of a movie was for his movie Robin Hood in 1922. While filming Robin Hood he was sued for $500 for accidentally shooting a tailor on the set in the rear end with a bow and arrow. His defense was that it accidentally went off while he was cleaning it. He and his wife Mary Pickford met Mussolini in Italy in 1926. Fairbanks told him, "I have seen you in the movies, but I like you better in real life." He was the first movie action hero, in The Black Pirate, 1926. He and his wife made only one movie together, The Taming of the Shrew, in 1929. They were Hollywood's first celebrity couple. He was the presenter at the first Academy Award ceremony in 1927, held at the Hollywood Roosevelt Hotel and attended by 200 people. He handed out all of the Oscars in 4 minutes and 27 seconds. He usually requested that his name be listed last in the credits of his movies. His physique was used as the model for the creation of Clark Kent and Superman in the Superman comic books. He and wife Mary Pickford never served alcoholic drinks at Pickfair but made an exception when they entertained a Duke and Duchess. "The best actors are children and animals." Signed his will three years before he died. His address at the time of this death was 705 Ocean Front, Santa Monica, California. He left half of his $2,000,000 estate to his wife, $600,000 to his son Douglas, Jr., $100,000 to his brother and $50,000 to be distributed among several unnamed friends. Last words: "Never felt better," to his caregiver who asked, "How are you?" He went back to sleep and died at home later that night. COD: Heart attack at home. He was the first person to receive an posthumous Honorary Oscar after his death. The University of California at Santa Barbara sports teams are called The Gauchos in honor of his role in The Thief of Bagdad.

William Farnum (Same)

b. 4 July 1876, d. 5 June 1953, = 76 yrs, 11 mos, 1 day. Made 146 movies. Married 3 times.

BKF: If I Were King, 1921. Younger brother of actor Dustin Farnum. Earned $10,000 per week in 1925. COD: Uremia and cancer. Buried in Glendale, California.

W. C. Fields (William Claude Dukenfield)

b. 29 Jan 1880, d. 25 Dec 1946, = 66 yrs, 10 mos, 26 days. Made 46 movies. Married 1 time.

NN: Whitey, The Boy Wonder and The World's Greatest Juggler (he is in The Juggling Hall of Fame). BKF: Movies with Mae West, a fondness for alcohol and a hatred of children. Oldest of five children. Worked in a clothing store and an oyster house. Was a stutterer but overcame it as he got older. Worked as a professional drowning victim, pretending to drown in the Atlantic Ocean so the lifeguard would save him. This would draw a crowd and increase business for their beachside concession stand. Billed as "The Distinguished Comedian" at age 19. He was one of the most popular jugglers and vaudeville performers in the year 1900, as well as being a circus elephant attendant. Earned $1,000 per week in 1914 for performing only two shows a week. Slept outdoors every day from age 11 to 15. Left-handed. Never won an Oscar. Worked for the Ziegfeld Follies in 1915. His first movie was Pool Sharks, made in England in 1915. First used the term 'My little Chickadee' in the 1931 film If I Had a Million. He was the first choice to play the Wizard of Oz, but turned it down. His screenwriting pen names were Charles Bogle, Mahatma Kane Jeeves and Otis Criblecoblis. When making a movie, he demanded total script approval, and he got paid handsomely for reviewing scripts. Accordingly, he would mail several scripts to himself that he had written under pen names and finally approved of one when he had collected enough money. Bragged that he was a 'reformed teetotaler.' His contract stipulated that his $5,000 per week salary be paid to him as $2,500 on Monday and $2,500 on Wednesday. Often jokingly referred to his non-existent son, Chester Fields. While on the set he was always sour, unapproachable and always ate alone. Starting in the mid-1930's he kept his money spread out in over 700 different banks throughout North America under fictitious names so he could have access to his money wherever he went. He even put $50,000 in a German bank "in case that little bastard (Hitler) wins." Most of the money is still there, drawing interest, and cannot be withdrawn because no one knows the fictitious names or account numbers. Kept his library in his bathroom. He spiked his co-star Baby Le Roy's milk with gin, causing filming to be stopped for the day. Paid $100,000 to make You Can't Cheat an Honest Man, 1939. Played himself in Never Give a Sucker An Even Break, 1941. He considered it to be his best movie. In 1941 Anthony Quinn, his wife Katherine De Mille and their three-year old son were visiting her father Cecil B. De Mille. The child wondered off and drowned in Fields' backyard lily pond. He had it filled in and quickly sold the house. Both men were so distraught that they could not attend the funeral and they never spoke of it again. Drank two quarts of gin per day. Spent a year in a sanitarium recovering from pneumonia and tuberculosis caused by drinking. When his landlord raised his rent in 1946, he just checked himself back into the sanitarium. He once thought his girlfriend was cheating on him, so he hired a detective to find out. She married the detective. "Never give a sucker an even break." "When life hands you lemons, make whiskey sours." "A woman drove me to drink and I never had the courtesy to thank her." "Women are like elephants. I like to look at 'em, but I wouldn't want to own one." "I believe in the tying the marriage knot, as long as it's around the woman's neck." "I was married once, in San Francisco. Then the great earthquake destroyed the marriage certificate--which proves that earthquakes aren't all bad." "I am free of all prejudices. I hate everyone equally." "I never vote for anyone; I always vote against." "Horse sense is good judgment, which keeps horses from betting on people." "I drink, therefore I am." "I never drink anything stronger than gin before breakfast." "I never met a kid I liked." "There's no such thing as a tough child. If you parboil them first for seven hours, they always come out tender." "Children should neither be seen nor heard from... ever again." "I always keep a flask of whiskey on hand in case I see a snake....which I also keep on hand." "A thing worth having is a thing worth cheating for." "A rich man is nothing but a poor man with money." He actually did not hate children, and he never famously said, "Any man who hates children and dogs can't be all bad." That line was said about him at a 1939 testimonial dinner. His New York City home was sold and razed in 1980 to make room for a children's nursery. In his autobiography he said the only type of person he really hated was singers. "Never work with kids or animals. They'll steal your best scene with their back to the camera." "Ah, the patter of little feet. There's nothing like having a midget for a butler." "Some things are better than sex, and some are worse, but there's nothing exactly like it." "After two days in the hospital I took a turn for the nurse." "Somebody left the cork out of my lunch." "Once on a trek through Afghanistan, we lost our corkscrew...and were compelled to live on food and water for several days." "Say anything about me except that I drink water." "Start every day off with a smile and get it over with. "I've never struck a woman in my life, not even my own mother." "The cost of living has gone up another dollar a quart." "I certainly don't drink all the time. I have to sleep, you know." "I've been on a diet for two weeks and all I've lost is two weeks." In an interview right before he died, he was asked, "If you had your life to live over, Mr. Fields, what would you change?" His answer was, "You know, I'd like to see how I would have gone without liquor." His last performance months before he died was an album recording of "The Day I Drank a Glass of Water." His codeword for going out to drink was, "I think I'll go out and milk the elk." He was once caught reading the Bible on his deathbed by his surprised friends. He explained, "I'm looking for a loophole." "There's no one in the world quite like Bill--thank God." Mae West. Last words: to his lifelong girlfriend: "God damn the whole friggin' world and everyone in it but you, Carlotta." He once suggested he'd like his epitaph to be "Here lies W.C. Fields. I would rather be living in Philadelphia." He does not have an epitaph because he was cremated. He never said, "On the whole, I'd rather be in Philadelphia," which is a line that first appeared in a Vanity Fair magazine in the 1920's. It wasn't attributed to him until after his death. COD: Stomach hemorrhage. He died on Christmas Day, a holiday he hated. Last words: "Merry Christmas to all my friends except two." He put his fingertips to his lips, smiled at his nurse and then died. His heirs were able to find $1,300,000 in assets when he died. His will stated that some of his money be used to establish a "W.C. Fields College for Orphan White Boys and Girls, where no religion of any sort is to be preached." Cremated, his ashes are interred at Forest Lawn Cemetery in Glendale, California. Signed his will three years before he died. His home address was 2015 De Mille Drive, Los Angeles, California. Worth about $800,000 when he died, he directed that he be cremated and be buried in an inexpensive coffin. He left a monthly stipend and his residual income to one brother and one sister and only $500 each to one other brother and sister. His wife, who he had married in 1900 and never divorced, contested the will and won. His likeness was on the cover of the Beatles' Lonely Hearts Club Band album, 1967. He was on a US postage stamp in 1980, to commemorate his 100th birthday. A medical condition called the "W.C. Fields syndrome" is named after him. It describes the rosacea (redness) of the nose due to alcohol consumption. One-third of the movies he made have been lost to history.

Barry Fitzgerald (William Joseph Shields)

b. 10 Mar 1888, d. 14 Jan 1961, = 72 yrs, 10 mos, 4 days. Made 50 movies. Never married.

BKF: Playing the priest in Going My Way, 1944. Attended college in Dublin, Ireland. Worked for the Irish Civil Service. Lived with his parents until he was 38. Changed his name when he started getting movies roles because he didn't want his bosses at his full time civil service job to know what he was doing. Only actor to be nominated for Best Actor and Best Supporting Actor for the same role in Going My Way in 1944. The Academy changed its rules after that. The night he won the Best Supporting Actor for Going My Way he accidentally destroyed his Oscar by playing around with it with his 4-iron at home. The Academy replaced it, making him, strictly speaking, the first actor to receive two Oscars for playing the same role. At this time, Oscars were made of plaster because of wartime metal shortages. He faced a vehicular homicide charge for killing an elderly woman in Hollywood in 1944. He was found not guilty at trial. He made seven movies with his actor brother, Arthur Shields. His last film was Broth of a Boy, 1959. "I never wanted to marry; I don't want any woman around. I'm a bachelor and I'm going to stay that way." "A golf course is nothing but a damned pool room moved outdoors." COD: Undisclosed. Died in a Dublin hospital. Eulogized as "The Greatest Comic Actor in the World," by playwright Sean O'Casey.

John Ford (John Martin Feeney)

b. 1 Feb 1894, d. 31 Aug 1973, = 79 yrs, 6 mos, 30 days. Directed 146 movies, acted in 23 movies, produced 43 movies. Married 1 time.

BNF: Directing epic westerns such as Stagecoach The Searchers and The Man Who Shot Liberty Valance. NN: Pappy, Coach, Uncle Jack. Youngest of 13 children. He played a KKK member in the 1915 classic The Birth of a Nation. Had only one good eye due to a hunting accident. Monument Valley in Utah is known as Ford Country, because he filmed so many movies there, beginning with the first one, Stagecoach, in 1939. The original negative prints of Stagecoach were lost until John Wayne discovered in 1970 he had copies in his possession, thus making a rerelease possible. WW2: Captain in the US Navy. Chief of the US Navy's Photographic Unit of the Office of Strategic Services. He was wounded by a Japanese fighter plane during the Battle of Midway. He landed at Normandy Beach on D-Day with the troops and filmed the invasion. He filmed the liberation of Nazi concentration camps across Europe. Awarded the Purple Heart and Legion of Merit for bravery on 17 September 1947. When he filmed My Darling Clementine in 1946, he claimed to have gotten the exact events at the gunfight at the OK Corral directly from the surviving Earps and Clantons themselves. He retired after WW2 but was called back to active duty for the Korean War in 1950. Directed John Wayne in 24 movies. When asked what brought him to Hollywood, he replied, "The train." "I love making pictures but I don't like talking about them." He was the first recipient of the American

Film Institute's Lifetime Achievement Award in 1973. He is the only director to win six Academy Awards and was a no-show for the first four awards. President Nixon personally went to his home in Beverly Hills to present him with the Presidential Medal of Freedom and a promotion to Admiral. The promotion was a temporary promotion that expired at the end of the day, but was nevertheless a genuine, bona fine, legal promotion. Last words: "May I please have a cigar?" COD: Stomach cancer. Buried in Culver City, California. His epitaph says, "Admiral John Ford."

William Frawley (William Clement Frawley)

b. 26 Feb 1887, d. 3 Mar 1966, = 79 yrs, 5 days. Made 134 movies. Married 1 time.

BKF: 180 episodes of playing Fred Mertz on the I Love Lucy Show, 1951 to 1957, 13 episodes of the Lucy-Desi Comedy Hour and 90 episodes as Bub on My Three Sons, 1960 to 1965. Stenographer for the Union Pacific Railroad in Omaha, Nebraska. Cafe singer in Denver, Colorado. He was the first performer to sing My Melancholy Baby, in 1912. It was he, and not Al Jolson, who first sang "My Mammy" in his vaudeville shows. His I Love Lucy contract said he could miss work if the New York Yankees were playing in the World Series. He missed two episodes of the show because he was at the game. He was a heavy drinker. Desi Arnaz saw to it that his contract also said that he'd be fired if he had more than three unexplained absences or showed up for work drunk. He never violated his contract. Desi was the only cast member who wanted him on the show. He complained about having too many lines to memorize at his age and frequently ripped up his scripts. He was paid $350 per week to play Fred Mertz. His on-screen wife, Vivian Vance, was livid and hated the fact that he was chosen to play her husband, because he was so much older than her, by 22 years. She complained frequently, openly and bitterly. When he learned that, he said, "She's one of the finest girls to come out of Kansas, but I often wish she'd go back there." They were offered a chance to have their own Fred and Ethel spin-off but she flatly refused to work with him. When she heard that he had died, she said, "Champagne for everybody!" Lived in the same bachelor apartment for forty years. He died of a massive heart attack while walking down the street after going to a movie in Los Angeles. He collapsed dead on the sidewalk only about 800 yards from his star on the Hollywood Walk of Fame. Nominated for an Emmy five times for I Love Lucy, with no wins. COD: Prostate cancer, heart attack. Buried in Mission Hills, CA. Worth $92,000 when he died, but his heirs have received millions in residuals for I Love Lucy.

Joe Frisco (Louis Wilson Joseph)

b. 4 Nov 1889, d. 12 Feb 1958, = 68 yrs, 3 mos, 8 days. Made 12 movies. It is not known if he ever married.

BKF: His trademark dance, which can be seen in Atlantic City, 1944. Vaudeville performer, dancer, singer, comedian. A stutterer, which he used to his comedic advantage. Illiterate. Always broke, his friend Bing Crosby gave him money. Once, when coming back to his hotel after a performance, the clerk (enforcing the 'blue laws' in existence at that time) disapprovingly told him, "Mr. Frisco, we understand you have a young lady in your room. His reply was, "T-t-t-then send up another G-g-g-gideon B-b-bible, please." "Hollywood is the only place where you can wake up in the morning and hear the birds coughing in the trees." COD: Cancer.

Mary Fuller (Mary Claire Fuller)

b. 5 Oct 1888, d. 9 Dec 1973, = 85 yrs, 1 mo, 26 days. Made 226 movies. Never married.

School teacher in Illinois. Author of eight screenplays that were made into movies. She was the star of the first serial, What Happened to Mary, in 1912. Was as popular as Mary Pickford in 1914. When her studio contract expired in 1917, she disappeared from the public view for decades. After a second nervous breakdown, she was a patient at Washington D.C.'s St. Elizabeth hospital for 26 years. COD: Unknown. No known relatives. Buried in Congressional Cemetery, Washington, D.C.

Hoot Gibson (Edmund Richard Gibson)

b. 6 Aug 1892, d. 23 Aug 1962, = 70 yrs, 17 days. Made 224 movies. Married 4 times.

NN: Hoot, and The Flying Cowboy. Got his nicknames from being an owl hunter in Nebraska and having a private pilot's license. He was a rodeo champion and accomplished horseback rider. His horse was a palomino named Goldie and he later had a horse named Mutt. He was the "World's All Around Champion Cowboy" at age 20. Got his big break when the star he was understudy for was hurt in an automobile accident. WW1: Sergeant in the US Army Tank Corps. Returned to movies after the war and his career took off with the help of fellow actor Tom Mix. He was injured when his plane crashed during the National Air Races in 1933. He was a greeter at a Las Vegas casino in the 1950's. He married Helen Gibson in 1913. They divorced and he married a different woman named Helen Gibson in 1922. Toured with the circus 1938-39 and then retired from acting to become a real estate investor. "I hired out to be an Indian in the morning and then turned cowboy and chased myself all afternoon. They paid me five dollars a day and two-fifty extra to fall off a horse. Make it ten dollars and I'll let the horse kick me to death." Died in the Motion Picture County House and Hospital in Woodland, Hills, California. Member of the Cowboy Hall of Fame, 1979. COD: Cancer. Buried in Inglewood, California. Earned over $6,000,000 during his life but died broke.

John Gilbert (John Cecil Pringle)

b. 10 July 1899, d. 9 Jan 1936, = 36 yrs, 5 mos, 30 days. Made 99 movies. Married 4 times.

BKF: The Big Parade, 1925. NN: The Perfect Lover and The Greatest Screen Lover (after the death of Valentino). As a teenager, he said he was "hungry enough to eat out of garbage cans." WW1: Tried to enlist in the US Navy was couldn't pass the physical. Rejected by the US Army Air Corps on educational grounds. Then he was drafted into the US Army on 11 November, 1918, the day the war ended. He was sent home the next day with an honorable discharge. He was Hollywood's highest paid actor in 1927, earning $10,000 per week. He was engaged to marry Greta Garbo in 1927, but she left him standing at the altar. His career faltered right after that because audiences laughed at his high-pitched voice, preventing him from making the transition to talkies. His 1929 MGM contract gave him $250,000 per picture at the rate of two pictures per year for your years. Marlene Dietrich attended his funeral. She walked up to the coffin and then fainted, collapsing on the floor in a very dramatic fashion. Being his former lover, she bought his bed sheets for $700 at auction. COD: Heart attack due to alcoholism. Cremated, ashes interred in Glendale, California. Worth $363,494 at the time of his death. Elton John is the current owner of his former mansion in Hollywood.

Lillian Gish (Lillian Diana Gish)

b. 14 Oct 1893, d. 27 Feb 1993, = 99 yrs, 4 mos, 13 days. Made 121 movies. Never married.

NN: The 1st Lady of American Cinema. BKF: Being the greatest actress of the silent era and her 75-year acting career. She was a childhood friend of Gladys Smith, who later became Mary Pickford. Her great-great grandfather came to America in 1733. She was a model, stage actor and related to President Zachary Taylor. She spoke fluent French,

German and Italian. She was the star of the first gangster movie in 1912, The Musketeers of Pig Alley, a 17 minute short. She contracted the flu during the Great Influenza Pandemic of 1918 but obviously survived. She and her actress sister looked so much alike that director D.W. Griffith had them wear a blue and red ribbon in their hair so he could tell them apart. She was an excellent sharpshooter. She was insured for $1,000,000 while making Way Down East in 1920. Made $5,000 per week in 1923. She was 93 years old when she made The Whales of August in 1987. She had the longest acting career of any actress--75 years from 1912 to 1987. Her last words on stage were, "Good night," in 1992. Claimed she went her entire life without ever having her hair cut. She left her $15,000,000 estate to her actress friend Helen Hayes, who survived her by only one month. "I have loved many men, but have never been in love with any of them. I never had the time." "Lionel Barrymore played my grandfather, later my father and finally my husband. If he'd lived, I'm sure I would have played his mother. That's the way it is in Hollywood. The men get younger and the women get older." "I've never been in style, so I can't go out of style." On her comedies: "I'm as funny as a barrel of dead babies." "She ought to know about close-ups. Jesus, she was around when they invented them! The bitch has been around forever." Bette Davis, when she was told how good Lillian Gish looked in a close-up. Buried next to her sister Dorothy in New York City. Autobiographies: The Movies, Mr. Griffith and Me, 1969. Dorothy and Lillian Gish, 1973. An Actor's Life For Me, 1987. The Smashing Pumpkins rock group named their first album Gish, (1991) after her. They said it was an album about spiritual ascension.

Samuel Goldwyn (Szmuel Gelbfisz)

b. 17 Aug 1879, d. 31 Jan 1974, = 94 yrs, 5 mos, 14 days. Made 1 movie, produced 140 movies. Married 2 times.

BKF: Being the founder of Hollywood motion picture studios. Creator of Leo the Lion, the lion who roars at the beginning of his movies. NN: Mr. Malaprop. Glove salesman. Salesman in the New York garment business. When told that he shouldn't acquire the rights to the Broadway hit "The Children's Hour" because it was about lesbians, he said, "So, we'll make them Albanians." "I don't want any yes-men around me. I want everyone to tell me the truth even if it costs them their jobs." "I read all of it part way through." "Never let that son of a bitch in the studio again--until we need him." "Spare no expense to make everything as economical as possible." "I'll give you a definite maybe." Being defensive about one of his movies that flopped: "Go see it and see for yourself why you shouldn't see it." Said that Wuthering Heights, starring Merle Oberon, was his favorite movie. "Anyone who goes to a psychiatrist should have his head examined." "When you're a star, you take the bitter with the sour." "A wide screen just makes a bad film twice as bad." "This new atom bomb is dynamite." "Our comedies are not be laughed at." "I never liked you, and I never will." "Why did you call you baby John? Every Tom, Dick and Harry is called John these days." "Don't pay any attention to the critics; don't even ignore them." "The scene is dull. Tell him to put more life into his dying." "For your information, I would like to ask a question." "Tell me, how did you love the picture?" "I want a story that starts out as an earthquake and works its way up to a climax." "You ought to take the bull between the teeth." "We've all passed a lot of water since then." "It's more than magnificent--it's mediocre." "If people don't want to go see a movie, nobody can stop them." "I challenge you to give me a frank, affirmative answer: yes or no." "You are partly one hundred percent right." "We've got twenty-five years worth of files out there, just sitting around. Now what I want you to do is to go out there and throw everything out--but make a copy of everything first." "If you won't give me your word of honor, will you give me your promise?" To a writer: "Let's have some more cliches. Let's bring it up to date with some snappy nineteenth century dialogue." "The reason so many people showed up at his (Louis B. Mayer) funeral was because they wanted to make sure he was dead." "The next time I send a damn fool for something, I go myself." "We're overpaying him, but he's worth it." "If I could drop dead right now, I'd be the happiest man alive!" "I don't think anyone should write his autobiography until after he's dead." "When someone else does something good, applaud! You will make two people happy." "I'm willing to admit that I may not always be right, but I am never wrong." "I want to make a picture about the Russian secret police--the GOP." "Don't worry about the war. It's all over but the shooting." "I am a rebel. I make pictures to please me. If it pleases me, there is a chance it will please others. But is has to please me first." "I read part of your book all the way through." "My wife's hands are so beautiful I had a bust made of them." "Too caustic? To hell with the cost--we'll make the picture anyway." "I can answer you in two words: im possible." "In this business it's dog-eat-dog and nobody's going to eat me." President Nixon went to his home in Beverly Hills to award him the Medal of Freedom on 27 March 1971. 1958 Jean Hersholt award winner and 1972 Cecil B. De Mille Award winner, making him the first person to win both awards. COD: Natural causes.

Ruth Gordon (Ruth Gordon Jones)

b. 30 Oct 1896, d. 28 Aug 1985, = 88 yrs, 9 mos, 29 days. Made 44 moves. Married 2 times.

BKF: Rosemary's Baby, 1968 and Every Which Way But Loose, 1978. 5' 0". Her photograph was used in the advertising for Mellin's Food for Infants and Invalids in the 1900's. Decided to go into acting when she received a personal reply to a letter she sent to a Broadway stage actress. Extremely bow-legged, she had them surgically corrected in the 1920's. "My legs were a liability, so I came to the hospital and had them broken to make them straight. Any woman who has bow-legs should be willing to suffer to have them right." Made Harold and Maude in 1971. Her husband, Garson Kanin, was 16 years younger than her. The movie didn't turn a profit until 1983. When she received a $50,000 royalty check in the mail, she almost threw it in the trash, thinking it was a fake sweepstakes check from Reader's Digest. Nominated for three Academy Awards for being a writer. Won an

Oscar for Rosemary's Baby at age 72, and in her 53rd year in the movie business, in 1969. She kissed her Oscar statuette and said, "Well, I can't tell you how encouragin' a thing like this is. The first money I ever earned was as an extra in 1915, and here it is 1969. I don't know what took me so long. Thank you Roman (Polanski). Thank you Bob. Thank you Mia (Farrow). Thank you Bill. And all of you who voted for me, thank you. And all of you who didn't, excuse me." The next morning she received the following telegram: "DEAR RUTH: WHAT DID TAKE YOU SO LONG? CONGRATULATIONS AND LOVE. MARY PICKFORD." Won an Emmy for a guest role on Taxi at age 83, in 1979. Nominated for Oscars for Best story three times and Best Screenplay three times. She played in The Matchmaker 1,078 consecutive times, without missing a single performance. "I think I can learn anything if someone will just take the trouble to teach me." "A little money helps but what *really,* gets it right is to *never,* I repeat, *never,* under any circumstances face the facts." "Get the knack of getting people to help you and also pitch in yourself." "The great have no friends. They merely know a lot of people." "The best impromptu speeches are the ones written well in advance." "You have to have a talent for having talent." "I'm in love in the past, but I'm having a love affair with the future." "To be someone, you must last." COD: Stroke.

Sydney Greenstreet (Sydney Hughes Greenstreet)

b. 27 Dec 1879, d. 18 Jan 1954, = 74 yrs, 22 days. Made 24 movies. Married 1 time.

BKF: Playing the club owner in Casablanca, 1942. NN: Tiny and The Fat Man. 5' 10" 280 lbs. He was a tea planter in Ceylon (now Sri Lanka) before he starting acting at age 61 and moved to Hollywood when the tea market went south. He earned an Oscar nomination for his first film. He could perfectly recite 12,000 lines of Shakespeare from memory. His studio contract required him to always weigh at least 250 pounds. He once got stuck in a studio phone booth, it had to be taken apart to get him out. His acting career lasted only from 1942 to 1949. Made nine movies with Peter Lorre. He was once trampled by a horse in Central Park. He said, "I was unhurt, but they had to destroy the horse." On retirement: "It's pure heaven to have a front door to unlock, a garden to grow, and a teapot to put on the table at four in the afternoon." COD: Bright's disease complicated by diabetes. Buried in Glendale, California. His likeness was the model for the look of Jabba the Hut in the Star Wars movies.

D. W. Griffith (David Llewelyn Wark Griffith)

b. 22 Jan 1875, d. 23 July 1948, = 73 yrs, 6 mos, 1 day. Directed 520 movies, acted in 44 movies, produced 96 movies, and writer of 228 movies. Made 141 films in 1909 alone. Married 2 times.

BKF: Directing The Birth of a Nation, 1915. NN: The Father of Film Technique, The Man Who Invented Hollywood, The Shakespeare of the Screen. Newspaper reporter, playwright. Discovered when he went to the Edison Company to sell a script and they hired him as an actor. Directed In Old California in 1910, which was the first film shot in Hollywood. Invented the close-up, the fade-out and the rapid cutting technique. Invented false eyelashes for actresses. He was the first director to use the now famous catchphrase, "Lights, camera, action!" in 1910. To Mary Pickford, "You're a little too old and a little too fat, but I might give you a job." "Movies are written in sand: applaud today, forgotten tomorrow." "Actors should never be important. Only directors should have power and place." "I have never really hated Hollywood except for its treatment of D.W. Griffith. No town, no industry, no profession, no art form owes so much to a single man." Lillian Gish. "He was the teacher of us all." Charlie Chaplin. "He was my day school, my adult education program, my university... but he was a very difficult man to know." Mack Sennett. Destitute, he lived in a single room in the Hollywood Knickerbocker Hotel. He died in the hotel lobby while on the way to see his doctor. Only one star showed up at his funeral--Lillian Gish. Elvis Presley later stayed in the same hotel, a few doors down from the room Griffith occupied.

This inspired him to write his hit "Heartbreak Hotel." COD: Cerebral hemorrhage. Buried in Centerfield, Kentucky.

Edmund Gwenn (Edmund John Kellaway)

b. 26 Sep 1877, d. 6 Sep 1959, = 81, yrs, 11 mos, 11 days. Made 95 movies. Married 1 time.

BKF: Playing Santa Claus (technically, Kris Kringle) in Miracle on 34th Street, 1947. He was evicted from his home as a teenager because he wanted to be a stage actor and would not change his mind. WW1: Infantry Officer in the British Army Supply Corps. While living in Hollywood during WW2, his home in London was completely destroyed by the German Luftwaffe. Always had a chauffer because he never learned to drive. He is the only actor to win an Oscar for playing Santa Claus, which he won at age 72. Miracle on 34th Street premiered in June. Accepting his Oscar, he said, "Now I know there is a Santa Claus." Last words, on his deathbed to his friend George Seaton, who said to him, "Oh, Teddy, it's (dying) awfully tough, isn't it?" To which he replied, "Yes, it's tough, but not as tough as doing comedy!" COD: Pneumonia after suffering a stroke. Cremated, ashes are in a vault in Los Angeles, California. The Santa costume he wore in Miracle on 34th Street sold for $41,000 at auction in 1996.

Alan Hale, Sr. (Rufus Edward MacKahan)

b. 10 Feb 1892, d. 22 Jan 1950, = 57 yrs, 11 mos, 12 days. Made 247 movies. Married 1 time.

BKF: Playing Little John in The Adventures of Robin Hood, 1939. Wrote obituaries for the New York Times. Sang with the Metropolitan Opera in New York City. He invented a theater chair that allowed the occupant to slide back instead of standing up to allow other patrons to get to their seats. He also invented the hand fire extinguisher and a greaseless potato chip. Appeared in 13 movies with Errol Flynn.

Played Little John in three Robin Hood movies. Father of Alan Hale, Jr., who played the Skipper in the 1960's sitcom Gilligan's Island. In this author's opinion, there are no other father/son actors who look as much like identical twins as these two. COD: Liver ailment and viral infection. Buried in Glendale, California.

Jack Haley (John Joseph Haley, Jr.)

b. 10 Aug 1897, d. 6 Jun 1979, = 81 yrs, 9 mos, 27 days. Made 56 movies. Married 1 time.

BKF: Playing The Tin Man in The Wizard of Oz, 1939. NN: Jack. Vaudeville performer. Hosted a radio show from 1937 to 1939. Got a serious eye infection from the same makeup that forced Buddy Ebsen to withdraw from playing the Tin Man. His singing in The Wizard of Oz was dubbed by Adriena Caselotti. Real estate agent in his semi-retirement. His son Jack married Liza Minnelli, who was Judy Garland's daughter. (The Tin Man's son married Dorothy's daughter.) The Tin Man's name in the original book was Nick Chopper. He donated so much money to the Catholic Church, that they made him a Knight of Malta, an honor held by only two other actors, Danny Thomas and Pat O'Brien. When someone suggested that it must have been fun to make The Wizard of Oz, he said, "Like hell it was. It was work!" and "It was awful. You couldn't have fun... I had to drag myself to work." His son Jack, Jr. (actually III, but known as Junior) said, "I didn't want to go into showbiz because I didn't want to clank in my father's footsteps." COD: Heart attack. Buried in Culver City, California. Autobiography: Heart of the Tin Man, 2000.

Juanita Hansen (Juanita C. Hansen)

b. 3 Mar 1885, d. 26 Sep 1961, = 76 yrs, 6 mos, 21 days. Made 46 movies. Never married.

BKF: A fifteen episode serial called The Phantom Foe in 1920. NN: The Original Mack Sennett Girl. Developed a cocaine addiction. Retired from movies after she was severely scalded in a bathroom accident in a New York City hotel. She won $118,000 in damages. Attempted suicide, but recovered and overcame her drug addiction. Like to drive fast, she was arrested several times for speeding. Toured the country preaching against drug abuse. Was a clerk for a railroad company and worked for the Works Project Administration (WPA) during the depression. COD: Heart failure due to years of drug abuse. Buried in Culver City, California.

Cedric Hardwicke (Cedric Webster Hardwicke)

b. 19 Feb 1893, d. 6 Aug 1964, = 71 yrs, 5 mos, 18 days. Made 110 movies. Married 2 times.

Wanted to become a doctor but could not pass the medical school entrance exams. WW1: Captain in the Judge Advocate's Office in the British Army serving in France. He was a member of the London Scottish Regiment, along with future actors Claude Rains, Herbert Marshall and Basil Rathbone. A British stage actor until the 1930's, when he became a major movie star in England and in Hollywood. Tried to get recalled to active duty during WW2 but the War Department told him, 'Your reserve status has been cancelled for reasons of your age." Knighted by King George V in 1934 at age 41, at that time the youngest actor to ever be knighted. After dubbing him a knight, the King misspoke and said, "Rise, Sir Cedric Pickwick." Narrated The Picture of Dorian Gray, 1945, and War of the Worlds, 1953. "I can't act. I have never acted. And I shall never act. What I can do is suspend my audience's power of judgment till I've finished." "I believe that God felt sorry for actors, so he created Hollywood to give them a place in the sun and a swimming pool. The price they had to pay was to surrender their talent." "Actors and burglars work better at night." "My temperament, a young actor needs to be mercurial." "Actors must practice restraint else think what might happen in a love scene." "Hollywood may be thickly populated, but to me it's still a bewilderness." His funeral was paid for by donations from various actor's charities. COD: Cancer, emphysema and chronic obstructive pulmonary disease (COPD).

Oliver Hardy (Norvell Hardy)

b. 18 Jan 1892, d. 7 Aug 1957, = 65 yrs, 6 mos, 20 days. Made 415 movies. Married 3 times.

BKF: The Laurel and Hardy comedy team from 1927 to 1951. NN: Babe. Got his nickname from his barber in Florida. The youngest of five children. His oldest brother drowned in the Oconee River. He pulled his brother from the river but was unable to save him. Went into acting because he thought he could do a better job than the actors he was watching. Opened the first motion picture theater in Millersville, Georgia in 1910. He was 6'2", 300 pounds. He was denied entry in to the US Army during WW1 because he was too tall. He was the first actor to play the Tin Man in The Wizard of Oz, a silent movie made in 1925. Along with Bing Crosby and Gary Cooper, he was a founding owner of the Del Mar Race Track in 1937. Laurel & Hardy won an Academy Award in 1932 for a new Academy Award category called Best Comedy Short for a short film called The Music Box. Early in their career as partners, Oliver & Hardy where known as "The Boys." Performed overseas with the USO during WW2. His catchphrase was, "Here's another nice mess you've gotten me into!" Wrote the scripts and gags and directed the Laurel & Hardy movies. Got paid twice what Stan Laurel did, which did not bother Stan at all. Made 107 movies with his partner Stan Laurel. Avid golfer. Had a heart attack in 1954 and suffered a stroke in September 1956, that left him paralyzed and unable to speak. "I don't know much, but I know a little about a lot of things." Last words: "Love you," to his wife. COD: Cerebral thrombosis. Died in his mother-in-law's home. Once having weighed 350 pounds, he weighed only 150 pounds when he died. His partner Stan Laurel was too sick to attend his funeral and said,

"Babe would understand." Cremated, his ashes interred in North Hollywood, California. His epitaph says, "A GENIUS OF COMEDY, His talent brought joy and laughter to all the world." His picture was on the cover of the Beatles' Lonely Hearts Club Band album in 1967.

Bobby Harron (Robert Emmett Harron)

b. 12 Apr 1893, d. 5 Sep 1920, = 27 yrs, 4 mos, 24 days. Made 220 movies. Never married.

BKF: True Heart Susie, 1919. COD: Depressed over being passed over for the lead in Way Down East by Richard Barthlemess, he suffered a gunshot wound to the chest when he dropped his gun on the floor in his hotel room. He adamantly insisted to the ambulance crew, the doctor and his friends that it was an accident, even though rumors of a suicide attempt have persisted to this day. He died four days after being shot.

William S. Hart (William Surrey Hart)

b. 6 Dec 1864, d. 23 Jun 1946, = 81 yrs, 6 mos, 17 days. Made 74 movies. Married 1 time.

BKF: Being the inventor of the adult Western and being the most popular Western star of the silent era. Worked at the US Post Office for three years to save up enough money to go to Hollywood to be an actor. He didn't make his first movie until age 49. He is the model for Uncle Sam for the WW1 military recruiting posters. Collected old western guns. He owned Billy the Kid's six-shooters. He was a friend to Wyatt Earp and Bat Masterson. His horse's name was Fritz, the first well-known horse star. Made only one talkie, which was a spoken prologue for the reissue of Tumbleweeds, in 1939. While several actors have high schools named after them, the entire school district in Newhall, California is named for him. COD: Heart attack.

Buried in Brooklyn New York. Autobiography: My Life East and West, 1929. Member of the Cowboy Hall of Fame, 1975.

Henry Hathaway (Marquis Henri Leopold de Fiennes)

b. 18 Mar 1898, d. 11 Feb 1985, = 86 yrs, 10 mos, 29 days. Directed 67 movies, produced 6 movies, acted in 1 movie. Married 2 times.

"To be a good director you've got to be a bastard. I'm a bastard and I know it." "There's a lot of nice guys walking around Hollywood but they're not eating." Wrote at least eleven western novels and short stories in retirement. COD: Heart attack. Bequeathed his home so that it could be converted into a park and museum. "When I was making pictures, the people gave me their nickels, dimes, and quarters. When I am gone, I want them to have my home." It is now a 265-acre park.

Sessue Hawakaya (Kintaro Hayakawa)

b. 10 Jun 1889, d. 23 Nov 1973, = 84 yrs, 5 mos, 13 days. Made 106 movies. Married 1 time.

BKF: Playing the prisoner of war Camp Commander Colonel Saito in Bridge on the River Kwai. Expelled from the Japanese Naval Academy because of a ruptured eardrum, he survived a suicide attempt at age 18. He then attended the University of Chicago and was the quarterback of the school's football team. He was once penalized for using Jujitsu to tackle an opponent. After graduation and on his way back to Japan in 1914, he took a detour to try acting. He got a starring role in The Typhoon, 1914. He earned $5,000 per week in 1915. He was an immensely popular leading man in the silent film era. He was also the first actor of Asian descent to become a leading man in Hollywood. He was 5'7", 155 pounds. Had a reputation for throwing the best, and wildest, parties in Hollywood. Once lost $1,000,000 in a single evening of gambling in Monte Carlo, and just shrugged it off.

Insanely popular in France, Russia and Germany, he was the first non-Caucasian movie star to become an international star and sex symbol. WW2: He was performing and subsequently trapped in France when the Germans quickly occupied the country. He joined the French Resistance. After retiring from acting he became an ordained Zen Buddhist priest. "My one ambition is to play a hero." COD: Cerebral thrombosis complicated by pneumonia. Died in Tokyo and buried in Japan. Died on the same day as actress Constance Talmadge. Autobiography: Zen Showed Me The Way, 1960.

Hays, Will H.

He became the head of the Motion Pictures and Producers and Distributors of America on 6 March 1922. He is the author of the Motion Picture Production Code, which studios had to follow. The Major studios were bound by this code from 1930 to 1968. They were required to submit all of their motion pictures to his office for screening to be seen if they were fit for an official approval from the office.

The Motion Picture Production Code. "Resolved, That those things which are included in the following list shall not appear in pictures produced by the members of this Association, irrespective of the manner in which they are treated:

1. Pointed profanity--by either title of lip-this included the words "God," "Lord," "Jesus,", "Christ" (unless they be use reverently in connection with proper religious ceremonies), "hell," "damn," "Gawd," and every other profane and vulgar expression however it may be spelled:
2. Any licentious or suggestive nudity-in fact or in silhouette; and any lecherous or licentious notice thereof by other characters in the picture;
3. The illegal traffic in drugs;
4. Any inference of sex perversion;
5. White slavery;

6. Miscegenation (sex relationships between the white and black races);
7. Sex Hygiene and venereal diseases;
8. Scenes of actual childbirth--in fact or in silhouette;
9. Children's sex organs;
10. Ridicule of the clergy;
11. Willful offense to any nation, race or creed.

And be it further resolved, That special care be exercised in the manner in which the following subjects are treated, to the end that vulgarity and suggestiveness may be eliminated and that good taste may be emphasized:

1. The use of the flag;
2. International relations (avoiding picturizing in an unfavorable light another country's religion, history, institutions, prominent people, and citizenry);
3. Arson;
4. The use of firearms;
5. Theft, robbery, safe-cracking, and dynamiting of trains, mines, buildings, etc. (having in mind the effect which a too-detailed description of these may have upon the moron);
6. Brutality and possible gruesomeness;
7. Technique of committing murder by whatever method;
8. Methods of smuggling;
9. Third-degree methods;
10. Actual hangings or electrocutions as legal punishment for crime;
11. Sympathy for criminals;
12. Attitude toward public characters and institutions;
13. Sedition;
14. Apparent cruelty to children and animals;
15. Branding of people or animals;
16. The sale of women, or of a woman selling her virtue;
17. Rape or attempted rape;

18. First-night scenes;
19. Man and woman in bed together; (a married couple could be shown on the screen in bed together as long as both of them had at least one foot on the ground);
20. Deliberate seduction of girls;
21. The institution of marriage;
22. Surgical operations;
23. The use of drugs;
24. Titles or scenes having to with law enforcement or law-enforcing officers;
25. Excessive or lustful kissing, particularly when one character or the other is a 'heavy."

George "Gabby" Hayes (George Francis Hayes)

b. 7 May 1885, d. 9 Feb 1969, = 83 yrs, 9 mos, 2 days. Made 192 movies. Married 1 time.

BKF: Being the sidekick to Hopalong Cassidy. Make 44 movies with Roy Rogers and 15 movies with John Wayne. NN: Gabby. Born in the hotel his father owned. Circus performer, vaudevillian. Semi-pro baseball player. His catchphrases were "yer durn tootin" and "young whipper snapper." Creator of the 'clean cuss,' such as "Dadblastit!" Already a millionaire, he retired from acting in 1925. The stock market crash of 1929 wiped him out. He went back to acting to earn a living. He later said that he never learned to ride a horse until he was almost 50 years old and that he particularly disliked making Westerns. "I hate them. Really can't stand 'em. They're always the same." His horse's names were Calico, Eddie and Blossom. "You have so few plots--the stagecoach holdup, the rustlers, the mortgage gag, the mine setting and the retired gunslinger." Starred in 78 episodes of the Gabby Hayes Show on television, 1950-1956. Made a nationwide personal appearance tour in the 1960's. COD: Cardiovascular disease. Buried in Los Angeles, California. Member of the Cowboy Hall of Fame, 2000.

Jean Hersholt (Jean Pierre Hersholt)

b. 12 Jul 1986, d. 2 Jun 1956, = 69 yrs, 10 mos, 21 days. Made 140 movies. Married 1 time.

BKF: The Jean Hersholt Award, established in 1956. Born in Denmark, he is a graduate of the Copenhagen Art School. He was on the board of directors of two Hollywood banks. Uncle of actor Leslie Neilsen. Founded the Motion Picture Relief Fund in 1939. He translated more than 160 of Hans Christian Andersen's books into English. Knighted by King Christian X of Denmark in 1948. Cecil B. De Mille Award winner, 1954. The Jean Hersholt Humanitarian Award was created in his honor in 1956. COD: Cancer. Buried in Glendale, California.

Hitchcock, Alfred (Alfred Joseph Hitchcock)

b. 13 Aug 1898, d. 29 Apr 1980, = 81 yrs, 8 mos, 16 days. Directed 70 movies, acted in 39 movies. Married 1 time.

BKF: Being one of the world's foremost filmmakers, his mastery of suspense, his cameos and 267 episodes of Alfred Hitchcock Presents television show, 1955-65. NN: The Master of Suspense, Hitch. He was born on the same day as actor Regis Toomey. Youngest of three children, said he could not remember ever having a playmate. "I was an uncommonly unattractive young man." Rejected by the British Army during WW1 for medical reasons. He was able to join the Royal Engineers, a noncombat unit. Had an extreme fear of eggs. He needed extras in his 1926 movie The Lodger, so he filled in himself. This began his tradition of cameos. Claimed he was a virgin when he married at age 27. He never learned to drive, claiming an intense fear of policeman and being stopped by one. Made the first British talking movie, which was 1929's Blackmail. When he made The Lady Vanishes in 1938, it was the only film he made that was not written by him or written specifically for him. The only one of the 70 films he directed to win Best Picture was Rebecca, 1940. He made patriotic anti-Nazi films during WW2 because, as he said, "I felt the need to make a little contribution to the war effort, and I was both overweight and overage for military service. I knew that if I did nothing, I'd regret it for the rest of my life." He has a cameo in Lifeboat, 1943, where a likeness of him appears in a newspaper ad for weight reducing pills. It was appropriate because he had just lost one hundred pounds. The shortest color film ever made (in a certain way) was his Spellbound in 1945. There is a two-frame red flash when the gun fires. His first movie in color was Rope, 1948. His daughter Patricia is in his movies Stage Fright (1950), Strangers on a Train (1951) and Psycho (1960). The first time Doris Day ever sang her hit song Que, Sera, Sera in public was in Hitchcock's 1956 thriller The Man Who Knew Too Much. He personally earned $15,000,000 from the 1960 thriller Psycho. The stabbing sound heard in the shower was made by stabbing a casaba melon. He never allowed nudity of profanity in his movies until 1972's Frenzy. He became a US citizen on 20 April 1955. When he made The Birds in 1963, he spent $200,000 trying to develop mechanical birds before abandoning the project and using real birds. Cecil B. De Mille Award winner, 1971. His production company was called Shamley Productions. He was knighted in 1980, after having declined a knighthood in 1962. When he was asked why it took so long to be knighted, he facetiously said, "I suppose it was a matter of carelessness." He was nominated 11 times for Best Director but never won. He actually passed on an offer to direct Rosemary's Baby. The theme song to his Alfred Hitchcock Presents TV show is called Funeral March of a Marionette, by Gounod. A man wrote him saying that after watching Psycho, his wife would no longer take a bath or a shower. Hitch wrote back, "Sir, have you considered sending your wife to the dry cleaners?" Had the habit of borrowing small amounts of money from friends, but repaid the loan only with coins. "The only thing wrong with the silent picture was that mouths opened, and nothing came out. The talking picture only partially soldved that problem." "Luck is everything...My good luck in life was to be a really frightened person. I'm fortunate to be a coward, to have a low threshold of fear, because a hero couldn't make a good suspense film." "The more outrageous a subject can get, the more I like it." "Conversation is the enemy of good wine and food." Advice to directors: "Stay out of jail." And, "Film your murders like love scenes, and film your love scenes like murders." "If I made Cinderella, the audience would immediately be looking for a body in the coach." "A good movie is when the price of admission, the dinner and the babysitter was well worth it." "The length of a movie should be directly proportional to the endurance of the human bladder." "What is drama, after all, but life with the dull parts cut out?" "There is no terror in the bang, only in the anticipation of it." On audiences: "Give them pleasure--the same pleasure they have when they wake up from a nightmare." And "Always make the audience suffer as much as possible." "No one can really like an actor." "I deny that I ever said actors are cattle; what I said was that actors should be treated like cattle." "Cary Grant is the only actor I ever loved in my whole life." "When an actor comes to me and wants to discuss his character, I say 'It's in the script.' If he says, 'But what's my motivation?', I say, 'Your salary.'" "Walt Disney has the best casting. If he doesn't like an actor, he just tears him up." "I'm not against the police; I'm just afraid of them." "Television has brought back murder into the home--where it belongs." "Some films are slices of life, mine are slices of cake." When asked why he doesn't make comedies: "But every film I made IS a comedy!" (He did make one comedy--Mr. and Mrs. Smith, 1941.) "One day he pulled up his shirt to show me his belly-button--which he didn't have. He'd had an operation and when they sewed him up they took it away! His belly-button was gone." Actress Karen Black. Last words: "One never knows the ending. One has to die to know exactly what happens after death, although Catholics have their hopes." "It is terribly embarrassing to be sick, and one's own death is so undignified." Died quietly at home surrounded by his friends, wife and daughter. COD: Renal failure. Cremated, ashes scattered over the Pacific Ocean. "There's is nothing quite so good as a burial at sea. It is simple, tidy, and not very incriminating." He appeared in 101 of his 119 films. Said his all-time favorite movie was Blazing Saddles. Signed his will one month before he died. His address was 10957 Bellagio

Road, Los Angeles, California. Left his entire $200,000,000 estate to his wife via a trust.

List of Known Hitchcock Cameos:

Title:	Year:	Time: H:M:S	Description:
The Birds	1963	0.2.18	Leaving the pet shop with two of his own terriers.
Blackmail	1929	0.10.25	Being pestered by a small boy as he reads a book on the London Underground. This is a long, 19 second cameo.
Dial M for Murder	1954	0.13.13	On the left side in the class reunion photo.
Easy Virtue	1928	0.21.15	Walking with a walking stick past a tennis court.
Family Plot	1976	0.40.00	In silhouette through the door of the Registrar of Births and Deaths.
Foreign Correspondent	1940	0.12.44	After Joel McCrea leaves his hotel, wearing a coat and hat and reading a newspaper.
Frenzy	1972	0.04.07	In the center of the crowd wearing a bowler hat; he is the only one not applauding the speaker, and a minute later, right after the body washes ashore, standing next to a gray-haired man with a gray beard.
I Confess	1953	0.1.33	Crossing the top of a flight of steps.
The Lady Vanishes	1938	1.32.31	In Victoria Station, wearing a black coat, smoking a cigarette and making a strange movement with his head.
Lifeboat	1944	0.25.0	In the before and after pictures in the newspaper ad for "Reduco Obesity Slayer."
The Lodger	1927	1.34.0	At a desk in the newsroom
The Man Who Knew Too Much	1956	0.25.12	As the McKennas watch the acrobats in the market place, he appears at the left and puts his hands in his pockets.
The Man Who Knew Too Much	1956	0.33.25	Walking across the road in a dark trench coat as a bus passes.
Marnie	1964	0.5.00	Entering from the left of the hotel corridor after Tippi Hedren passes by, and clearly breaking the fourth wall by looking the audience straight in the eye.

Mr. & Mrs. Smith	1941	0.42.57	Passing Robert Montgomery in front of the building.
Murder!	1930	0.59.45	Walking past the house where the murder was committed, with a female companion.
North by Northwest	1959	0.02.09	Missing a bus just after his credit passes off screen during the title sequence.
Notorious	1946	1.04.44	At the part in Claude Rains' mansion drinking champagne and then quickly departing.
Number Seventeen	1932	0.51.25	On the bus with the other passengers, in a dark coat and hat, facing away, he bounces up and down for about four seconds.
The Paradine Case	1947	0.38.00	Leaving the train carrying a cello case
Psycho	1960	0.06.59	Seen through an office window wearing a Stetson cowboy hat Just as Janet Leigh comes through the door.
Rear Window	1954	0.26.12	Winding the clock in the songwriter's apartment.
Rebecca	1940	2.06.57	Walking near the phone booth just after George Sanders makes a call.
Rope	1948	0.55.00	In the background as a flashing red neon sign of his trademark profile.
Sabotage	1936	0.08.56	Just after the lights come back on in front of the Bijou, looking up just as he crosses the crowd.
Saboteur	1942	1.04.45	Standing in front of "Cut Rate Drugs" just as the saboteurs' car stops.
Shadow of a Doubt	1943	0.16.27	On the train to Santa Rosa, playing cards, back to the camera.
Spellbound	1945	0.38.50	Coming out of an elevator at the Empire State Hotel, carrying a violin case and smoking a cigarette.
Stage Fright	1950	0.39.49	Turning to look back at Jane Wyman in her disguise as Marlene Dietrich's maid.
Strangers on a Train	1951	0.10.34	Boarding a train with a double bass as Farley Granger gets off in his hometown.
Suspicion	1941	0.03.25	Walking a hose across the screen at the hunt meet.
		0.44.58	Mailing a letter at the village postbox.
The 39 Steps	1935	0.06.56	He is the man tossing a white cigarette box while the bus pulls up for Robert Donat and Lucie Mannheim to leave the theater.

To Catch a Thief	1955	0.09.40	Sitting next to Cary Grant on the bus.
Topaz	1969	0.32.27	Being pushed in a wheelchair in the airport. He gets up from the chair, shakes hands with a man, and walks off to the right.
Torn Curtain	1966	0.08.00	Sitting in the Hotel d'Angleterre with a baby on his knee. The music playing at this point in the film is an adaptation of Charles Gounod's Funeral March of a Marionette, a song now associated with Hitchcock due to it being used as the theme song for his television series Alfred Hitchcock Presents.
The Trouble With Harry	1955	0.22.14	Seen outside of the window--the man walking past the parked limousine of an old man who is looking at paintings.
Under Capricorn	1949	0.02.11	In the town square during the new governor's speech, wearing a blue coat and brown hat.
		0.12.17	One of the three men on the steps of Government House.
Vertigo	1958	0.11.40	In a gray suit walking in the street with a trumpet case.
The Wrong Man	1956	0.00.18	Seen in silhouette narrating the film's prologue. His biographer says that Hitchcock chose to make this an explicit appearance in the film, rather than a cameo, to emphasize that, unlike his other movies, The Wrong Man was a true story about an actual person.
Young and Innocent	1937	0.00.16	Outside the courthouse, holding a camera.
Alfred Hitchcock Presents (TV)	1958	0.05.15	In an episode called "Dip in the Pool" on the cover of a magazine being read by Philip Bournauf.

Jack Holt (Charles John Holt, Jr.)

b. 31 May 1888, d. 18 Jan 1951, = 67 yrs, 2 mos, 18 days. Made 200+ movies. Married 1 time.

BKF: Being one of the most popular cowboy stars of his time. NN: The Granddaddy of the Western Serial. San Francisco, 1936. Expelled from Virginia Military Academy for bad behavior. Gold miner in Alaska, railroad and civil engineer, mailman, cowpuncher in Oregon, laborer, prospector, trapper, stagecoach driver, cattle hand, surveyor in San Francisco. Joined a theatrical company which toured in Hollywood in 1913. As a stuntman, he rode a horse off a 30-foot cliff into a river, which got him a starring role in the company's next movie, Salomy Jane. He was the star of Liberty, a Daughter of the USA, which was the first completely Western-themed serial. His horse's name was Robin Hood. He is one of the original founders of the Academy of Motion Picture Arts and Sciences (AMPAS). The comic strip character Dick Tracy is based on his granite-jawed profile. Could not enlist during WW1 due to frostbite he suffered during his time in Alaska. He enlisted in the US Army as a private at age 54 during WW2 following a personal request from General George C. Marshall. He bought horses for the US Army and was promoted to Major within two years. He was Margaret Mitchell's choice to play Rhett Butler in Gone With the Wind. COD: Heart attack. Member of the Cowboy Hall of Fame, 1991. Father of actor and Western star Tim Holt.

Hedda Hopper (Elda Furry)

b. 2 May 1885, d. 1 Feb 1966, = 80 yrs, 8 mos, 30 days. Made 150 movies. Married 1 time.

BKF: America's best-known Hollywood Gossip Columnist. NN: Queen of the Quickies. Unable to make it as a stage actress or movie actor, Florenz Ziegfeld called her a "clumsy cow." She married DeWolf Hopper in 1913, whose previous wives' names were Ella, Ida, Edna and Nella. Being named Elda, he often called her by the wrong name. She changed her name to Hedda after paying $10 for the advice of a numerologist. She said, "It was the best money I ever spent." Published her first gossip column in the Los Angeles Times in 1938. Hedda Hopper and Louella Parsons together had about 75,000,000 readers in 1950. The population of the United States at that time was 151,325,798. She called her home in Beverly Hills "The House That Fear Built." Actress Joan Bennett once mailed Hedda Hopper a skunk with a note that read, "Won't you be my valentine? Nobody else will.

I stink and so do you." Spencer Tracy kicked her in the ass when she revealed his secret affair with Katherine Hepburn in her column. "Two of the cruelest, most primitive punishments our town deals out to those who fall from favor are the empty mailbox and the silent telephone." "Go figure those two. Hedda Hopper was a homophobic, and her only child was a homosexual. Louella was anti-Semitic, yet she was born Jewish, then converted. They were a demented pair, and Hollywood was even more demented for allowing them to have so much power over people's careers and lives." Gale Sondergaard. "Her virtue was that she said what she thought. Her vice was that what she thought didn't amount to much." Peter Ustinov. Her son William Hopper became famous for playing Detective Paul Drake on the Perry Mason television show. Her guest starring in Gilligan's Island in 1965 made it the highest rated episode ever. It was named #62 of TV Guide's 100 Greatest Episodes of All Time in 1997. COD: Double pneumonia. She and Buster Keaton died on the same day. He was her co-star in The Stolen Jools, 1931, Speak Easily, 1932, and Sunset Boulevard, 1950. Buried in Altoona, Pennsylvania. Autobiography: The Whole Truth and Nothing But, and From Under My Hat, 1963.

Leslie Howard (Leslie Howard Stainer)

b. 3 Apr 1893, d. 1 Jun 1943, = 50 yrs, 1 mo, 29 days. Made 33 movies. Married 1 time.

BKF: Playing Ashley in Gone With the Wind in 1939 and as Professor Higgins in Pygmalion, 1938. He was the second actor (after Lyle Talbot in The Thirteenth Guest, 1932) to say the word 'damn' on the movie screen. WW1: Officer in the British Army. WW2: Made documentaries for the BBC. His daughter's name is also Leslie. While filming Gone With the Wind, he told his daughter, "Yesterday I put on my Confederate uniform for the first time and looked like a fairy doorman at the Beverly Wilshire--a fine thing at my age (46)." Along with Hattie McDaniel, he was the only major star of Gone With the Wind to not attend the Atlanta premier of the movie. He had gone to

England to enlist in the Royal Air Force. She could not attend because she was black. Known as a ladies' man, he said that he "Didn't chase women but...couldn't always be counted on to run away." "I can't think of anything more exciting than trying to be an actor." COD: Shot down while on civilian Pan Am Flight 777 from Lisbon to Bristol, UK by Luftwaffe fighter planes. He had boarded the flight in the pre-dawn hours with his agent, who resembled Winston Churchill in the dark. There were 17 'souls on board.' The German fighter pilots expected that they were participating of the assassination of Prime Minister Winston Churchill, they photographed the attack and the subsequent debris. They sent the pictures to Howard's family after the war. He and Noel Coward were the only two Hollywood actors to work for British Intelligence during WW2--that British Intelligence would confirm. Left his Beverly Hills home to his secretary, but she died six months before he did.

Moe Howard (Moses Harry Horwitz)

b. 19 Jun 1897, d. 4 May 1975, = 77 yrs, 10 mos, 15 days. Made 245 movies. Married 1 time.

BKF: Being the leader of The Three Stooges. Dropped out of the 9th grade. Performer on a Mississippi River showboat. He was only 5'3'. The only film to include all three Howard brothers was Hold That Lion, in 1947. The Three Stooges appeared in more movies together than any other comedy team, making 190 movies. Joe Besser, who played Curly, was the only stooge who could hit Moe back. He claimed that he never missed a single date, appointment or curtain call in sixty years of performing. Real estate salesman in retirement. "We're not nearly as violent as the Westerns." Owned a restaurant called Stoogeburgers after he and Curly retired. COD: Lung cancer. Buried in Los Angeles, California. Autobiography: Moe Howard and the Three Stooges, 1977.

Shemp Howard (Samuel Horwitz)

b. 11 Mar 1895, d. 22 Nov 1955, = 60 yrs, 8 mos, 11 days. Made 184 movies. Married 1 time.

BKF: The 3rd of The Three Stooges. NN: The Ugliest Man in Hollywood. The Forgotten Stooge. Skipped school so much that his mother spent a lot of time in the principal's office answering for it. When he finally graduated, the joke was that he didn't graduate--his mother did. Vaudeville performer, usually in blackface. Never had a driver's license due to a lingering fear from having had a driving accident as a teenager. He drove his car through the front of a barbershop. Completely recovered from a stroke in 1952. After he died in 1955, they filmed four more episodes with his double, seen only from the back. "There's a thousand reasons why I shouldn't drink... but I can't think of one right now." COD: Heart attack while riding in a car with friends. He was returning home with friends from a boxing match in a taxi cab when he died in the middle of telling a joke while lighting a cigar. Buried in Los Angeles, California.

Walter Huston (Walter Scott Huston)

b. 5 Apr 1883, d. 7 Apr 1950, = 67 yrs, 2 days. Made 56 movies. Married 3 times.

BKF: The Treasure of the Sierra Madre, 1948. Trained as an engineer. Managed electric power station in Nevada, Missouri. Hit and killed a pedestrian while driving on Sunset Boulevard in 25 September 1933. He was cleared of any wrongdoing in an inquest. Was the first person to sing September Song in 1938. Had an un-credited role in The Bandwagon, 1953. Became an Irish citizen in 1964. His son John directed him to a Best Supporting Oscar for The Treasure of the Sierra Madre in 1948. He deliberately refused to wear his false teeth for the film. Accepting his Oscar,

Walter said, "Many years ago I raised a son and I said to him, "If you ever become a writer or a director, please find a good part for your old man." His son John also won an Oscar for Treasure of the Sierra Madre. "Hell, I ain't paid to made good lines sound good. I'm paid to make bad lines sound good." "Son, give 'em a good show, and always travel first class." "You need about twenty million dollars to live properly. My life span would probably be lengthened if I had that much. It's only *trying* to make twenty million dollars that cuts short a man's years. Spending it would be healthy." 1983 American Film Institute Lifetime Achievement Award. COD: Aortic aneurysm in his hotel room in Beverly Hills. Cremated, ashes buried in Fresno, California.

Thomas Ince (Thomas Harper Ince)

b. 16 Nov 1880, d. 19 Nov 1924, = 44 yrs, 3 days. Produced and directed more than 800 movies. Acted in 9 movies. Married 1 time.

BKF: One of the founding fathers of early Hollywood. NN: The Father of Western Movies. COD: Shot in the head, probably by William Randolph Hearst, who probably mistook him for Charlie Chaplin. Hearst thought Chaplin was having an affair with his wife.

Rex Ingram (Same)

b. 20 Oct 1895, d. 19 Sep 1969, = 73 yrs, 10 mos, 30 days. Made 58 movies. Married 1 time.

BKF: The Thief of Bagdad, 1940. Was born on the riverboat Robert E. Lee near Cairo, Illinois. Earned a Bachelor's Degree in Medicine from Northwestern University and was the first African-American man to receive a Phi Beta Kappa key from Northwestern. Discovered in 1918 while literally just standing on the street corner by a casting director looking for actors for a Tarzan of the Apes movie. He was also the first African-American to have a contract role in a soap opera, The

Brighter Day, in 1962. The show was cancelled before production began. "My career as an actor was quite by chance. I was standing on a Hollywood corner waiting to cross the street when I was discovered by a movie talent scout. I was persuaded that I was just what was needed to play a native in the jungles in the first Tarzan movie." COD: Heart attack, shortly after filming The Bill Cosby Show. Buried in Hollywood Hills, California.

Emil Jannings (Theodor Fredrich Emil)

b. 23 July 1884, d. 2 Jan 1950, = 65 yrs, 5 mos, 10 days. Made 72 movies in Hollywood and about 10 movies in Germany during WW2. Married 3 times.

BKF: Winning the first Best Actor Academy Award in 1929. NN: The Greatest Screen Actor of All time. Actually born in Switzerland and not Brooklyn as advertised by his studio. Had a heavy German accent. Left immediately for Germany after being photographed with the Oscar in hand three days before the awards. The results had been leaked. He was also the first no-show Oscar winner at the awards a few days later. When he won the Best Actor Oscar he was actually second in the voting. The winner who got disqualified was...Rin Tin Tin. His very thick, almost undecipherable German accent killed his career when he tried to make a talkie. Made The Blue Angel in 1930, the first talkie made in Germany. He was head of the Film Studio for the Third Reich during WW2. Won several awards for the Nazi propaganda films he made for Germany during WW2. This includes being named "Artist of the Year for 1941" by Joseph Goebbels. He was unemployable after WW2. In the months following the end of the war, he carried his Oscar with him to prove who he was. He is the only German to have won the Best Actor Oscar. Reportedly kept his cash in his pillow. "We can only realize the shadows of our dreams." COD: Liver cancer, buried in Salzburg, Austria.

Al Jolson (Asa Yoelson)

b. 26 May 1886, d. 23 Oct 1950, = 64 yrs, 4 mos, 27 days. Made 207 movies. Married 4 times.

BKF: The Jazz Singer, 1927. NN: Jolie and The World's Greatest Entertainer. Voted The Most Popular Male Vocalist, beating out Frank Sinatra, Bing Crosby and Perry Como. Born in Russia. His parents wanted him to become a cantor but he ran away from home and became a Vaudeville star. He had an equally talented, successful and look-alike brother whom he paid $150 per week to stay out of show business. Started his blackface act in 1906. Made $2,000 per week in 1916. Entertained the troops during The Spanish-American War in 1898 and during the Korean War in 1950. Wrote a 1920 Republican Harding-Coolidge ticket theme song called "Harding, You're the Man For Us." Paid $75,000 to make The Jazz Singer. He said, "I got my salary and that's all. I haven't made a penny out of this picture racket, not compared to what I used to make on the stage. Of course, I only started the whole talkie business and put the company on its feet." There are fewer than 435 spoken words in The Jazz Singer, all of which were improvised by the actors. He sang while on one knee and outstretched arms because he had a painful ingrown toenail and performing in this pose relieved the pain. He left his knee prints in the cement at Grauman's Chinese Theater, in a recreation of the pose he used when singing Mammy. His catchphrase was, "You ain't heard nothing yet, folks!" These were also the first words spoken in The Jazz Singer. He was the highest paid and most famous entertainer of the 1930's. He was the first actor to go overseas to entertain the troops at a military base, in 1942. He performed in the jungles of Central America and in Great Britain. He contracted malaria and had one lung surgically removed. One of the last songs he recorded was Are You Lonesome Tonight?, which was then famously covered by one of his fans who idolized him, Elvis Presley. "Neither a Broadway reputation nor Mammy songs on the Vitaphone nor a good story can conceal the painful fact that Al Jolson is no movie star." Unnamed critic. He was forced to do a screen test in 1945 to determine if he could play himself in Jolson Sings Again, 1945. He failed the test and actor Larry Parks got the role. Had more than 150 coats in his closets when he died. He was the first vocalist to sell 10,000,000 records. "It was easy enough make Al Jolson happy at home. You just had to cheer him for breakfast, applaud wildly for lunch and give him a standing ovation for dinner." George Burns. He was the first Hollywood celebrity to sing for the troops in Korea, 1950. Last words: "This is it. I'm going. I'm going." COD: Heart attack while playing poker in his hotel suite. Buried in Los Angeles, California. This third wife, Ruby Keeler, refused to allow her name to be used in The Jolson Story in 1946. Broadway lowered their lights on the day he died.

Buck Jones (Charles Fredrick Gebhart)

b. 12 Dec 1891, d. 30 Nov 1942, = 50 yrs, 11 mos, 18 days. Made 168 movies. Married 1 time.

BKF: Being the most popular movie cowboy of the silent era. NN: King of the Cowboys and The Poor Man's Tom Mix. Voted #1 Favorite Cowboy in 1936, in the first such poll of its kind. Enlisted in the US Army at age 16 years and one month. His mother swore to the army on his behalf that he was 18. Wounded in combat in the Philippines in 1909. Test driver for the Marmon Motor Car Company. Cowhand in Montana. Worked for the Barnum & Bailey Circus and the 101 Wild West Show. Stunt double for Tom Mix. His horse's name was Silver in 50 of 73 westerns and he rode White Eagle and Sandy in other westerns. When he died, Sunset Carson got his horse and renamed him Cactus. Did commercials for Post Grape-Nuts Flakes. He was the first Hollywood Western star to be famous in the Orient. COD: Fire burns. He was one of the 492 victims of the Cocoanut Grove fire in Boston. He was there because he was the honoree at a testimonial dinner that evening. His studio advanced the story that he could have survived but for the fact that he made several trips into the burning building to rescue victims and, the third time he went back in, the roof collapsed on him. This story is a categorically untrue story put out by the Hollywood studio. His body was found still seated at his table and was so badly burned that he had to be identified by the FBI through his fingerprints. Had a fan club--more than 2,000,000 boys were "Buck Jones Rangers."

Boris Karloff (William Henry Pratt)

b. 23 Nov 1887, d. 2 Feb 1969, = 81 yrs, 2 mos, 10 days. Made 205 movies. Married 5 times. A prolific serial adulterer, professional biographers and researchers claim he was most likely married 7 or 8 times.

BKF: Playing the monster in Frankenstein, 1931 and The Mummy in 1932 and for a career in horror films. NN: Billy, The Uncanny. Youngest of nine children. Attended King's College in London but did not graduate. The plan was for him to go into the British Foreign service with his brothers in China. Farm worker in Canada. Rejected by the British Army during WW1 due to a heart murmur. Claimed he chose his screen name from a 17th century Russian ancestor, which was later proven to be not true. He was one of the 12 founding members of the Screen Actors Guild and his membership number was 9. He turned down the role that went to Claude Rains in The Invisible Man because he didn't want to be unseen until the end of the picture. He was 44 years old when he played Frankenstein. His name was not in the credits, even though he played the lead role. It was his 80th movie. The studio credited him as "The Monster--?" because the publicity would help the box office receipts. His name was not revealed until the next year. He was the second star, after Greta Garbo, to be billed by his last name only, in 1933. It took 7 1/2 hours to apply the makeup for The Bride of Frankenstein in 1935. The costume and makeup weighed 62 pounds and made him 18 inches taller. The Frankenstein makeup was a copyrighted recipe. He lost twenty pounds filming the movie. The back brace he wore caused him to have several back operations later in life. He made eight movies with Bela Lugosi. He and Lugosi both married a woman whose last name was Hope. While filming Son of Frankenstein and still in full makeup, he rushed to the hospital for the birth of his daughter, who was born on his birthday, "scaring the hell out of the hospital staff." He always carried a roll of dimes with him to make phone calls because he believed his phone was tapped. He had all false teeth and was a chain smoker. Played an Indian Chief in Unconquered, 1947, co-starring with Gary Cooper. When his wife kept from him the fact that he was going to be ambushed to be the guest on an episode of This Is Your Life in 1952, he said, "She sold me out for a washer and dryer!" Won $32,000 on The $64,000 Question in the category of children's stories. He then voluntarily quit the game because he didn't want to pay taxes on the next higher prize. He had a pet pig named Violet. His hobbies were gardening and writing poetry. Did a commercial for A-1 Steak Sauce. Had a 53 year career. In the 1960's, he suffered from emphysema, only half of one lung functioned and he required oxygen between takes. Directors would allow his character's scenes to be shot in a wheelchair. Retired to England in 1955. He was the inspiration for and the model for the creation of The Incredible Hulk. "It's not true that I was born a monster. Hollywood made me a monster." "When I was nine, I played a demon king in Cinderella and it launched me on a long and happy life of being a monster." "My wife has good taste. She has seen very few of my movies." "My dear old monster. I owe everything to him. He's my best friend." "Certainly I was typed. But what is typing? It is a trademark, a means by which the public recognizes you. Actors work all their lives to achieve that. I got mine with just one picture. It was a blessing." Never legally changed his name. He signed his contracts as "William H. Pratt, a.k.a. Boris Karloff." Last words: To his wife, "Walter Pidgeon." COD: Pneumonia and bronchitis. Cremated, ashes buried in Guilford, England. Died on Groundhog Day. The poster for the 1931 Frankenstein movie sold for $453,000 in 1977.

Buster Keaton (Joseph Frank Keaton)

b. 4 Oct 1895, d. 1 Feb 1966, = 70 yrs, 3 mos, 28 days. Made 149 movies. Married 4 times.

BKF: The General, 1926. NN: The Great Stone Face. Got his Nickname Buster from the pratfalls he was so good at. They were called busters. Harry Houdini gave him the nickname when he saw him fall down a flight of stairs. His right index finger was amputated at the first knuckle when he was three years old. It can best be seen in 1920's The Garage when he holds Fatty Arbuckle's head. Never attended any school. WW1 US Army infantryman in France. Got an ear infection that permanently impaired his hearing. Once broke three vertebrae in his neck performing a gag onstage. He finished the scene and walked off stage. Did not discover he had a broken neck until he got an X-ray years later. He was ambidextrous. His popularity was such that he was as recognizable as Abraham Lincoln. His MGM contract stipulated that he could not smile in public. After finishing a film called What, No Beer?, his contract with MGM was terminated due to his excessive drinking. His first television appearance was on the Ed Wynn Show in 1947. Played himself in a cameo in Sunset Boulevard, 1950. He had only one line and was paid $1,000. Appeared with Charlie Chaplin in Limelight in 1952. It was the only time they appeared together in the same film. He had a cameo in Around the World in 80 Days. His last film was a posthumous appearance in A Funny Thing Happened on the Way to the Forum in 1967. He died in 1966, on the same day as Hedda Hopper. His last public appearance was a tribute to Stan Laurel hosted by Dick Van Dyke in November, 1965. He was diagnosed with lung cancer a month before he died, but his doctors told him it was a severe case of bronchitis. "I always want the audience to out-guess me, and then I double-cross them." "The law reads that a child can't do acrobatics, walk a wire, juggle...a lot of those things, but there's nothing in the law that says you can't kick him in the face or throw him through a piece of scenery. On that technicality, we were allowed to work, although we'd get called into court every other week." COD: Lung cancer. Died at home in his sleep, shortly after playing cards with his wife. Buried in Los Angeles. Autobiography: My Wonderful World of Slapstick, 1964.

Guy Kibbee (Guy Bridges Kibbee)

b. 6 Mar 1882, d. 24 May 1956, = 74 yrs, 2 mos, 18 days. Made 114 movies. Married 2 times.

BKF: The Scattergood Baines series at RKO Studios and playing Governor Hopper in Mr. Smith Goes to Washington, 1939. Riverboat entertainer, Broadway star. Was 49 years old when he made his first movie, Man of the World. Made 20 movies in 1932. COD: Parkinson's disease. He lived in the Home for aged and Destitute actors in East Islip, New York.

Rod La Rocque (Roderick LaRocque de la Rou)

b. 29 Nov 1898, d. 15 Oct 1969, = 70 yrs, 10 mos, 16 days. Made 114 movies. Married 1 time.

BKF: Being Married to actress Vilma Bankey and playing Dan McTavish in The Ten Commandments, 1923. Worked as a stage hand in Chicago and New York theater until he was discovered by Samuel Goldwyn and taken to Hollywood. He was 6'3". Talkies killed his career. Voluntarily retired from acting in 1941 and became a real estate agent. COD: Undisclosed.

Carl Laemmle (Karl Lammle)

b. 17 Jan 1867, d. 24 Sep 1939, = 72 yrs, 8 mos, 7 days. Produced 400+ movies. Married 1 time.

BKF: Founder of Universal Studios. NN: Uncle Carl. Nickelodeon operator and salesman. Became a US citizen 1889. Manager of a clothing store in Oshkosh, Wisconsin in early 1920's. Produced The

Hunchback of Notre Dame, 1923, and Phantom of the Opera, 1925. Said his name is pronounced 'lem-lee.' COD: Heart disease. Buried in Beverly Hills.

Bert Lahr (Irving Larheim)

b. 13 Aug 1895, d. 4 Dec 1967, = 72 yrs, 3 mos, 21 days. Made 51 movies. Married 2 times.

BKF: Playing The Cowardly Lion in The Wizard of Oz. NN: Leo, because it was also his astrological sign. Dropped out of school to go into Vaudeville at age 15. Even though Judy Garland's rendition of Over the Rainbow was the big hit of The Wizard of Oz, she got to sing only one song in the movie. Bert Lahr got to sing two songs: If I Only Had the Nerve, and If I Were King of the Forrest. He was the actor who first appeared in Lay's Potato Chip commercials saying, "Betcha' can't eat just one." "That was my one big Hollywood hit, but, in a big way, it hurt my picture career. After The Wizard of Oz, I was typecast as a lion, and there aren't all that many parts for a lion." "If you want to be a success in Hollywood, be sure and go to New York." "Hollywood is the only community in the world where the entire population is suffering from 'rumouritis.'" Last words: "Mildred, why aren't all my clothes laid out?" He was not told he was dying of cancer at the time of his death. COD: Pneumonia and cancer. Buried in Queens, New York.

Charles Laughton (Same)

b. 1 July 1899, d. 15 Dec 1962, = 63 yrs, 5 mos, 14 days. Made 65 movies. Married 1 time.

BKF: Playing Captain Bligh in Mutiny on the Bounty, 1935, and Ruggles of Red Gap, 1935 which he said was his favorite movie. 5' 8 1/2". Worked in his family's inn. WW1: Member of Britain's 7th North Hampshire Regiment. Suffered from poison gas during the war. He was the first actor to play Agatha Christie's detective Hercule Poirot. He won the first Best Actor Oscar for a British-made film, The Private Life of Henry VIII, in 1933. It was the first British film to become an international hit. While filming The Hunchback of Notre Dame, he went home after filming still wearing the hunchback. That was so he could jump in his pool and use it as a flotation device for several hours of swimming. Lived in a London house once owned by Karl Marx. While working in Chicago during WW2, he learned that his house in London had been destroyed by a German dive bomber. He sold $500,000 worth of war bonds during WW2 by reading The Bill of Rights on Wall Street. On closing his war bond drive on the radio at midnight, he said, "It is a duty and a privilege to buy bonds--the last chance to save the flickering flame of democracy. God help you and your children if that flame dies out." "He had a face that faintly resembled a large wad of cotton wool." Josef Von Sternberg. Toured with the USO in the US and Europe during WW2. One of his best jokes was: "Q: Isn't this a bloody awful war? A: Oh, I don't know, It's better than no war at all." Became a US citizen in 1950. On the cover of Time Magazine, 31 March 1952. When Elvis Presley made his first of three appearances on the Ed Sullivan Show on 9 September 1956, Charles Laughton was the guest host. Ed Sullivan was recovering from a automobile accident. He and his wife Elsa Lanchester were both nominated for Best Acting Oscars in the same year, in 1957, for Witness For the Prosecution. He was the guest on What's My Line? not once, but twice. He discovered actress Maureen O'Hara at age 18 and put her in her first movie with him. His wife disliked her so much that she said, "She always looked as if butter wouldn't melt in her mouth--or anywhere else, either." He turned down the role that went to Alec Guinness in Bridge on the River Kwai and he turned down the role that went to Leslie Howard in Pygmalion. A closet homosexual, his wife didn't learn of it until years after they were married. They stayed together because of their mutual interests like gardening, cooking, acting and, as he said, "young men." She said of their open marriage, "We both needed each other's company. I met his young men and I had a young man around, and Charles didn't even argue." He said the worst thing about being famous was going to a restaurant, and instead of getting his order, being served by yet another Captain Bligh imitation by the waiter. "I have a face like the behind of an elephant." "I have a face that would stop a sun dial and frightens young children." "Method actors give you a photograph. Real actors give you an oil painting." "They can't censor the gleam in my eye." You can't direct a Laughton picture. The best you can hope for is to referee." Alfred Hitchcock. His last film was Advise and Consent, 1962. COD: Renal cell carcinoma (kidney cancer) and spinal cancer. Buried in Hollywood Hill, California.

Stan Laurel (Arthur Stanley Jefferson)

b. 16 Jun 1890, d. 23 Feb 1965, = 74 yrs, 8 mos, 7 days. Made 186 movies. Married 5 times, twice to the same woman.

BKF: Being the shorter and thinner member of The Laurel & Hardy Comedy duo and 25 pictures with Oliver Hardy. Came to the US from England on the same boat as the equally unknown Charlie Chaplin in 1910. Passed through Ellis Island. He was Chaplin's understudy. He changed his name because he didn't want a name with thirteen letters in it. Got a deferment from military service in WW1 due to being slightly deaf. It was Laurel & Hardy, and not the Marx Brothers, who appeared in the first Duck Soup movie, a short made in 1927. He removed the heels from his shoes when filming all of his movies. He thought it made him walk funnier. The house destroyed in Big Business in 1929 was the wrong house. It was supposed to have been the house next door. He appeared in the movie Jitterbugs in drag dressed as a woman. At an alimony hearing in open court, his wife claimed that he invited his ex-wife along on their honeymoon and threatened to bury her alive in their back yard. When Oliver Hardy died in 1957 he was too sick to attend the funeral, saying, "Babe would understand." He was so thankful for his good luck and success in life that he never turned down an autograph request. He also made sure his home phone number (OXford-0614) was in the phone book so fans could reach him. When asked why he would do that, he said, "How will people find me if I don't?" Turned down an offer of a cameo in It's a Mad, Mad, Mad, Mad World in 1963 because he didn't want his fans to see how old he looked. He was a heavy smoker until four years before he died. When asked if he had any bad habits, he said, "Yes, and I married them." On the films he and Oliver Hardy made at 20th C. Fox: "We had no say on those films and it sure looked it." "People have always loved our pictures. I guess that's because they saw how much love we put into them." "If anyone at my funeral has a long face, I'll never speak to him again." Last words: "I'd rather be skiing than doing this. [Do you ski, Mr. Laurel?] No, but I'd rather be doing that than doing this." "Chaplin wasn't the funniest, I wasn't the funniest, this man was the funniest." Buster Keaton, at his funeral. COD: Heart attack, which he had four days earlier. His eulogy was delivered by Dick Van Dyke. Cremated, ashes buried in Hollywood Hills, California. His epitaph reads: "A master of comedy/His genius in the art of comedy/Brought gladness/To the world he loved." His likeness is on the cover of the Beatles' Lonely Hearts Club album cover. In 1975, a New York judge ruled that the names, images and merchandising rights of Laurel and Hardy belonged to their wives, and not to the Hal Roach Studios.

Florence Lawrence (Florence Annie Bridgwood)

b. 2 Jan 1886, d. 28 Dec 1938, = 52 yrs, 11 mos, 26 days. Made 302 movies. Married 3 times.

BKF: Being The First Movie Star. NN: The First Movie Star. Baby Florence, The White Wonder, The Vitagraph Girl, The Biograph Girl, The IMP Girl, Queen of the Screen. One reviewer said, "We do not know the lady's name." Studios refused to name their actors, fearing that the more popular ones would demand bigger salaries. But when they learned that more popularity meant more money for the studio, then relented. She is the first movie star to get a screen credit with her real name, in 1910's The Broken Oath. When she appeared in person in St. Louis in 1910, she drew a much larger crowd than President Taft did a week before. In 1910 a newspaper erroneously reported that she had died in a streetcar accident. She was the first movie star to be interviewed; by Motion Picture Magazine in 1911. She was the most popular movie star in the world from 1910 to 1912. She was badly burned in a studio fire trying to save someone else. She invented the 'auto signaling arm' which became the turn signal and the 'full stop' sign which became brake lights on automobiles. She neglected to get a patent for either one. COD: Suicide by eating ant paste poison five days before her next birthday.

Gertrude Lawrence (Gertrude Alice Dagmar Klasen)

b. 4 July 1898, d. 6 Sep 1952, = 54 yrs, 2 mos, 2 days. Made 13 movies. Married 2 times.

BKF: London and New York stage actress and The Glass Menagerie, 1950. NN: Gertie, Cinders, short for Cinderella. 1951 Hasty Pudding Woman of the Year. COD: Liver and abdominal cancer. She was the first actor to have all the lights on Broadway dimmed on the occasion of their death. Autobiography: A Star Danced, 1945.

Beatrice Lillie (Beatrice Gladys Lillie)

b. 29 May 1894, d. 4 Feb 1987, = 94 yrs, 7 mos, 12 days. Made 7 movies. Married 1 time.

BKF: Thoroughly Modern Millie, 1967. NN: Funniest Woman in the World. Vaudeville and stage actress. She was a candidate for the role of the Good Witch in The Wizard of Oz, but was ultimately rejected because she was considered to be too well known for her comedy. She married Sir Robert Peel and was known as Lady Peel. While performing for the troops during WW2, and about to go on stage, she was told that her son had been killed in action. She insisted on performing, saying, "I'll cry tomorrow." Her decades-long companion, John Huck, who was thirty years younger than her, died thirty-one hours after she did. Had a cameo in Around the World In 80 days. Had two strokes in 1973. COD: Alzheimer's disease. Buried in Blackburn, England.

Elmo Lincoln (Otto Elmo Linkenhelt)

b. 6 Feb 1889, d. 27 Jun 1952, = 63, yrs, 4 mos, 21 days. Made 81 movies. Married 2 times.

BKF: Tarzan of the Apes, 1918. Train engineer. Law man in Arkansas. He was the first actor to portray Tarzan as an adult on the silver screen. (The first actor ever to play Tarzan on the silver screen was successful child actor Gordon Griffith, who appeared in the same movie, but appeared earlier in the film as a 10-year-old Tarzan.) He got to replace the original actor, Stellan Windrow, when he was called to active duty for WW1. Tarzan of the Apes was released on 21 Jan 1918. Variety said it is "a freak picture that will cause talk." It was one of the first five movies to earn more than $1,000,000 when released. Had a small part in Carrie in 1952. COD: Heart attack. Buried in Glendale, California.

Harold Lloyd (Harold Clayton Lloyd)

b. 20 Apr 1893, d. 8 Mar 1971, = 77 yrs, 10 mos, 16 days. Made 213 movies. Married 1 time.

BKF: Along with Charlie Chaplin and Buster Keaton, being one of the three top comedians of the silent era. NN: The King of Daredevil Comedy. Worked for Thomas Edison in his motion picture company. With a choice of either New York or California on a coin flip, his father took him to California where he got a job as an extra. Lost his right thumb and forefinger when a fake publicity bomb turned out to be real and exploded in 1919. He always wore gloves after that. He made more movies and more money than Chaplin did in the 1920's.

That's him hanging onto the hands of the clock on the outside of the building and above a busy street in Safety Last, in 1923. He is credited with creating movie previews and cutting and reshooting movies based on test audience results. His trademark glasses were the model for the glasses wore by Clark Kent (Superman). Made The Milky Way in 1936 and was a flop when released. It has since become a must-see classic. His personal collection of hundreds of his silent films was destroyed by a house fire in 1943. He survived only because his wife pulled his unconscious body out of the house just in time. He was a 33rd degree Scottish Rite Mason. President Harry Truman attended his installation ceremony on 25 July 1945. He received an Honorary Academy Award for being a 'master comedian and good citizen' in 1953. He was the honoree on This Is Your Life on 14 Dec 1955. He said if a movie of his life were ever made, he wanted no one but Jack Lemmon to play him. He is not as well known as he could be today because he kept the copyrights to all of his films and demanded $300,000 per picture for two showings. "My character represented the white-collar middle class that felt frustrated but was always fighting to overcome its shortcomings." His Beverly Hills estate was called Greenacres and is now on the National Registry of Historic Places. It was the location of the filming of the movie Westworld. COD: Prostate cancer. Buried in Glendale, California. Worth $12,000,000 at the time of his death.

Bela Lugosi (Bella Ferenc Deszo Blasko)

b. 20 Oct 1882, d. 16 Aug 1956, = 73 yrs, 9 mos, 27 days. Made 116 movies. Married 5 times.

BKF: Playing Dracula in 2 movies and starting the Zombie trend in horror films. Born in Transylvania on the same day as Margaret Dumont, costar of the Marx Brothers comedies. 6' 1". Mine and factory worker. Named himself after his hometown of Lugos, Hungary. He added the i. His first role on stage was as Romeo in Romeo and Juliet. He also played Jesus Christ on stage before coming to America.

During WW1 he was an infantryman in the Austro-Hungarian Army, becoming Captain of the Ski Patrol. He was wounded three times in action on the Russian front. Arrived in the United States (New Orleans) by working as a seaman on a merchant marine ship. He was a charter member of the Screen Actors Guild. He was chosen to be the first on screen Frankenstein but turned down the role when the makeup and screen test revealed that he would not be able to show his great profile or have any dialogue other than grunts. His wife filed for divorce in 1924, naming Clara Bow (!) as the other woman. Made six movies with Boris Karloff. He was paid $500 for the seven weeks it took to make Dracula, 1931. His career took a nosedive when horror films were banned in Britain in 1936. His fifth wife, and Boris Karloff's fifth wife, were both named Hope. In all his movies, he only had one romantic scene where he got to kiss his female co-star. It was in The Midnight Girl, 1925. His face was used as a model for Satan's in Walt Disney's Fantasia, 1940. His heavy German accent limited the roles he could play. Had a popular nightclub act in Las Vegas in 1954. His third wife left him after three days. In a questionnaire he answered later in life, he said his boyhood ambition was to be a highway bandit and his favorite screen star was Mickey Mouse. He is the star of what critics universally agree is the worst movie ever made, Plan 9 From Outer Space. Died before he could begin work on his final movie, ironically titled The Final Curtain. His fifth, and final, wife was a fan who wrote him encouraging letters when he was in the hospital being treated for drug addictions. "I'll be truthful. The weekly paycheck is the most important thing to me." COD: Heart attack at home while his wife was out grocery shopping. Buried in Culver City, California. His epitaph says "Beloved Father." His funeral was paid for by Frank Sinatra. He was buried in his Dracula cape. At his funeral his wife said, "He was just terrified of death." Johnny Depp bought his house and moved in with his collection of insects and guns. His heirs lost a lawsuit in 1979 when they claimed that Universal Studios unfairly exploited his image as Dracula by licensing it to appear on merchandise. They regained the rights to his publicity through a new California law passed in 1988. His personal cane sold for $10,000 at auction in 2015.

Paul Lukas (Pal Lukacs)

b. 26 May 1891, d. 15 Aug 1971, = 80 yrs, 2 mos, 20 days. Made 131 movies. Married 3 times.

BKF: Academy Award winning performance in Watch on the Rhine, 1943. 6' 1/2". Born on a train near Budapest, Hungary. Had a successful stage and film career in Europe. Came to the US in 1927. When he won the Best Actor Oscar in 1943, he was told that that would mark the height of his career. He said, "I know. That's why I voted for myself." He beat Humphrey Bogart in Casablanca. In retirement, he voluntarily worked six hours a week at New York's Memorial Hospital as an orderly. COD: Heart attack. Died in Morocco, while looking for a retirement home. Buried in Spain.

Moms Mabley (Loretta Mary Aitken)

b. 19 Mar 1894, d. 23 May 1975, = 81 yrs, 2 mos, 4 days. Made 3 movies. Never married.

BKF: Her stand-up comedy. NN: Moms, because she was known to be a mother role for other entertainers on the Chitlin' Circuit in the 1950's. NN: The Funniest Woman in the World. She was one of the first openly gay comedians, coming out in 1921 at age 27. Had six children. Chose the name Mabley to honor her friend Jack Mabley. "Jack was my first boyfriend. He took a lot off me and the least I could do was take his name." Had a 60-year career. Earned $10,000 per week in the 1960's. At age 75, she became the oldest living person to have a Top 40 hit with Abraham, Martin and John in 1969. "Love is like playing checkers. You have to know which man to move." "A woman is a woman until the day she dies, but a man's a man only as long as he can." "There ain't nothing an old man can do for me except bring me a message from a young one." "The teenagers ain't all bad. I love 'em if nobody else does. There ain't nothing wrong with young people. Jus' quit lyin' to 'em." COD: Heart failure.

Marjorie Main (Mary Tomlinson Krebbs)

b. 24 Feb 1890, d. 10 Apr 1975, = 85 yrs, 1 mo, 17 days. Made 89 movies. Married 1 time.

BKF: Playing Ma in 10 Ma and Pa Kettle movies, 1947-1955. Vaudeville. Chose her stage name to keep her father from being embarrassed of her. Made 6 films with Wallace Beery in the 1940's. Raised $500,000 in war bonds during WW2. "Most of the time I played mothers. That's acting!" Ma and Pa Kettle movies: 1. The Egg and I, for which she was nominated for a Best Supporting Actress Oscar, 2. Ma and Pa Kettle, 3. Ma and Pa Kettle Go To Town, 4. Ma and Pa Kettle Back on the Farm, 5. Ma and Pa Kettle on Vacation, 6. Ma and Pa Kettle at the Fair, 7. Ma and Pa Kettle at Waikiki, 8. Ma and Pa Kettle at Home, 9. The Kettles in the Ozarks, 10. The Kettles on Old MacDonald's Farm. COD: Lung cancer and heart attack. Buried in Hollywood Hills, California. Epitaph: Mary Tomlinson Krebbs with "Marjorie Main" underneath.

Frederic March (Ernst Frederick McIntyre Bickel)

b. 31 Aug 1897, d. 14 Apr 1975, = 77 yrs, 7 mos, 14 days. Made 86 movies. Married 2 times.

BKF: Dr. Jeckyl and Mr. Hyde, 1931, and The Best Years of Our Lives. Because he considered the number 12 to be his lucky number, he shortened his name to Fredric and his mother's name from Marcher to March to become Fredric March. WW1 Lieutenant in the US Army Artillery Corps. Banker, but changed to part time acting after an appendectomy. His nurse was a former actress who talked him into acting. During WW2 he traveled 40,000 miles with the USO to entertain the troops. Studied to be an economist, earning a Bachelor's Degree in Economics from the University of Wisconsin. He was the first actor to be brought to Hollywood from the New York stage when talkies were invented. He is the only actor to win a Best Actor Oscar for playing a monster, Dr. Jekyll and Mr. Hyde and the first actor to win for a horror film. It wouldn't happen again until Anthony Hopkins won for Silence of the Lambs in 1991. In 1946 he won the Best Actor Oscar for The Best Years of Our Lives and the Best Actor Tony Award for his role in Years Ago, making him the only actor to win the highest stage and screen awards in the same year. Also he is the only actor to win two Best Actor Oscars and two Tony awards for Best Actor in a Play. He said his work on television was "an awful experience." In retirement he liked to swim, play tennis, ride horseback, golf, read and travel. "An actor has no more right to be temperamental than a bank clerk." "Keep interested in others; keep interested in the wide and wonderful world. Then in a spiritual sense, you will always be young." When Audrey Hepburn won her Academy Award in 1954 she kissed him and he said, "I'll take a dozen of those." He suggested his epitaph read "This is just my lot," COD: Prostate cancer. Cremated, ashes buried under his favorite tree on his farm in Connecticut. His Beverly Hills mansion is now owned by Madonna.

Chico Marx (Leonard Marx)

b. 22 Mar 1887, d. 11 Oct 1961, = 74, yrs, 6 mos, 19 days. Made 22 movies. Married 2 times. Got his nickname Chico from being called a 'chick' chaser.

BKF: Being one of the Marx Brothers. The Marx Brothers had an older brother named Manfred who died in infancy. Chico is the oldest to survive and the first to die. He was raised in a brothel. In 1917, he was a pianist in Manhattan's City Theater, earning $25 per week. He quit after one show and was replaced by George Gershwin. In 1931, he was severely injured in a car accident that held up filming of Horse Feathers for ten weeks. He had a photographic memory, being able to memorize stunningly large amounts of information and photos in perfect detail. He was the Marx Brother who negotiated the first-ever contract with MGM that gave a star a percentage of the movie's profit. He got the deal by losing at gin rummy on purpose with a studio executive and winning after making a five-movie deal on the hand. When mobster Bugsy Siegel was shot and killed in Los Angeles, a check written to him by Chico was found in his wallet. He was interrogated and convinced the police that the check was payment for a gambling debt. Groucho said, "It's a good thing Bugsy was dead. If he had tried to cash that check it would have bounced and he would have killed Chico." Because he couldn't handle his own money, his brothers took his money and put him on an allowance in the later part of his life. He is the one who said, "Well, who you gonna believe, me or your own eyes?" which is often erroneously attributed to Groucho. "Ask my brother Groucho how much he's made and that's how much I've lost (at gambling)." "There were three things Chico was always on--a phone, a horse or a broad." Groucho Marx. "I wasn't kissing her, I was whispering in her mouth." Because he gambled away all of his money, he was forced to play in second-rate venues to earn a living. "He was such a gambler that in order to get him to read a movie script, you'd have to slip it in between his racing forms." To his wife: "Remember don't forget what I told you. Put in my coffin a deck of cards, a mashie niblik, and a pretty blonde!" COD: Heart disease. Buried in Glendale, CA

Groucho Marx (Julius Henry Marx)

b. 2 Oct 1890, d. 19 Aug 1977, = 86 yrs, 10 mos, 17 days. Made 33 movies. Married 3 times. NN: Got his nickname Groucho from always carrying his money around in a grouch bag. "My own name--I never did understand."

BKF: Being the lead Marx Brother, his quick wit and one-liners. Hosting 529 episodes of You Bet Your Life from 1950 to 1961. It was the first game show to have its reruns syndicated. The Marx Brothers made 13 movies together. Drove a grocery wagon in Colorado in the 1910's. Vaudeville performer. In 1912, Variety called the Marx Brothers "A lively set of youngsters, with four comedians. One of them is a harpist, and a good one." Groucho lost $240,000 in the stock market crash of 1929. He did not like actor John Wayne. Consequently, he named his dog Duke. His radio and television show theme song was "Hooray For Captain Spaulding," which was first sung in Animal Crackers, 1930. The five Marx Brothers were on the cover of Time Magazine on 15 August 1932. Groucho and his brother Chico were convicted in US District Court in 1937 of stealing material used in another performer's radio show act the previous year. They paid $1,000 in fines and $7,500 in civil penalties. It was the first Hollywood case of criminal plagiarism. The name of the fictional country in Duck Soup, 1933, was Freedonia. When the residents of the real Freedonia, New York complained, he said, "You change your name. It's hurting our movie." His character's name in A Day at the Races, 1937, was changed from Dr. Quackenbush to Dr. Hackenbush after it was discovered that there were dozens of bona fide, real Dr. Quackenbushes across the United States who just might sue him. The Marx Brothers were delighted when the movie was banned in the Republic of Latvia as being "worthless." Just so you know: There were 15 people crammed into the stateroom in the movie A Night At the Opera: Groucho, Chico, Harpo, Ricardo Baroni, two maids, an engineer, a manicurist, a girl looking for her aunt Minnie, a washwoman and four stewards. Margaret Mitchell suggested, in jest, that he play Rhett Butler in Gone With the Wind. He had an unaccredited role in Will Success Spoil Rock Hunter? He sold war bonds on tour during WW2 but he was virtually unknown and unrecognizable without his trademark props bushy eyebrows, mustache and glasses. One night he was actually prevented from getting back into his hotel room by the policeman on duty. The 13 Marx Brothers Movies: 1. The Cocoanuts, 1929, 2. Animal Crackers, 1930, 3. Monkey Business, 1931, 4. Horse Feathers, 1932, 5. Duck Soup, 1933, 6. A Night at the Opera, 1935, 7. A Day at the Races, 1937, 8. Room Service, 1938, 9. At the Circus, 1939, 10. Go West, 1940,

11. The Big Store, 1941, 12. A Night in Casablanca, 1946, 13. Love Happy, 1949. Groucho is well known for the time his guest on You Bet Your Life had 19 children. He asked her, "Why do you have so many children?" to which she replied, "I love my husband," to which Groucho replied, "Well, I love my cigar too, but I take it out of my mouth once in a while." Thing is--this never actually happened. It's just an example of the kind of thing that Groucho would say that over the years was accepted as truth. Groucho said, "I get credit for a lot of things I didn't say." The secret word on You Bet Your Life was worth $100. Claimed he didn't eat his first bagel until he was eighty-one years old. Said that when he once visited a Havana cigar factory, "There were four hundred people there rolling cigars, and when they saw me, they all stood up and applauded." His daughter Melinda made her screen debut playing opposite Ronald Colman in The Story of Mankind, 1957. The only time all five Marx Brothers were on television together was on Tonight! America After Dark, hosted by Jack Lescoulie on 18 February 1957. In 1971, at age 81, the FBI listed him as a "threat to the life of President Richard Nixon." "Whoever named it necking was a poor judge of anatomy." "I find television very educating. Every time somebody turns on the set, I go into the other room and read a book." "Home is where you hang your head." "Those are my principles. If you don't like them, I have others." "My mother loved children. She would have given anything if I had been one." "Politics is the art of looking for trouble, finding it everywhere, diagnosing it incorrectly and applying the wrong remedy." "I drink to make other people more interesting." "There is no sweeter sound that the crumbling of one's fellow man." "Anyone who says he can see through women is missing a lot." "The ideal woman is short and tall, slim and stout, and blonde and brunette." "Quote me as saying I was mis-quoted." "The funny thing about her (Margaret Dumont) is that she never understood the jokes." "Behind every successful man is a woman; behind her is his wife." "I was married by a judge. I should have asked for a jury." "The husband who wants to have a happy marriage should learn to keep his mouth shut and his checkbook open." "I made a killing on Wall Street a few years ago--I shot my

broker." "In Hollywood, brides keep the bouquet and throw away the groom." "I wish to be cremated. One tenth of my ashes shall be given to my agent, as written in our contract." Sometimes guest host of The Tonight Show, With Johnny Carson. When he was about to die in the hospital, a nurse with a thermometer told him, "I want to see if you have a temperature." He said, don't be silly--everybody has a temperature." Later that night his last words were, "This is no way to live!" COD: Pneumonia. He died three days after Elvis Presley. He signed is will three years before he died. Worth about $2,000,000, he left $50,000 to his only surviving brother Zeppo, $150,000 to his "secretary/companion" and his country club membership to his son. The rest went to a trust. He has no epitaph but he once suggested it be, "Excuse me, I can't stand up." He also suggested his epitaph be, "Here lies Groucho Marx, and lies and lies and lies. He never kissed an ugly woman." His ashes were scattered in Mission Hills, CA. Autobiographies: Groucho and Me, 1959. Memoirs of a Mangy Lover, 1963. The Groucho Letters, 1967. Beds, 1977.

Harpo Marx (Adolph, later changed to Arthur, Marx)

b. 23 Nov 1888, d. 28 Sep 1964, = 75 yrs, 10 mos, 5 days. Made 23 movies. Married 1 time. Got his nickname Harpo from playing the harp, which he unknowingly at first played from the wrong side.

BKF: Being the one Marx Brother who did not speak on film. He was terrible at having to memorize his lines so he decided at the outset of his movie career that he just wouldn't speak. Quit school at age 8 after failing the 2nd grade twice. He was raised in a brothel. Newspaper boy, butcher shop boy, office errand boy. Bellhop at New York City's Plaza Hotel. Vaudeville performer. Mime artist. Performed in Moscow in the late 1930's and carried secret messages between the US State Department and the US Embassy in Moscow. He did speak in his first movie which, ironically, was the 1925 silent movie Too Many Kisses. After tying up the bad guy, he asks him, "Are you sure you can't move?" You can read his lips and besides, that's what the cue card said. He was left-handed. He had four adopted children. When Bob Hope asked him, "How many more children are you going to adopt," he said "I want one child for each window in my house. That way, when I leave home someone is waving goodbye from every window." The Marx Brothers incorporated themselves on 3 April 1933, with Groucho as President. He spoke before an audience (not in a movie) for the first time in twenty-five years at a playhouse in Pennsylvania in July 1941. The line was: "I can feel the hot blood pounding through your varicose veins." WW2: He performed for stateside troops, traveling more than 200,000 miles back and forth across the country. In 1946 he was offered $55,000 to say just one word--"Murder!" in the Marx Brothers movie A Night in Casablanca. He declined. "I am the most fortunate self-taught harpist and non-speaking actor that ever lived." "Harpo Marx was probably the sweetest man you would ever want to meet." Jack Benny. COD: Heart attack. Actress Geneane Garafalo was born on the day he died. Upon his death, he donated his harp to the state of Israel. Cremated, his ashes were spread on a golf course in Rancho Mirage, California. Autobiography: Harpo Speaks!, 1961.

Zeppo Marx (Herbert Manfred Marx)

b. 25 Feb 1901, d. 30 Nov 1979, = 78 yrs, 9 mos, 5 days. Made 6 movies. Married 2 times. Got his nickname Zeppo from a chimpanzee act, which he did not like being reminded of.

BKF: Being the youngest Marx Brother and the last to die. Owned a company that supplied machine parts the US military. Made only six movies, the first five being with his brothers. Left the act to become a talent agent and engineer in 1934. The fist Marx Brothers movie without him was A Night at the Opera, 1935. He invented a wrist-worn pulse rate monitor that alerted the patient when his pulse became irregular. His other engineering inventions made him a multi-millionaire. His father Frenchie appeared as a extra in Monkey Business in 1931. "There just wasn't room for another funny Marx

Brother. But offstage he was the funniest one of us." Groucho Marx. COD: Heart attack. Cremated, ashes scattered in the Pacific Ocean. (Author's note: Even though he was born in 1901, I included him in this edition to keep all of the Marx brothers together.) The rock band Queen named two of their albums after The Marx Brothers movies, A Night at the Opera, 1975, and A Day at the Races, 1976.

Raymond Massey (Raymond Hart Massey)

b. 30 Aug 1896, d. 29 July 1983, = 86 yrs, 10 mos, 29 days. Made 86 movies. Married 3 times.

BKF: Abe Lincoln In Illinois, 1941, and playing Dr. Gillespie in 191 episodes of Dr. Kildare, 1961-1966. Also played James Dean's father in East of Eden, 1955. His ancestors arrived in America in 1629. Sold farm equipment. Served in WW1 in the Canadian Expeditionary Force, field artillery unit, in Siberia. Later wounded in action in France. He had a contract to join the US Marine Corps as an Intelligence Officer at the beginning of WW2, when he received the following telegram from the Canadian Minister of Defense: "Breathes there a man with a soul so dead to never to himself to hath said 'this is my own land?' Please phone me." He made the call and was commissioned a Major in the Canadian Army and put in charge of what he said was, "recreation, entertainment and athletics." He resigned his commission a year later and went back to Hollywood. He played Abraham Lincoln in several movies and television shows, causing him to complain that he was "the only actor to be typecast as a president." A fellow actor said that Massey thought his portrayal of Lincoln was so good that it wouldn't be complete unless someone assassinated him. His younger brother was the first Canadian-born Governor General of Canada (1952-59). He was one of the first four inductees into the Canadian Motion Picture Hall of Fame, 1973. COD: Pneumonia. He and David Niven died on the same day. Buried in New Haven, Connecticut.

Ken Warren

Louis B. Mayer (Lazar Meir, later Louis Burt Mayer)

b. 12 July 1884, d. 29 Oct 1957, 73 yrs, 3 mos, 17 days. Produced thousands of movies. Married 2 times.

BKF: Founder of Metro-Goldwyn-Mayer (MGM) Studios. Could not remember his birth date in Russia, so he claimed July 4th. Scrap dealer. Owned a burlesque house and several small movie theaters. Was the owner of Busher, the greatest money-winning filly in racing history. He was the first person in America to receive a $1,000,000 annual salary. He earned $1,300,000 per year from 1937 to 1946. Suffered a broken pelvis from a fall from a horse in August 1944. "Never be afraid to hire a fellow smarter than you are. You'll only learn from them." "I want to make beautiful pictures about beautiful people." Last words: "Nothing matters. Don't let them worry you. Nothing matters." And then he added, "It wasn't worth it." "The only reason so many people showed up at his funeral was because they wanted to make sure he was dead." Samuel Goldwyn. Jeannette MacDonald sang, Oh, What Sweet Mystery of Life at his funeral. COD: Leukemia. Buried in East Los Angeles, California.

Tim McCoy (Timothy John Fitzgerald McCoy)

b. 10 Apr 1891, d. 29 Jan 1978, = 86 yrs, 9 mos, 19 days. Made 93 movies. Married 2 times.

BKF: Being one of Hollywood's earliest cowboys. He was the star of the first movie filmed in Hollywood in 1911, which also starred Joan Crawford in the female lead. Was on the cover of Wheaties cereal boxes. Made eight Rough Rider films with Buck Jones. in the 1930's. He was a US Army Colonel during WW1, serving as an artillery officer. Adjutant General of Wyoming as a Brigadier General at age 28, making him possibly the youngest General ever in the US Army. Earned a Bronze Star with the US Army Air Forces in WW2. He was such a renowned expert on American Indian sign language that his

120

Arapaho name was High Eagle. He was one of the few white men who could converse in Indian sign language. His horse's names were Pal, Barron and Ace. Host of The Tim McCoy Show in Los Angeles in 1952, a show to teach children about American Indians. Inducted into the Cowboy Hall of Fame in 1973. COD: Undisclosed. Died in Arizona, cremated. Ashes buried in his family plot in Saginaw, Michigan. Autobiography: Tim McCoy Remembers the West, 1977.

Hattie McDaniel (Same) AKA: Joanna Rose

b. 10 Jun 1893, d. 26 Oct 1952, = 59 yrs, 4 mos, 16 days. Made 300+ movies but is credited in only about 80 of them. Married 4 times.

BKF: Playing Mammy in Gone With the Wind. NN: Hi-Hat Hattie, The Colored Sophie Tucker, Mamie. (5'-2") Youngest of 13 children. Her father was a slave, who eventually was freed and fought in the US Civil War with the 122nd United States Colored Troops. Extremely wealthy by 1929, she lost everything in the 1929 stock market crash and had to start over as a washroom attendant. She was the first black woman to sing on the radio in 1930. Sang a duet with Will Rogers in Judge Priest in 1934. She was not only the first black woman to win an Oscar, she was also the first black woman to even be nominated and attend the Academy Award Ceremony. Clark Gable threatened to boycott the premier of Gone With the Wind in Atlanta unless she was allowed to attend, but she urged him to attend, saying that she would find another way to protest and insisted that he still attend. During the Academy Award Ceremony in 1940, she and a guest were seated in the back of the venue near the kitchen. When her name was called, she yelled out "Hallelujah!" She got the heavily contested role in Gone With the Wind even though First Lady Eleanor Roosevelt lobbied the producer to give her personal maid the part. Accepting her Oscar, she said: "Academy of Motion Picture Arts and Sciences, fellow members of the motion picture industry and honored guests: This is one of the happiest moments of my life, and I want to thank each one of you who had a part in selecting me for one of their awards, for your kindness. It has made me feel very, very humble; and I shall always hold it as a beacon for anything that I may be able to do in the future. I sincerely hope I shall always be a credit to my race and to the motion picture industry. My heart is too full to tell you how I feel, and may I say thank you and God bless you." Gone With the Wind was not her first movie with Clark Gable--they were both in Saratoga in 1937. She was also the first black American to star in her own radio show, which was the comedy Beulah in 1951. WW2: She was chairman of the Negro Division of the Hollywood Victory Committee and performed at USO shows and bond drives. Raised money for the American Red Cross. "Why should I complain about making $700 a week playing a maid when I could be a maid for $7 a week?" She earned $1,000 per week for making Gone With the Wind. COD: Breast cancer, an earlier heart attack and a mild stroke. Her will stated: "I desire a white casket and a white shroud; white gardenias in my hair and in my hands, together with a white gardenia blanket and a pillow of red roses. I also wish to be buried in the Hollywood Cemetery." The cemetery owner refused to allow her to be buried there because of racial segregation, so she was buried at her second choice, and became the first African-American to be buried in Rosedale Cemetery. She left her Oscar to Howard University and she was worth less than $10,000 at the time of her death, despite earning millions during her lifetime. Her will left her husband only $1. Her Oscar disappeared in the mid-1960's and is still missing today. She was the first of 7 African-American actresses to receive an Academy Award. The others are: 2. Whoopi Goldberg for Ghost in 1990, 3. Halle Berry for Monster's Ball in 2001, 4. Jennifer Hudson for Dream Girls in 2006, 5. Mo'Nique for Precious in 2009, 6. Octavia Spencer for The Help in 2011, and 7. Viola Davis for Fences in 2016. The year given as her date of birth on her epitaph--1895--is incorrect. She was the first black Oscar winner to be honored on a US postage stamp, in 2006.

Victor McLaglen (Victor Andrew de Bier Everleigh McLaglen)

b. 10 Dec 1886, d. 7 Nov 1959, = 72 yrs, 10 mos, 18 days. Made 124 movies. Married 3 times.

BKF: Best Actor winner in Star of the Informer, 1935. NN: The two-fisted man of action. Wrestler, boxed under the name Sharkey, circus barker, vaudeville performer. Joined the London Guards at age 14. He wanted to fight in the Boer War but was discharged when his true age was discovered. He was Provost Marshal of Baghdad, Iraq. Prospected for gold in Canada in the early 1900's. He was bodyguard for an Indian rajah. He was promoted to food taster after being accidentally shot during a hunting expedition. The rajah died of food poisoning--right after he quit the job. Fought heavyweight champion Jack Johnson in a non-title fight on 10 March 1909 in Vancouver, British Columbia. Went six rounds, no decision. He said, "He never knocked me down...but he sure beat the be-Jesus out of me." He was heavyweight champion of the British Army in 1918. He was discovered in 1920 when a producer who needed a boxer for a movie saw him boxing at a sporting club. Although he was well known for playing Irish drunks, he was actually English. Became a US citizen in 1933. He was paid $62,000 for making Gunga Din in 1939. Played John Wayne's First Sergeant in Fort Apache (1948), She Wore a Yellow Ribbon (1949) and Rio Grande (1950). He was the first actor to win an Oscar for his role in a remake. The Informer, made in 1935, was a remake of the 1929 movie by the same title. He was nominated for a BSA in 1952 for The Quiet Man, making him the first actor to be a BA winner to be nominated for a BSA. His motto was Stand Up and Fight. Had a cameo in Around the World in 80 Days. "Acting never appealed to me, and I was dabbling in it solely as a means of making money. I rather felt that the greasepaint business was somewhat beneath a man who was once a reasonably useful boxer." "I have no illusions about acting and certainly I have none about myself. Long ago I came to the conclusion that actors are victims of luck and circumstance. If the role you are in fits the size of your head and some inherent quality in yourself, you do it well." Died on the same day his last movie, Sea Fury, was released. COD: Undisclosed. Died after filming an episode of Rawhide, which was directed by his son. His eulogy was delivered by actor Donald Crisp. Ashes interred at Forrest Lawn Memorial Park, Glendale, California.

Adolphe Menjou (Adolphe Jean Menjou)

b. 18 Feb 1890, d. 29 Oct 1963, = 73 yrs, 8 mos, 11 days. Made 150 movies. Married 3 times.

BKF: Being the best-dressed ladies' man in Hollywood. He and Edward Arnold were born on the same day. He is a cousin to author James Joyce. (5' 8", 145 pounds.) WW1 US Army Captain, in the Ambulance Service. Saw action in Italy and France. He began his film career as an extra in 1912. He was the star of the first film shown in a drive in theater, Wife Beware, on 6 June 1933 in Camden, New Jersey. Admission was 25 cents per car and an additional 25 cents for each passenger. Very popular co-star of The Sheik, with Rudolph Valentino. Always on the world's 'best dressed' lists, being named the Best Dressed Man in the United States nine times. Was fluent in six languages, which helped keep him employed after the stock market crash of 1929. His second wife divorced him because, as she said in court, "He loved money more than anything else." Entertained the troops overseas, making extensive use of his ability to speak the native tongue wherever he went. The Menjou mustache was named for him. His favorite golfing partner was Clark Gable. Made television commercials for Drewrys Beer in the 1950's. He was so fearful that a Democrat in the White House would wipe out his wealth, he said, "I've got gold stashed in safety deposit boxes all over town...they'll never get an ounce from me." "All Communists should be taken out and shot, regardless of whether they were American citizens or not." "My success has been as full of luck as a crapshooter's dream." "It was my mustache that landed jobs for me. In those silent film days it was the mark of a villain. When I realized they had me pegged as a foreign nobleman type I began to live the part, too. I bought a pair of white spats, an ascot tie and a walking stick." COD: Hepatitis. Died at home surrounded by his wife and family. Buried in Glendale, California. Autobiography: It Took Nine Tailors, 1948. Worth $700,000 at the time of his death.

Tom Mix (Thomas Hezikiah Mix)

b. 6 Jan 1880, d. 12 Oct 1940, d. 60 yrs, 9 mos, 6 days. Made 291 movies, with only 9 of them being talkies. Married 5 times.

BKF: Being Hollywood's first Western Star. NN: King of the Cowboys. Born in Mix Run, Pennsylvania. According to his studio publicity, he was one of the Rough Riders during the Spanish-American War in 1898, he fought in the Boer War and he was a deputy US Marshal in Oklahoma. None of this was true. What is true is that he enlisted in 1898 in the US Army and went AWOL in 1902 but was apparently never missed, court-martialed or discharged. He knew he was a deserter and kept it a closely guarded secret, which wasn't known until after his death. He was a bartender and Sheriff of Dewey, Oklahoma in 1911. He was a national riding and roping contest winner in 1909 and 1910. He accidentally shot himself at home while handling his gun in 1924. Ten years later, he revealed that he was in fact shot by his wife, who claimed he beat her. At $20,000 per week, he was the highest paid movie star from 1921 to 1925. He was the first actor to play Harry Destry and The Lone Ranger. When he tried, and failed, to get more money from studio boss Joseph P. Kennedy, he called him a "tight-assed, money-crazed son-of-a-bitch." Whenever he would eat at his favorite restaurant, The Musso and Frank Grill at 6667 Hollywood Boulevard and has been open since 1919, he always chose a seat at the window so his fans could see him. He had his name in neon lights on the roof of his house, giant monograms over his fireplace, front door and front gate. He also had the letters T and M engraved in his car's tires so that he left a trail of TM's in the dust wherever he drove. He was seriously hurt many times because he insisted on doing his own stunts, but later had to admit in court in 1933 that most of his stunts were done by stuntmen. His horse's name was Tony, the Wonder Horse, who lived from 1899 to 1942. He is the cowboy who started the tradition of the good guys wearing white hats. He always wore an all-white suit to all social an formal occasions. He was a pall bearer at Wyatt Earp's funeral in 1929. He made only 9 talking movies because, after years of doing his own stunts, he was physically unable to make any more. Also, his voice was unusable because of a previous bullet wound to his throat and several broken noses. He was Gene Autry's hero and he modeled his cowboy image after Mix. Mix's screen code was "NO drinking, smoking, swearing and killing, *unless* it was absolutely necessary." He described most of his movie plots as "getting into trouble when doing the right thing for somebody else." He was designated an Honorary Texas Ranger in 1935. He was so jealous of John Wayne's rising career status that he called him a "no-talent upstart." When he brought his Tom Mix Circus to Germany in 1939, Adolph Hitler welcomed him in a telephone conversation. Mix told him, "I would like to visit my fans in Germany again, but only over your dead body." "I like to make the pictures so that when a boy pays, say, 20 cents to see it, he will get 20 cents worth, not 10. If I drop, you see, it would be like putting my hand in his pocket and stealing a dime." COD: Severe head injuries suffered in a one-car accident. He was killed in his Cord Roadster in Arizona while attempting to cross a flooded section of road. His car flipped over and a suitcase containing cash and jewels hit him in the back of the head, breaking his neck. The site is now known at Tom Mix Wash. It is on State Route 79 near Florence. His horse Tony later died two years to the day that he died. His horse Tony has a star on the Hollywood Walk of Fame. He earned over $6,000,000 during his career, (which is worth $108,000,000 in 2018) but died nearly broke. Buried in Glendale, California. Rudy Valee sang Empty Saddles at his funeral. He was such a well-known celebrity that the US Army swallowed their pride over the fact that he was still a deserter and gave him a full military funeral. His picture is on the cover of the Beatles' Lonely Hearts Club Band album cover, 1967.

Colleen Moore (Kathleen Morrison)

b. 19 Aug 1899, d. 25 Jan 1988, = 88 yrs, 5 mos, 6 days. Made 64 movies. Married 4 times.

BKF: Her western movies with Tom Mix. NN: The Screen's First Flapper, The Typical American Girl. Had one blue eye and one brown eye, known as heterochromia. She is the actress that popularized the bobbed haircut. Her first starring role, as a novice actress, was as Annie in Little Orphan Annie in 1918. Made $12,500 per week and became very wealthy through wise investments. She was the star who discovered Loretta Young, and not Mervyn LeRoy who later falsely made that claim. On fellow flapper Clara Bow: "I like Clara. A very warm, sweet, generous girl. What great potential! But she wasn't a finisher. Her mind was like a sponge, but she didn't have the concentration or ability to see it through. She was quite ingenious. People would go into shock over her salty language." Talkies killed her career. Worked for the Merrill Lynch investment company and authored the book How Women Can Make Money in the Stock Market, 1969, and married two stockbrokers. Her last appearance on screen was in the TV mini-series Hollywood in 1980. Autobiography: Silent Star: Colleen Moore Talks About Her Hollywood, 1968. COD: Cancer. Buried in Paso Robles, California.

Frank Morgan (Francis Phillip Wuppermann)

b. 1 Jun 1890, d. 18 Sep 1949, = 59 yrs, 3 mos, 17 days. Made 100 movies. Married 1 time.

BKF: Playing the Wizard of Oz in The Wizard of Oz. (5' 8") Youngest of 11 children. His mother was a Mayflower descendant. Sold toothbrushes door-to-door, real estate agent, cowpuncher on a western ranch, a hobo and a stoker on a New Orleans-to-New York tramp steamer, and then Broadway actor. Played five different characters in The Wizard of Oz: 1. The Wizard of Oz, 2. Professor Marvel, 3. The Gateman, 4. The driver of a horse of a different color, and 5: The Wizard's Guard. W.C. Fields was the first choice to play the Wizard of Oz, and he had the contract sewn up except for the fact that he would not negotiate on his fee for the part. The part was offered to Ed Wynn and only after he turned it down did Morgan get the role. The Wizard's name was Oscar Zoroaster Phadrig Isaac Norman Hinkle Emmanuel Abroise Diggs. His and Judy Garland's given names were Francis and Frances. In one of the most amazing coincidences ever positively confirmed, he bought a worn, ragged coat from a second-hand shop in Los Angeles. Years later he noticed that it had a nametag sewn into the inside of it, obviously of the original owner. The name was Frank L. Baum, the original owner of the coat and author and creator of The Wizard of Oz. He was in a serious auto accident in New Mexico in 1939, which injured his wife and killed his chauffeur. His hobby was yacht racing, one having won a race from Los Angeles to Honolulu in 1947. Had a drinking problem and would usually bring a black suitcase to work with him, containing a fully-equipped mini-bar. However, he kept his drinking to himself and did not allow it to affect him while working or his temperament on the set. COD: Heart attack. Died with his boots on while filming Annie Get Your Gun. Died before The Wizard of Oz was broadcast on television in 1956, making him the only major cast member to not know what a huge success it was to become. Buried in Brooklyn, New York. His pallbearers were Clark Gable and Pat O'Brien.

Ralph Morgan (Raphael Kuhner Wuppermann)

b. 6 July 1883, d. 11 Jun 1956, = 72 yrs, 11 mos, 5 days. Made 110 movies. Married 1 time.

BKF: Playing soft-talking villains. Older brother of Frank Morgan. Their mother was a Mayflower descendant. Graduate of Columbia

University with a Law Degree. Founder, charter member and President of the Screen Actors Guild, 1933, 1938-1940. His wife Georgiana played Nora Charles in the radio show The Thin Man. COD: Heart attack at home. Buried in Brooklyn, New York.

Alan Mowbray (Alfred Ernest Allen)

b. 18 Aug 1896, d. 25 Mar 1969, = 72 yrs, 7 mos, 7 days. Made 189 movies. Married 1 time.

BKF: Topper, 1937. (6' 0") Served with distinction in the British Army during WW1, earning their equivalent of the Silver Star for bravery and the French Croix De Guerre. Came to the US in 1923. Claimed he went into acting because he had no other skills. Member of the Royal Geographic Society. Personally funded the Screen Actors Guild when it was formed in 1933 and was its first vice-president. He was also a founder of the Hollywood Cricket Club. Had a major role in Around the World in 80 Days. COD: Heart attack. Buried in Culver City, California.

Carmel Myers (Same)

b. 4 Apr 1889, d. 9 Nov 1980, = 81 yrs, 7 mos, 5 days. Made 94 movies. Married 3 times.

BKF: Playing the Egyptian vamp in Ben-Hur, 1925. Had nose surgery. She was robbed in her apartment in 1932 and two masked gunmen made off with $20,000 in jewels. Hosted The Carmel Myers Show in 1951. Founded Carmel Myers, Inc, which distributed French perfumes. Had a cameo in Won Ton Ton, the Dog Who Saved Hollywood, 1976. Hobbies were swimming, tennis and chess. "Talking pictures have done a lot of things to this industry, one of the most important being the placement of a value on brains. Brains never mattered before as far as an actor or actress was concerned. But now we must learn our lines." COD: Natural causes. Cremated, ashes strewn in the rose Garden at Pickfair.

Nita Naldi (Mary Nonna Dooley)

b. 13 Nov 1894, d. 17 Feb 1961, = 66 yrs, 3 mos, 4 days. Made 29 movies. Married 1 time.

BKF: Playing opposite Rudolph Valentino in Blood and Sand, 1922. NN: The Dumb Duse. Vaudeville and Broadway actress. Artist's and coat model. (5'-7") Never made a talkie. She was Rudolph Valentino's most frequent co-star. Declared bankruptcy in 1932. "We were all as blind as bats. Theda Bara couldn't see a foot ahead of her and poor Rudy (Valentino) groped his way through many a love scene and I really mean groped. They all use big reflectors to get extra light from the sun--that's how we acquired that interesting Oriental look. We didn't have any censors in those days, but we did have our own eyelashes...And we never took ourselves seriously." COD: Heart attack in her hotel room at the Wentworth Hotel on West 46th Street in New York. Buried in her family plot in Queens, NY.

Alla Nazimova (Marem-Ides Adelaida Yakovlevna Leventon)

b. 3 Jun 1879, d. 13 July 1945, = 66 yrs, 1 mo, 10 days. Made 23 movies. Married 1 time.

BKF: The title role in Camille (1921), with Rudolph Valentino. NN: The Woman of 1,000 Moods. Major star in Russia and Europe before moving to the US in 1905. Earned $13,000 per week in 1917. Credited with creating the phrase 'sewing circle' as a euphemism for lesbian activities. Became a US citizen in 1927. She was instrumental in promoting the careers of actresses Jean Acker and Natacha Rambova, both of who were Rudolph Valentino's ex-wives. She was also a close friend of actress Edith Luckett, who was the mother of future US First

Lady Nancy (Davis) Reagan, and she was Nancy Davis' godmother. She had a swimming pool that was the first to have underwater lighting and shaped like the Black Sea in her native Crimea. It was the first known pool to have underwater lighting. When she lost her palatial mansion on Sunset Boulevard, it was turned into a hotel and she rented a room there, where she lived for the rest of her life. When she met the then unknown Rudolph Valentino for the first time, she said, "How dare you bring that gigolo to my table? How dare you introduce that pimp to Nazimova?" "I wish I could burn every inch of my films. I'm ashamed of them." Survived breast cancer in the 1930's. COD: Coronary thrombosis. Buried in Glendale, California.

Pola Negri (Barbara Apolonia Chalupiec)

b. 3 Jan 1897, d. 1 Aug 1987, = 90 yrs, 6 mos, 29 days. Made 68 movies. Married 3 times.

BKF: A Woman Commands, 1932. NN: The Movie's Greatest Vamp. She and actress Marion Davies were born on the same day. Famous as an actress in Poland and Germany, she signed with Paramount Pictures in 1922, thus making her the first-ever European actor to have a Hollywood contract. She announced her engagement to Charlie Chaplin without telling him about it first. The newspapers billed it as "The Queen of Tragedy to Wed the King of Comedy." He read about it the newspapers. They did not get married. She did eventually marry a baron, a count and a prince. She was Maid of Honor and Rudolph Valentino was Best Man at Mae Murray's wedding to Prince David Mdivani. She was one of the richest women in Hollywood and her Los Angeles home was built to resemble the White House. She started the fashion trends of red painted toenails, fur boots and turbans. Her movies were described as "slink and mink." While attending Rudolph Valentino's funeral in 1926, she 'fainted' several times and it was claimed in the newspapers that she had had an arrangement of flowers placed on his coffin which spelled out P-O-L-A. However, photos of the funeral show this to not be true. This was a publicity stunt designed to increase her presence in the press but it backfired with the public. Could not make the transition from silent movies to talkies because audiences laughed at her Polish accent and she returned to Europe. A French magazine claimed in a 1936 interview that she had an affair with Adolph Hitler. It was untrue, she sued for libel and won. She was asked to play the role of Norman Desmond in Sunset Boulevard in 1950 and turned it down. Became a US Citizen in 1951. Walt Disney coaxed her out of retirement to make The Moon Spinners in 1964. Sister-in-law of Barbara Hutton. "I don't care whether I'm beautiful or not. I want a chance to act." "I consider my work great, as I am a great artist." "Love is disgusting when you no longer possess yourself." "It is difficult for a foreigner coming to America...I had been told so much what not to do. It was particularly difficult for me, a Slav. My emotion seemed exaggerated to Americans. I cannot help that I haven't the Anglo-Saxon restraint and tact." COD: Pneumonia and brain tumor. Autobiography: Memoirs of a Star, 1970.

Mable Normand (Mabel Ethelreid Normand)

b. 9 Nov 1892, d. 23 Feb 1930, = 37 yrs, 3 mos, 14 days. Made 220 movies. Married 1 time.

BKF: The title role in Mickey, 1918. NN: Queen of the Mack Sennett Lot. Madcap Mabel and Keystone Mabel. The First Great Comedienne. 5' 3". Diagnosed with tuberculosis at age 10 in 1902. She was a model for postcards illustrated by Charles Dana Gibson, the creator of the Gibson Girl image. Star of the first Keystone comedy movie, Bangville Police in 1912. She is also the 'girl tied up on the railroad tracks' in the advertising clip used to represent silent movies. Was the first person to throw a pie in the face of another actor on screen. The victim was Fatty Arbuckle in A Noise From the Deep, 1913. She was also the first actress to get a pie in the face, thrown by Ford Sterling in 1913. By 1914, she was the first woman to both write and direct films. Made $3,500 per week in 1917. Made 12 films with Charlie Chaplin and 17 films with Fatty Arbuckle. Her career suffered greatly when Fatty Arbuckle was tried three times for rape and manslaughter because his films were banned. A large portion of her body of work was in those films. She was the last person to see William Desmond Taylor alive before his murder on 1 February 1922. Impulsively married her friend Lew Cody at 2am, at the end of a night of drinking and partying. When asked what her hobbies were: "I don't know. Say anything you like, but don't say I love to work. That sounds like Mary Pickford, that prissy bitch. Just say I like to pinch babies and twist their legs. And get drunk." (She was being facetious about Mary Pickford, as they were close friends.) COD: Pulmonary tuberculosis. Buried in Los Angeles, California.

George O'Brien (Same)

b. 19 Apr 1899, d. 4 Sep 1985, = 86 yrs, 4 mos, 16 days. Made 85 movies. Married 1 time.

BKF: Sunrise: A Song of Two Humans, 1927. NN: The Chest. His father, as Chief of Police of the city of San Francisco, ordered the arrest of Fatty Arbuckle in connection with the death of Virginia Rappe in 1921. WW1: Served on a submarine chaser in the US Navy. Decorated for bravery. Lightweight boxing title holder of the Pacific Fleet. He took part in 15 invasions of Japanese-held islands. Retired in 1962 as a Captain, having been passed over for the rank of Admiral four times. Popular leading man for most of the major female stars of the 1920's and successful western star. His horse's name was Mike. COD: Stroke suffered four years before he died.

Pat O'Brien (William Joseph Patrick O'Brien)

b. 11 Nov 1899, d. 15 Oct 1983, = 83 yrs, 11 mos, 4 days. Made 149 movies. Married 1 time.

BKF: Playing Knute Rockne in Knute Rockne, All American, 1940 and uttering the phrase, "win just one for the Gipper (played by Ronald Reagan). Also played Father Duffy in The Fighting 69th. NN: Hollywood's Irishman In Residence. Boyhood friend of Spencer Tracy. They enlisted in the US Navy together during WW1 and shared a room while attending acting school after the war. WW1 US Navy but was too old to enlist for WW2. His agent was Myron Selznick, brother of studio head David O. Selznick. Toured with the USO during WW2. When told that his USO camp was near a village of known cannibals, he said, "We were lucky it was Lent." Also entertained the troops in Vietnam with the USO in February, 1969. Made nine movies with James Cagney. They were said to be part of the Irish Mafia. Three of his four children were adopted. His final on-screen performance was on a 1982 episode of Happy Days. "Women's pictures are talky pictures. Their use of the cigarette and the telephone break to talk, talk, talk of soap-opera storytelling." "I'm not a loner; not a solitary. I liked people, crowds, activities, so I didn't stay in dark corners. I made friends." COD: Heart attack following prostate surgery. James Cagney knew him for 60 years and called him his "dearest friend." Buried in Culver City, California. Autobiography: The Wind at My Back, 1964.

Warner Oland (Johan Verner Ohlund)

b. 3 Oct 1879, d. 6 Aug 1938, = 58 yrs, 10 mos, 3 days. Made 97 movies. Married 1 time.

BKF: Playing Charlie Chan in 16 movies, particularly in Charlie Chan at the Opera, 1936. Vaudeville stage performer. Once taught at Harvard. Discovered by Alla Nazimova, who saw him in a Shakespeare play in 1907. He had a major role in Don Juan in 1926, which was the first film with synchronized sound. He played Al Jolson's father in The Jazz Singer, 1927. (5'-8") Went to China to learn how to speak Chinese for the Charlie Chan role. He was a Swede who played a Chinaman but claimed he could pass as a Chinaman due to his alleged Mongolian ancestry. There is no evidence that this was true and it was probably just studio propaganda, as his ancestry has been traced back five generations and there is no evidence of any Asian heritage. He was the first actor to play Dr. Fu Manchu, in 1929 and he was the first actor to play a werewolf in a Hollywood film (A Werewolf in London), in 1935. His Charlie Chan movies are credited with keeping Fox Studios from going under until Shirley Temple was signed. Earned $30,000 for his later Charlie Chan movies. His hobby was breeding miniature schnauzers. He walked off the set in the fall of 1938 and was never seen in public again. It was later learned that he went to Italy and then to Sweden to be with his mother, where he died. The director of his Charlie Chan movies, John G. Blystone, died the same day he did. "Life is a circle that looks for a straight line." "Everywhere I went, people addressed me in Chinese. I was always introduced as 'Mr. Chan'." Owned a 7,000 acre island off the west coast of Mexico. COD: Bronchial pneumonia, aggravated by emphysema. Cremated, his ashes were brought back to the US by his ex-wife and buried in Southborough, Massachusetts.

Maria Ouspenskaya (Maria Alekseyevna Ouspenskaya)

b. 29 July 1876, d. 3 Dec 1949, = 73 yrs, 4 mos, 4 days. Made 25 movies. Married: Not known.

BKF: The Perils of Pauline serial, which had 14 episodes. (5-1 1/2") Stage performer in Russia. Made six silent films in Russia. Founding member of the First Studio, the forerunner of the Moscow Art Theater. Defected and came to the United States in 1922. Founded the School of Dramatic Art in New York City. Anne Baxter was an early student. Founded the Maria Ouspenskaya School of Dance in Los Angeles. Marge Champion was an early student. In 1936, became the first actress, along with Gale Sondergaard, to be nominated for a Best Supporting Actress Academy Award in their screen debut, for Dodsworth. She appeared in the movie for only four minutes. Later nominated for another Best Supporting Actress for Love Affair, in which she appeared for only ten minutes. Chainsmoker. COD: Stroke caused by severe burns from a house fire, which she caused by smoking in bed. Her headstone gives her date of birth as 1887, instead of the correct year 1876.

Louella Parsons (Louella Rose Oettinger)

b. 6 Aug 1881, d. 9 Dec 1972, = 91 yrs, 4 mos, 3 days. Made 7 movies. Married 3 times.

BKF: Being America's first movie columnist. NN: Lolly, The Goddess of Flack, The Queen of Hollywood and Queen of the Quickies. Born in Freeport, Illinois, only 38 miles from Tampico, where Ronald Reagan was born. They both lived in Dixon, Illinois at the same time. In fact, she held a reception at her home for Ronald Reagan and Jane Wyman when they married in 1939. Later in life she changed her date of birth to 1893, but that would have been impossible because her father died in 1890. Part-time writer for the Dixon Star, making her the first female journalist in Dixon. Her first movie review column first appeared in the Chicago-Record Herald in 1913. Wrote the nation's first gossip column in the Chicago-Record Herald in 1914. In 1925 she was diagnosed with tuberculosis, given six months to live, and advised to move to Arizona, which she did. In 1942, the circulation of her column was 20,000,000 compared to only 6,000,000 for rival Hedda Hopper. Her last byline appeared on 1 December 1965. "Listen, Dearie. I was on the Top when you were a has-been practicing to be a never-was." On her rival Hedda Hopper. "Hedda Hopper and Louella Parsons. They were bitches." Elizabeth Taylor. "Louella was stronger than Samson. He needed two columns to bring the house down. Louella can do it with one." Samuel Goldwyn. Lived in a nursing home until her death. Has two stars on the Hollywood Walk of Fame, one for radio and one for motion pictures. Godmother to actress Mia Farrow. Autobiography: The Gay Illiterate, 1942, and Tell It to Louella, 1961. COD: Heart disease.

Jack Pickford (John Charles Smith)

b. 18 Aug 1896, d. 3 Jan 1933, = 36 yrs, 4 mos, 16 days. Made 130 movies. Married 3 times.

BKF: Being Mary Pickford's brother. NN: The Ideal American Boy. He and his older sister Mary Pickford were both named Smith at birth. Got a job at Biograph because it was required by his sister's acting contract. Enlisted in the US Navy during WW1 and was assigned to service in New York Harbor. Due to his celebrity status he was able to abuse his position to procure women for the officers above him and change the duty assignments of other enlistees, deciding for himself who did and did not have to go overseas to fight in combat units. He and his ring of coconspirators were caught. Hearing of this, his mother had a private meeting with President Woodrow Wilson after which he received a general discharge and was sent home. Everyone else involved received three years in prison and dishonorable discharges. The Secretary of the Navy later denied all knowledge of the incident. All three of his wives were Ziegfeld Girls at one time. COD: Multiple neuritis due to alcoholism and drug use.

Mary Pickford (Gladys Louise Smith)

b. 8 April 1892, d. 29 May 1979, = 87 yrs, 1 mo, 21 days. Made 245 movies. Married 3 times.

BKF: Being a pioneer in the early motion picture business and her immense popularity. NN: America's Sweetheart, Queen of the Movies. The Little Girl With Curls, Little Mary, Our Mary. Also known at her studio as The Bank of America's Sweetheart, for the huge income her movies generated. "America's Sweetheart" was born in Canada. She had only 6-7 months of formal schooling before dropping out. She was the child star of the Toronto Opera House at age 5. Originally billed as 'Baby Gladys Smith.' She was released from her first film contract with IMP because she was a minor at signing. D.W. Griffith told her, "You're a little too fat but I might give you a job." Made 51 movies in 1909 alone. She was the most popular woman in the world in the 1910's. She was the first movie star to win acclaim on stage in 1912. Made $10 per day in 1909, made $175 per week in 1910, $275 per week in 1911, $500 per week in 1913, $2,000 per week in 1914, $4,000 per week in 1914 and $10,000 per week and 50% of the profits in 1916. Made $250,000 per movie in 1918. Made $10,000 per week, plus expenses in the 1920's. She was the first bankable movie star. Her curls were the first fashion fad taken from a movie star. She was exactly 5' 0" tall. She contracted influenza during the epidemic that swept the world in 1918, but obviously survived. Got the nickname America's Sweetheart during a military ceremony during WW1 when Sid Grauman told her, "American is a great country and you're America's Sweetheart." She was an Honorary US Army Colonel and the US Navy dubbed her "Little Sister." Got a quickie Nevada divorce from husband Owen Moore in 1920. At age 27, she played a 10-year-old in The Hoodlum. She and husband Douglas Fairbanks were the first two stars to have a star on the Hollywood Walk of Fame, 30 April 1927. They were also the first two stars to create their own production company, which we now know as United Artists. While filming Pride of the Clan off the New England coast in 1916, she was knocked down by a wave and began to drown. Director Maurice Tourneur saved her life. She did bond drives and charity work during WW1. When Albert Einstein visited the Fairbanks at Pickfair, he tried to explain his theory of relativity to them by using the silverware and china as props. Their china was a set than Napoleon had given Josephine on their wedding day. She bought the rights to Coquette so she could campaign for the 1928 Best Actress Oscar. It worked. Both she and her husband Jack Pickford were named Smith at birth. When she went on vacation to Russia in 1922, a Russian filmmaker named Sergei Komanov used newsreel footage of her public appearances to make a movie out of it, without her knowledge or permission. This incident was the inspiration of the movie Bowfinger in 1991. She bobbed her hair in 1928 and her career took a nosedive and never recovered. Her third husband, Buddy Rogers, was 11 years younger than her. She was at one time the mother-in-law to Joan Crawford. She made only one movie with husband Douglas Fairbanks, The Taming of the Shrew (a talkie), in 1929. It was the first sound film of a Shakespeare play. She was the first female Grand Marshall of the Rose Parade, in 1933. After 1965, she became a recluse, speaking to Pickfair visitors only through a house phone. She was one of the first four inductees into the Canadian Motion Picture Hall of Fame. "I was forced to live far beyond my years when I was just a child, now I have reversed the order and I intend to remain young indefinitely." "If you make mistakes, even serious mistakes, there is always another chance for you. You may have a fresh start any moment you choose, for this thing we call failure is not the falling down, but the staying down." "Adding sound to movies would be like putting lipstick on the Venus de Milo." On her voluntary retirement: "I wanted to stop before I was asked to stop." "No one can convince me that the modern girl cares for nothing but cocktails, cigarettes and jazz." 1925. On her retirement: "I'm not satisfied but I am grateful." "I never really liked any of my films in its entirety." "It took longer to make one of Mary's contracts than it did to make one of her movies." Samuel Goldwyn. She wanted all of her more than 235 films destroyed when she died but was talked out of it. COD: Cerebral hemorrhage. Worth $50,000,000 when she died. Her mansion, Pickfair, was originally a hunting lodge, had 50 rooms on 18 acres and cost $37,261.77 when purchased by Jack Pickford for his new wife in 1919. He installed an Olympic-sized kidney-shaped pool, which was the first pool in Beverly Hills. After she died it was purchased by sports personality Jerry Buss for $5,362,500. It was then purchased by Pia Zadora in the 1980's for $7,000,000 and was promptly demolished. She kept the swimming pool and built an exact replica of the original on the site for $11,000,000. It was then purchased by actor George Hamilton. Autobiography: Sunshine and Shadow.

Walter Pidgeon (Walter Davis Pidgeon)

b. 23 Sep 1879, d. 25 Sep 1984, = 87 yrs, 2 days. Made 138 movies. Married 2 times.

BKF: Mrs. Miniver and Madame Curie. Bank teller. Studied law and drama at the University of New Brunswick. 6' 2". Lied about his age to get into the Canadian Army during WW1. He was severely injured when two 500-pound gun cartridges fell on him and he spent seventeen months in the hospital. Tried to join the Royal Canadian Mounted Police after the war but was disqualified due to his war injuries. Moved to Boston after the war and became a bank runner. Discovered by Fred Astaire, who got him an agent. His first wife died in childbirth. His second wife was his secretary. He was a classically trained baritone singer with the New England Conservatory of Music in Boston. Played the title role in The Gorilla, 1926. Became an American citizen on 24 December 1943. Couldn't remember names so he called everyone Joe. Accordingly, his chairs on the movie sets were labeled Joe Pidgeon. Had an encyclopedic memory of dirty limericks, which he loved to recite frequently. He is one of only three Canadians to be nominated for Best Actor (Raymond Massey and Ryan Gosling are the other two). Screen Actors Guild President, 1952-1957. Said the best films he ever made were the ones he made with Greer Garson. PIDGEON/Garson movies: 1. Blossoms in the Dust, 1941, 2. Mrs. Miniver, 1942, 3. The Youngest Profession, 1943, 4. Madame Curie, 1943, 5. Mrs. Parkington, 1944, 6. Julia Misbehaves, 1946, 7. That Forsythe Woman, 1949, 8. The Miniver Story, 1950, 9. Scandal at Scourie, 1953. On being a star: "You didn't need to carry money. Your face was your credit card--all over the world." "It takes a lot of work to appear easy going and I tried to avoid being stuffy." "I was like a kept woman during my 21 years at MGM." "I didn't demand any vetoes over the films I didn't like, as they do today. I asked nicely and discovered a secret that has stayed with me for my entire career--that a request spoken softly usually brings results and demands rarely do." COD: A series of strokes. Donated his body to the UCLA School of Medicine.

ZaSu Pitts (Eliza Susan Pitts)

b. 3 Jan 1894, d. 7 Jun 1963, = 69 yrs 5 mos, 4 days. Made 220 movies. Married 2 times.

BKF: Playing Elvira on 126 episodes of The Gale Strom Show, 1956-60. NN: The Greatest Dramatic Actress. Named after her father's sisters Eliza and Susan. She said her name is pronounced "Say Zoo." Star of Greed, 1924, considered to be one of the greatest films ever made. Specialized in comedies and 'B' movies. Had a six-month contract with Charlie Chaplin in the 1920's but she was never called upon to make a film. Made a movie called The Greatest Thing in Life in 1918. After the film was completed all of the scenes with her in it were cut out because Director D.W. Griffith said she looked too much like Lillian Gish, who was the star of the movie. She responded by saying, "Of course I was flattered but I was out of a job again." Years later she added, "Being told that I looked like Lillian Gish was the nicest thing anyone ever said to me." Played the switchboard operator in It's a Mad, Mad, Mad, Mad World, which was released after she died. Professional candy maker, wrote a book titled Candy Hits in 1963. COD: Cancer.

William Powell (William Horatio Powell)

b. 29 July 1892, d. 5 Mar 1984, = 91 yrs, 7 mos, 5 days. Made 96 movies. Married 3 times.

BKF: Playing Nick Charles in six of The Thin Man films with Myrna Loy. 5' 11". Graduate of the American Academy of Dramatic Arts in 1912. He was engaged to marry Jean Harlow and after her death in 1926, but was so distraught that he spent a month in seclusion on Ronald Colman's yacht. He paid for her $30,000 funeral. Married to

Carole Lombard from 1931 to 1933, six years before she was married to Clark Gable. In Love Crazy, he appeared in drag as a woman. Diagnosed with cancer in 1937. He kept it a secret and lived another 47 years. Made 14 movies with Myrna Loy and because of that, the public thought they were really married. They usually had to change their hotel reservations from one room to two separate rooms because hotel clerks assumed they were married. His only child, a son, committed suicide in 1968 due to ill health. His last film was the critically acclaimed Mr. Roberts in 1955. Said his role as Nick Charles was more like his real personality than any other role. On his slim physique: "I highly recommend worrying. It's much more effective than dieting," and "I give my swimming pool a long and piercing look every morning. I think a lot about tennis and talk a lot about golf. I find I keep fit best by worrying about what I'm going to do next." On retirement: "When an offer comes I ask myself 'why would I do it?' For the glory? The ham in me burned out years ago. I'd just be in a higher tax bracket. So I've said 'no' for about twenty-five years." "Dessert is probably the most important stage of the meal, since it will be the last thing your guests remember before they pass out all over the table." "There is more money in being liked by an audience than in being disliked by it." "Money: The aphrodisiac which fate brings you to cloak the pain of living." "He has grace, style, wit and technique. He was not absolutely handsome, so that he was believable as a leading man or as a villain." Bette Davis. COD: Heart failure.

Claude Rains (William Claude Rains)

b. 10 Nov 1889, d. 30 May 1967, = 77 yrs, 6 mos, 20 days. Made 78 movies. Married 6 times but had only one child.

BKF: Playing Police Chief Captain Renault in Casablanca and the line, "Round up the usual suspects." NN: 5' 7". One of 12 children. His father was a famous stage actor in London. Suffered from stuttering so bad that he could only pronounce his own name as 'Willie Wains.' Dropped out of the second grade. Came to the United States in 1913.

Served in WW1 as a Captain in the London Scottish Regiment with future fellow actors Cedric Hardwicke, Basil Rathbone, Ronald Colman and Herbert Marshall. Suffered from a gas attack that left him blind in one eye. Became a US citizen in 1939. Bette Davis said he was her favorite co-star. Became a father for the first time at age 49. He is the voice of the unseen man in The Invisible Man (1933). The suit he wore in The Invisible Man sold for $34,000 in 2003. He flunked his screen test for The Invisible Man, saying, "It was the worst in the history of moviemaking." The director said, "I don't care what he looks like; that's the voice I want." Made $5,000 per week for filming Casablanca, $1,500 more per week than Humphrey Bogart. Played an angel in Here Comes Mr. Jordan in 1941 and played a devil in Angel on My Shoulder in 1946. He never attended a premiere of any of his movies. Always pretended to be broke and cashless, which was not the case. Five roles he is famous for turning down: 1. Professor Higgins in Pygmalion, 1938. 2. Qasimodo in The Hunchback of Notre Dame, 1939. 3. Harry Potter in It's a Wonderful Life, 1946. 4. Klaatu in The Day the Earth Stood Still, 1951. 5. Mr. Doolittle in My Fair Lady, 1961. He was the first actor to earn a $1,000,000 salary for a film, Caesar and Cleopatra, which was filmed in England in 1945. In retirement he was a gentleman farmer who owned a 380-acre farm near Coatsville, Pennsylvania. He was John Gielgud's acting teacher in England. Gielgud said, "He inspired us all. Claude Rains. I don't know what happened to him, I think he failed and went to America." John Gielgud. Nominated four times for Best Supporting Actor, no wins. "God felt sorry for actors, so he gave them a place in the sun and a lot of money. All they had to do was sacrifice their talent." "Often we'd secretly like to do the very things we discipline ourselves against. Isn't that true? Well, here in the movies, I can be as mean, as wicked as I want to--all without hurting anybody. Look at that lovely girl I've just shot!" "I learn the lines and pray to God." On his acting range: "I can play the butcher, the baker and the candlestick maker." "He was a great influence on me." John Gielgud. COD: Abdominal hemorrhage. Designed his own tombstone and epitaph, which reads: "All things once, Are things forever, Soul, once living, lives forever."

His daughter said, "And, just like most actors, he died waiting for his agent to call."

Virginia Rappe (Virginia Caroline Rappe)

b. 7 July 1891, d. 9 Sep 1921, = 30 yrs, 2 mos 2 days. Made 9 known movies, plus an unknown number of lost movies. Never married.

BKF: Being the actress who died four days after having sex with Fatty Arbuckle. NN: Best Dressed Girl in Pictures. Had a bit part in Over the Rhine with Rudolph Valentino. Appeared on the cover of the original sheet music of "Let Me Call You Sweetheart." Last words: "I'm dying. I'm dying...he hurt me!" referring to Fatty Arbuckle. COD: Acute peritonitis caused by a ruptured bladder. She was pregnant and had syphilis at the time of her death. Eptitaph: "VIRGINIA RAPPE/1895--1921

Basil Rathbone (Philip St. John Basil Rathbone)

b. 13 June 1892, d. 21 July 1967, = 75 yrs, 1 mo, 8 days. Made 125 movies. Married 2 times.

BKF: Playing Sherlock Holmes in 14 movies. NN: The Greatest Villain in the History of Cinema. 6' 1". Direct descendant of King Henry IV of England on his mother's side. Born in South Africa, his family had to flee because his father was accused of being a British spy. Distant cousin of US Army Major Henry Rathbone, who was present at Lincoln's assassination. Insurance salesman. Captain in the British Army Military Intelligence Division during WW1. Member of the Scottish London Regiment along with future actors Cedric Hardwicke, Claude Rains, Herbert Marshall and Ronald Colman. Spotted enemy positions from behind enemy lines. Won the British Military Cross for Valor. Arrested in 1926 on a morals charge for being a member of a play, The Captive, which dealt with homosexuality. Charges were later dropped. His Sherlock Holmes movies, all co-starring Nigel Bruce: 1. The Hound of the Baskervilles, 1939. 2. The Adventures of Sherlock Holmes, 1939. 3. Sherlock Holmes and the Voice of Terror, 1942. 4. Sherlock Holmes and the Secret Weapon, 1943. 5. Sherlock Holmes in Washington, 1943. 6. Sherlock Holmes Faces Death, 1943. 7. The Spider Woman, 1944. 8. The Scarlett Claw, 1944. 9. The Pearl of Death, 1944. 10. The House of Fear, 1945. 11. The Woman in Green, 1945. 12. Pursuit to Algiers, 1945. 13. Terror by Night, 1946. 14. Dressed to Kill, 1946. He was Margaret Mitchell's first choice to play Rhett Butler in Gone With the Wind. Did a 1960's television commercial for Getz Exterminators. His slogan was, "Getz gets 'em, since 1888!" Was a contestant on several 1960's game shows. Actor Nigel Bruce also appeared in all 14 of his Sherlock Holmes films. Made Comedy of Terrors in 1963. It was the only movie made with the 'Big 4' of horror films: Vincent Price, Basil Rathbone, Boris Karloff and Peter Lorre. "When you become the character you play, it's the end of your career as an actor." Last film credit is The Great Mouse Detective, 1986, where his voice is used 19 years after he died. COD: Heart attack. Has three stars on the Walk of Fame, one each for Film, Radio and Television. Autobiography: In and Out of Character, 1967

Wallace Reid (William Wallace Halleck Reid)

b. 15 Apr 1891, d. 18 Jan 1923, = 31 yrs, 9 mos, 3 days. Married 1 time.

BKF: Being the Premiere 1920's matinee idol. NN: The Screen's Most Perfect Lover. Stage performer at age 4. Cowboy, civil engineer, reporter, hotel clerk, poet, musician, movie stunt man, composer and motion picture director. He never wanted to be an actor. Came to Hollywood with his playwright father, wanting to be a cameraman. He was forced into acting because the directors said he was too good looking to be behind the camera. In 1915, he had the first Hollywood house to have a below ground swimming pool. He wanted to enlist during WW1 but the studio bosses talked him out of it. He received a severe scalp injury while filming a movie in 1919 and was given morphine for the pain so he could keep working. He became addicted to the morpine which led to his early death. An avid semi-professional race car driver, he unsuccessfully tried out for the 1922 Indianapolis 500. Died in a sanitarium at 1pm. Before entering the sanitarium for treatment, he said, "Either I'll come out cured or I won't come out." Last words: "God...I...please!" His was the first Hollywood drug death. His unexpected death at age 31 was partly responsible for the creation of The Hayes Code. COD: Morphine addiction.

Paul Robeson (Paul Leroy Bustill Robeson)

b. 9 Apr 1898, d. 23 Jan 1976, = 77 yrs, 9 mos, 14 days. Made only 12 movies. Married 1 time.

BKF: His rendition of Ol' Man River in the 1936 Movie Showboat, his political views and for being America's #1 Entertainer in 1946. NN: Robey. 6' 3". He was the first black All-American college football player, Rutgers, 1915. Phi Beta Kappa and class valedictorian. Graduated with four letters in football, basketball, baseball and track and field. New York Law School graduate and became a New York Attorney in 1923. Spoke French, German, Russian, Swahili and about fifteen other languages. He was one of the first black performers to refuse to play live for segregated audiences. Playwright Eugene O'Neill personally asked him to play the lead in several of his plays, which he did. In 1942 he refused to make any more movies until there were better roles for blacks. WW2: Made an anti-venereal disease training film for the US War Department called "Get Easy." Made for black soldiers, he urged them to "stay clean." In 1940, along with a Chinese co-author, he wrote a song that eventually became the current Chinese National Anthem. After the Chinese co-author died in a Chinese prison in 1968, he continued to send song royalties to the man's family. In 1943 he became the first African American to play the title role of Othello with an all-white cast on Broadway. When questioned by the US Senate Committee on the Judiciary in 1947 about his Communist beliefs, he replied, "Some of the most distinguished and brilliant Americans are about to go to jail for the failure to answer that question, and I am about to join them, if necessary." In 1948, he had to travel overseas to work and earn an income because his stateside engagements were being cancelled by the secret, behind the scenes, efforts of the FBI. Won the Stalin Peace Prize in 1952 for his pro-Soviet opinions. US Senator Joseph McCarthy had his passport revoked in 1950 due to his support of the Soviet Union and criticism of the US Government, which consisted of his condemnation of President Truman's refusal to support legislation outlawing lynching. He was the first black performer to sing at St. Paul's Cathedral in 1959. In 1960 he was the first black performer to sing at the construction site of the future Sydney Opera House. Suffered from bipolar depression and attempted suicide by cutting his wrists in Moscow in 1961. The Hollywood Chamber of Commerce refused in July of 1978 to honor him in the Hollywood Walk of Fame because "he's not a household word" and not because of his leftist politics. They reversed themselves three weeks later, after a huge public outcry and what they called "additional information." "My weapons are peaceful, for it is only by peace that peace can be obtained." On Australian Aborigines: "There is no such thing as a backward human being; there is only a society which says they are backward." "The artist must take sides. He must elect to fight for freedom or slavery. I have made my choice. I have no alternative." COD: Complications of a stroke. One of his pallbearers was Harry Belafonte. Autobiography: Here I Stand, 1958. The FBI has 31 pages on him. College Football Hall of Fame, 1995. American Theater Hall of Fame. Lifetime Achievement Grammy Award on his 100th birthday, 1998. US Postal Service 37-cent stamp in 2004. Has a variety of black tomato named after him.

Bill "Bojangles" Robinson (Luther Robinson)

b. 25 May 1877, d. 25 Nov 1949, = 72 yrs, 6 mos. Made 18 movies. Married 3 times.

BKF: Tap Dancing with Shirley Temple in her movies and his signature 'Stair Dance' tap routine. NN: Mr. Bojangles. Fought his brother for the name Bill at age 8. He won. His brother then changed his name to Percy. Sold newspapers, danced in beer gardens. He was the first black star in white vaudeville shows. Served in the US Army during the Spanish-American War in 1898. Suffered an accidental gunshot wound. Served in the US Army as a rifleman during WW1 at age 40. Held world records in backwards running: 50 yard dash 6.0 seconds. 75 yard dash 8.2 seconds. 100 yard dash 13.2 seconds, a record which stood from 1907 to 1977. He was the star of the first all-black Hollywood movie, Harlem is Heaven, 1932, in which he played the Mayor of Harlem (how prophetic). He coined and helped popularize the word 'copacetic', which was in use starting in 1919 and added to Webster's Dictionary in 1934. He was the best man at baseball player's Satchel Page's wedding. Taught Shirley Temple how to dance in The Little Colonel, 1935. He was the first black to be in a Hollywood film as one of an interracial dance team. He was the first black to be a solo act, breaking vaudeville's 'two-color' rule, which required black actors to work in pairs. Used wooden instead of steel taps on his shoes. Persuaded the Dallas Police Department to hire their first black policemen in the 1930's. He was the mascot of the New York Giants Baseball team. Refused to fly after his best friend Will Rogers was killed in a plane crash. When Jackie Robinson took the field to play first base and thus become the first black pro non-Negro League baseball player on April 15 1947, Bill Robinson was allowed to tap dance on top of the Brooklyn Dodgers dugout. Honorary Mayor of Harlem from 1935 until his death in 1949. Founder of The Negro Actors Guild. Said his hobby was ice cream, because he ate at least one gallon every day. Never smoked, drank or owned a dog. He was the highest-paid black entertainer of the first half of the 20th century. His last public appearance was on Ted Mack's The Original Amateur Hour, 1949. "What success I achieved in the theater is due to the fact that I have always worked just as hard when there were ten people in the audience as when there were thousands. Just as hard in Springfield, Illinois as on Broadway." "Bill Robinson treated me as an equal, which was very important to me. He didn't talk down to me like a little girl. And I like people like that. And Bill Robinson was best of all." Shirley Temple. "He changed the course of my life." Ann Miller COD: Heart attack. Harlem schools closed for the day so the kids could listen to his funeral on the radio. One million people lined Broadway when his body was moved from Harlem to Times Square. Earned $2,000,000 but died penniless. His funeral was paid for by Ed Sullivan. In 1989, Congress declared May 25th to be National Tap Dance Day in his honor.

Edward G. Robinson (Emmanuel Goldenberg)

b. 12 Dec 1893, d. 26 Jan 1973, = 79 yrs, 1 mo, 14 days. Made 12 films. Married 2 times.

BKF: Gangster roles and playing Rico in Little Caesar, 1931. NN: Eddie and Manny. 5' 6". Born in Romania. When he arrived in the US, he was fluent in Romanian, French, German, Russian, Yiddish and Hebrew, but couldn't speak a word of English. After learning English, he became a public speaker for various political candidates, particularly William Randolph Hearst. He wanted to become a criminal defense attorney but discovered acting instead. Earned a Master's Degree from Columbia University. Took his stage name from a play called The Passerby. He once played seven different roles in a stage play. Said his middle initial stood for "God only knows or Gangster." It actually stands for his original surname, Goldenberg. Said that if he could do it over again, he would not choose Robinson because it takes too long to sign autographs. Became a father for the first time at age 39. Enlisted in the US Navy during WW1. He said, "I learned more about ships and navigation and the fleet from a picture I made years later--Destroyer, with Glenn Ford, than I ever learned at Pelham Bay." Made one silent film, Bright Shawl, in 1928. Turned down for WW2 due to his age--48. Instead, the War Department assigned him as Special Representative based in London. His job was to radio broadcast in six languages to Nazi-occupied countries.

He donated $100,000 of his own money to the USO and $250,000 to various charities during WW2. Also toured to sell war bonds. He was the first entertainer to land on Normandy Beach after D-Day, on July 4th, 1944. Shot to death in six movies: 1. Little Caesar, 1931, 2. Silver Dollar, 1932, 3. I Love a Woman, 1933, 4. Barbary Coast, 1935, 5. Bullets On Broadway, 1936, and 6. Kid Galahad, 1937. He hated guns so much that his eyes had to be taped open to keep him from closing them during the shooting scenes in Little Caesar. His movie Confessions of a Master Spy was banned in 18 countries. Made five films with Humphrey Bogart. Played himself in It's a Great Feeling, 1949. He was a delegate to the 1960 Democratic Convention that nominated John F. Kennedy for President. Fell asleep at the wheel and crashed his car while driving in Beverly Hills on 8 June 1966. It took four hours of surgery to save his life. His face had to be reconstructed by plastic surgery. Had a role in Planet of the Apes but had to drop out due to heart problems, heavy makeup and long hours of filming. Made movies from 1916 to 1972. His last movie was Soylent Green, 1972. Died twelve days after filming ended. Said his role in Double Indemnity, 1944, was his favorite. Never nominated for an Academy Award. He was scheduled to receive an Honorary Academy Award but died two months before the awards ceremony. Collected art, cigar bands and cigarette cards. "No cigar anywhere was safe from me. My father, my uncles and all their friends turned their lungs black trying to satisfy my collector's zeal." "I have not collected art. Art collected me. I have never found painting. Paintings found me. I have never owned a work of art. They owned me." "Paintings never really belong to any one of us. If we are fortunate, as I have been, we are allowed at most a lovely time of custody." "Some people have youth, some have beauty--I have menace." "The sitting around the set is awful. But I always figure that's what they pay me for. The acting I do for free." Owned art works by Cezanne, Van Gough, Gauguin, Renoir and Toulouse-Lautrec. After he died an art gallery in New York bought them for $5,100,000. COD: Bladder cancer. A memorial service was held in Los Angeles with Charlton Heston delivering the eulogy. It was attend by 1,500 friends and 500 more people outside the church.

Signed his will eleven months before he died. Left his art and book collections to his son and daughter, his piano to the University of California and 5% of his estate to various local charities. "If any person other than my son Edward shall claim to be a child of mine or the descendant of a child of mine...I direct the Executors to resist such claim; but if any court shall nevertheless determine that such person is a descendant of mine, I give to such person the sum of Ten Dollars ($10.00) and no more." From his will. Autobiography: All My Yesterdays, 1973. On a US Postal Service stamp in 2000. Chief Wiggum of The Simpsons is modeled after him.

Will Rogers (William Penn Adair Rogers)

b. 4 Nov 1979, d. 15 Aug 1935, = 55 yrs, 9 mos, 11 days. Made 50 silent films, 21 talkies. Married 1 time.

BKF: His humor and apolitical social commentary. NN: The King of the Cowboys, The Cherokee Kid. Born the last of 8 children, and is 9/32nds Cherokee Indian. Born a Cherokee citizen in the Cherokee Nation, Indian Territory (now Oklahoma) in a house that was part frame and part logs. When he was born, his mother delivered him in the log portion of the house so she could say he was born in a log cabin like her hero, Abraham Lincoln. Dropped out of the 10th grade. A poor student, he said, "I studied the Fourth (grade) Reader for ten years." Worked as a gaucho in Argentina. Worked transporting pack animals from Argentina to South Africa in support of the Boer War. Began performing his rope and lasso trick act as part of Texas Jack's Wild West Circus in South Africa. Performed at the 1904 St. Louis World's Fair. Ran for President in 1928 on the Anti-Bunk ticket. His horse's name was Soapsuds. Rode another horse named Teddy in vaudeville and another named Comanche for riding engagements. Wrote more than 4,000 syndicated columns. His "Will Rogers Says" column had 40,000,000 readers in the mid-1920's. Made more than three dozen silent movies before he made his first talkie. Mayor of Beverly Hills, California. He was the announcer of the 1933 Academy

Awards ceremony. He was the #1 box office star of 1934. His most famous quote, in its entirety, is: "When I die, my epitaph is going to read, 'I joked about every prominent man of my time, *but I never met a man I didn't like.*'" "I'm not a real movie star--I've still got the same wife I started out with twenty-eight years ago." "I don't make jokes. I just watch the government and report the facts." "There ain't nothing but one thing wrong with every one of us, and that's selfishness." "Swingin' a rope's alright...if your neck ain't in it." "A humorist entertains, a lecturer annoys." "So get a few laughs and do the best you can." "I don't know what humor is." "Even if you're on the right track, you'll get run over if you just sit there." "My most important duty as the Mayor of Beverly Hills is directing folks to Mary Pickford's house." "The best part about the talkies is that when I say somethin', I say it and it sticks." "Pictures are the only business where you can sit out front and applaud yourself." "The best thing about this group of candidates is that only one of them can win." "A remark generally hurts in proportion to its truth." "When the Okies left Oklahoma and moved to California, it raised the IQ of both states." "Make crime pay. Become a lawyer." "Always drink upstream from the herd." "The man with the best job in the country is the Vice President. All he has to do every morning is wake up and say, 'How's the President?'" "The trouble with practical jokes is that they very often get elected." "When you put down the good things you ought to have done, and leave out the bad ones that you did do--that's Memoirs." "Be thankful we're not getting all the government we're paying for." "If we got one-tenth of what was promised us in these state of the union speeches, there wouldn't be any inducement to go to Heaven." "You can't say civilization don't advance...in every war they kill you a new way." "Good judgment comes from experience, and a lot of that comes from bad judgment." "I might have gone to West Point, but I was too proud to speak to a congressman." "It's not what we don't know that hurts, it's what we know that ain't so." "There's two theories to arguing with a woman. Neither one of them works." "A difference of opinion is what makes horse races and missionaries." "Never miss a good chance to shut up." "I am not a member of an organized political party. I am a Democrat." "It's not knowing that he's a grandfather that makes a man feel old--it's knowing that he's married to a grandmother." COD: Airplane crash near Point Barrow, Alaska. "The American Nation, to whose heart he brought gladness, will hold him in everlasting remembrance." FDR. The Will Rogers Memorial in Claremont, Oklahoma, gets more than 2,000,000 visitors per year. The international airport in Oklahoma is named for him. The Barrow, Alaska airport is known as the Wiley Post-Will Rogers Memorial Airport. Buried at the Will Rogers Memorial in Claremore, Oklahoma. He once said, "When I die, my epitaph, or whatever you call those signs on gravestones is going to read: I joked about every prominent man of my time, but I never met a man I dident (sic) like. I am so proud of that, I can hardly wait to die so it can be carved." His actual epitaph reads: "If You Can Live Life Right, Death is a Joke as Far as Fear is Concerned." He was the first actor to have his portrait on a US postage stamp, a 3-cent stamp in 1948,and then again on a 15-cent stamp in 1979. Rogers County, Oklahoma is named after his father Clement, and not him. Thirteen public schools in Oklahoma are named after him and the iconic US Route 66 (Chicago to Los Angeles) is known as The Will Rogers Highway. A statue of his likeness is in the US Capital building. He insisted that it face the House Chamber, "So I can keep an eye on Congress." His son Will Rogers, Jr. played him in Look For the Silver Lining in 1949 and in The Story of Will Rogers, 1952. Wrote five books but no autobiography. Has two stars on the Hollywood Walk of Fame. The FBI has eight pages of material on him. "It's the fellow who knows when to quit that the audience wants more of."

Randolph Scott (George Randolph Crane Scott)

b. 23 Jan 1898, d. 2 Mar 1987, = 89 yrs, 1 mo, 7 days. Made 108 movies. Married 2 times.

BKF: Western movie star of the 1940's and 1950's. NN: Randy and The Gentleman From Virginia, for his dignified personal conduct.

6'3". Has two adopted children. Learned to ride horses in fox hunts as a child in Virginia. Lied about his age and served in the US Army in France during WW1 at age 15. Served as an enlisted artillery observer. Later commissioned a 2nd Lieutenant in the Artillery Corps. Earned in Bachelor's Degree in textile manufacturing and engineering from the University of North Carolina. Accountant. Got his first roles as a movie extra by playing golf with Howard Hughes. Voice coach for Gary Cooper in The Virginian, 1929. He was so tall that he could not find a big enough bed in Hollywood until the equally tall Howard Hughes supplied him with one. Earned $400 per week in 1932. He was Margaret Mitchell's first choice to play Ashley Wilkes in Gone With the Wind (Leslie Howard got the part). Star of The Desperadoes, 1943, which was the first movie filmed in Technicolor. Once married to the heiress to the DuPont fortune. Rejected by the US Marine Corps during WW2 because of a back injury. Toured with the USO in a comedy act with Joe DeRita, who later became Curly Joe of The Three Stooges in 1958. Shootout At Medicine Bend, 1957, was his last movie filmed in black and white. His horse was a Palomino named Stardust. Sixty of his movies were Westerns. Designed in 1960, his likeness was used as the model for the Oakland Raiders pro football team. Invested his movie income in tungsten and uranium mines, which earned him more than $50,000,000 in dividends in the 1950's. Voluntarily retired in 1962, saying the making movies no longer interested him. Said his favorite movie was To the Shores of Tripoli. Member of the Cowboy Hall of Fame, 1975. "My five sisters took my mother to see me in a movie and she said, "Oh, no! That can't be Randolph. This feller's older than Randy and not so good-looking." "My father went to see all my films--not because he had a son starring in them, but because he thought I looked like Wallace Reid, his favorite actor." "Randy Scott is a complete anachronism. He's a complete gentleman. And so far the only one I've met in this business." Director Michael Curtiz. COD: Heart and lung failure. Buried in Charlotte, NC just four blocks from his boyhood home. Worth more than $100,000,000 at the time of his death. Died only two months after his lifelong best friend Cary Grant. Cried uncontrollably when he heard the news.

Mack Sennett (Mikall Sinnott)

b. 17 Jan 1880, d. 5 Nov 1960, = 80 yrs, 9 mos, 19 days. Produced more than 1,115 movies, directed 311 movies, wrote 96 movies. Never married.

BKF: Creating the Keystone Kops, The Bathing Beauties and bringing slapstick comedy to the screen. NN: King of Comedy. Born in Canada. He wanted to be an opera singer but was talked out of it by Northampton, Connecticut Mayor (and future US President) Calvin Coolidge. He was the first American actor to play Sherlock Holmes in the movies, in The $500 Reward, in 1911. He was the first producer to hire beginning actor Charlie Chaplin. "Go hire some girls, any girls, as long as they're pretty, especially around the knees." Became a US citizen on March 25th, 1932. Forced to declare bankruptcy in 1933 due to the Great Depression. In 1934 he was in an auto accident in Mesa, Arizona that killed his friend, blackface performer Charles Mack. When he went out in public and didn't want to be recognized, he used the name Walter Terry. Received an Honorary Academy Award in 1938 "For his lasting contribution to the comedy technique of the screen, the basic principles of which are as important today as when they were first put into practice, the Academy presents a Special Award to that master of fun, discoverer of stars, sympathetic, kindly, understanding comic genius--Mack Sennett." Appeared on This Is Your Life, 1954. Paid $1,000 to appear in Abbot and Costello's Meet the Keystone Kops in 1955. "Pioneers are seldom from the nobility. There were no dukes on the Mayflower." "We never made fun of religion, politics, race or mothers. A mother never gets hit with a custard pie. Mothers-in-law, yes. But mothers, never!" "I called myself The King of Comedy, but I was a harassed monarch. I worked most of the time. It was only in the evenings that I laughed." Has a star on Hollywood's Walk of Fame, 1960, and the Canadian Walk of Fame, 2014. COD: Undisclosed. Died on the same day as Ward Bond. Buried in Culver City, California.

C. Aubrey Smith (Charles Aubrey Smith)

b. 21 July 1863, d. 20 Dec 1948, = 85 yrs, 4 mos, 29 days. Made 113 movies. Married 1 time.

BKF: Playing Colonel Zapt in The Prisoner of Zenda, 1937, and his "officer and a gentleman" roles. NN: Round the Corner Smith, from his time as a professional cricket bowler. 6' 2". On the London stage in 1895. Graduate of Cambridge University. While prospecting for gold in South Africa 1889, he was mistakenly pronounced dead of pneumonia. Internationally known professional cricket player in England. Made dozens of silent films, didn't make his first talkie until age 67 in 1930. He was a founding member of the Screen Actors Guild in 1933. Founded the Hollywood Cricket Club of Hollywood, consisting entirely of British actors such as team Captain NIgel Bruce, David Niven, Laurence Olivier, Leslie Howard and Boris Karloff. Too old to serve in the military right before WW2, he strongly criticized British actors who did not return to the United Kingdom to enlist. Knighted by King George VI in 1944. His last appearance on screen was posthumously as Mr. James Laurence in Little Women, 1949, the year after he died. "It is an almost everyday occurrence to see a London audience give an ovation to some player who has been a favorite for years and years. In American, favorites pass more quickly. Life is faster in the States. Britishers don't like to be hurried in the American manner." Star on the Hollywood Walk of Fame, 1960. He was the inspiration for the character Commander McBragg on Tennessee Tuxedo and His Tales, 1963. COD: Pneumonia. Cremated, buried in his mother's grave in Sussex, UK.

Gale Sondergaard (Edith Holm Sondergaard)

b. 15 Feb 1899, d. 14 Aug 1985, = 86 yrs, 5 mos, 30 days. Made 56 movies. Married 2 times.

BKF: Playing the King's wife in Anna and the King of Siam, 1946. NN: None. Studied at the School of Music and Dramatic Arts (they did not have drama department) at the University of Minnesota, where her father was a professor. She was the first actress to win the first Best Supporting Actress Oscar in 1936, for Anthony Adverse. She was also the first actress (along with Maria Ouspenskaya) to be nominated for an Academy Award for their screen debut. The roles she most excelled in were classified as manipulative, cunning and sinister. She was the first choice to play the Wicked Witch of the West in The Wizard of Oz. She did screen tests costumed as an ugly witch and then as a beautiful witch. She got the role as the ugly witch but turned it down because it would typecast her and harm her career. The role went to Margaret Hamilton. Her career took a dive when her husband, Herbert Biberman, was named one of the "Hollywood 10." She was blacklisted for refusing to testify before Congress. Didn't make another movie for 28 years. Appeared on Get Smart in 1970, in the Rebecca of Funny-Folk episode. Her likeness was the model for the Evil Queen in Snow White and the Seven Dwarfs. "Go figure those two. Hedda Hopper was a homophobic and her only child (the actor who played Paul Drake on Perry Mason) was a homosexual. Louella (Parsons) was anti-Semitic, yet she was born Jewish, then converted. They were a demented pair, and Hollywood was even more demented for allowing them so much power over other people's careers and lives." COD: Cerebrovascular thrombosis, following several strokes. Admitted to the hospital in 1982, died there in 1985. Cremated, remains scattered in the Pacific Ocean.

Gloria Swanson (Gloria May Josephine Svensson)

b. 27 Mar 1899, d. 4 Apr 1993, = 94 yrs, 8 days. Made 82 movies. Married 6 times.

BKF: Playing Norma Desmond in the 1950 movie Sunset Boulevard and the line, "All right, Mr. DeMille, I'm ready for my close-up. 4' 11 1/2". She was an only child. Her father was in the US Army and she spent most of her childhood growing up in Puerto Rico, where she learned fluent Spanish. Discovered when she was chosen at random from a Chicago audience to be a movie extra. Earned $13.50 per week in 1914 as a Mack Sennett extra. At $10,000 per week, she was the highest-paid actress in Hollywood in 1925. Married 31-year-old Wallace Beery on her 17th birthday. In her autobiography she says he raped her and later forced her to drink a potion that induced an abortion. Married to him for only three weeks. Remarried and sued for divorce by her husband in 1923, claiming that she had committed adultery with fourteen different men, including some of the most prominent names in Hollywood. Because of this, her contract was amended to include the first morals clauses in any Hollywood actor's contract. Later married a marquis, which made her a genuine marquise. She was caught in bed with her financial backer, Joseph P. Kennedy, by his 10-year-old son, John F. Kennedy, while on his yacht. The kid was so distraught that he jumped overboard and had to be rescued. Made her first color film in 1925 in Stage Struck. She did not make another film in color until 1952, when she made Three For Bedroom C. Became a lifelong vegetarian in 1928. Earned and spent an estimated $8,000,000 in the 1920's alone. Because of her fondness for extravagant wardrobes and accessories she became known as Hollywood's first clothes horse. When nominated for Best Actress for Queen Kelly in 1929, she refused to attend the Academy Award ceremony, saying, "It was like comparing apples to oranges." Turned down $1,000,000 per year to renew her studio contract in the 1930's. Never wore the same dress twice. Many of her silent films have been lost. In 1938, and in anticipation of WW2, she moved to New York City and formed a company called Multiprises. The company mission was to rescue Jewish scientists and inventors from the war in Europe and bring them safely to the United States. In 1948, she hosted one of the first live television series, The Gloria Swanson Hour. She was on the cover of the first edition of what was later to become TV Guide on June 14th 1948. She was the fourth choice to play Norma Desmond in Sunset Boulevard, after Mae West, Mary Pickford and Pola Negri all turned down the role. She was a mystery guest on What's My

Line twice. Testified at John Lennon's immigration hearing in New York City in 1960, helping him to become a permanent resident. She played herself on an episode of The Beverly Hillbillies in 1966. Actress Irene Ryan, as Granny, said she was her favorite actress because, "We lookalikes, y'know." The first film shown at the Roxy Theater in New York City was her Love of Sunya, in 1922. When the theater was demolished in 1961, she posed for photos while standing in the rubble. She was a guest on The Dick Cavett show in 1970, along with Janis Joplin, who died one year later. Rededicated the HOLLYWOOD sign on its fiftieth anniversary, 14 September 1973. Wrote newspaper columns, painted, sculpted and was a traveling advocate of health and nutrition. In 1980 she was Chairperson of the New York Chapter of Seniors for Reagan-Bush. Never won an Oscar. Wanted desperately to be a guest star on the Batman television show but no appropriate role could be found. "I am big. It's the pictures that got small." "Fame was thrilling only until it became grueling. Money was for only until you ran out of things to buy." "I've given my memoirs far more thought than any of my marriages. You can't divorce a book." "Never say never, for if you live long enough, chances are you will not be able to abide by its restrictions. Never is a long, undependable time and, life is too full of rich possibilities to have restrictions placed on it." "I have decided that while I am a star, I will be every inch and every moment a star. Everyone from the studio gateman to the highest executives will know it." "As I felt my feet leave the ground, I could tell that someone behind me was standing on my train, so I screamed for one of the horsemen to pick it up. I was not completely horizontal, face down, like a battering ram, and that is the way they carried me through the crowd and into the theater lobby." On being transported by the police through a mob at the premiere of The Trespasser, 1929. "I've given my memoirs far more thought than any of my marriages. You can't divorce a book." "It's amazing to find so many people, who I thought really knew me, could have thought that Sunset Boulevard was autobiographical. I've got nobody floating in my swimming pool." Suggested epitaph: "When I die, my epitaph should read: 'She Paid the Bills'. That's the story of my private life." "Two of the more tired topics I never discuss are my marriage (of three weeks) to Wallace Beery and those frozen dinners which have become famous with my name on them." "All they had to do was put my name on the marquee and watch the money roll in." On Marlene Dietrich: "Her legs may be longer than mine, but unlike me, she doesn't have seven grandchildren." "All creative people should be required to leave California for at least three months every year." "Damned if she didn't keep on getting married! I got her into an awful bad habit." Wallace Beery. On her role in Airport 1975, which was her final movie and she played herself: "I was holding out for a picture I could take my grandchildren to see, something exciting and contemporary without senseless violence." "I think all this talk about age is foolish. Every time I'm one year older, everyone else is too." COD: Heart ailment. Cremated, ashes interred at the Church of Heavenly Rest in New York City, the same church that held the funeral for President Chester A. Arthur. Jacqueline Logan, her co-star in her 1929 movie Hollywood, died on the same day she did. Signed her will twenty months before she died. Married to her sixth husband when she died, he received nothing. She earned $10,000,000 in her lifetime, worth $1,440,000 at the time of her death. Left 80% of her estate to her two daughters. Instructed that "there be no public funeral or display of any sort." Autobiography: Swanson on Swanson, which she published in 1975 to rebut several critical comments Rose Kennedy made in her 1974 autobiography. Her autobiography was an international bestseller, being translated into French, Italian and Swedish.

Blanche Sweet (Sarah Blanche Sweet)

b. 18 Jun 1896, d. 6 Sep 1986, = 90 yrs, 2 mos, 19 days. Made 164 movies. Married 2 times.

BKF: Anna Christie, 1923. NN: The Biograph Blonde. On stage at 18 months old and dancing by age 4. She was raised by her grandmother, who was a stage performer. She made 150 silent films and only three talkies. Her voice killed her career. Before Biograph started revealing the names of their stars, she was billed as Daphne Wayne. She was Mary Pickford's chief rival for her looks and types of movies she made. Earned $10,000 per week in 1926. Had no children. Worked in a Los Angeles department store after retiring. Became a film historian. In her last movie she played the role of a washed-up silent film star in Show Girl of Hollywood, 1930. "It never occurred to me that I was different from other children. My wonderful grandmother was both mother and father to me." COD: Stroke. Ashes scattered in Brooklyn Botanical Gardens, New York.

Norma Talmadge (Same)

b. 26 May 1894, d. 24 Dec 1957, = 63 yrs, 6 mos, 28 days. Made 300+ movies. Married 3 times.

BKF: Smilin' Through, 1922, the greatest romance movie of the silent era. NN: The Lady of the Great Indoors. Older sister of Constance Talmadge. Made $10,000 per week in 1923. Made $250,000 per film in 1924. Her appearance in 1930's DuBarry, Woman of Passion, abruptly ended her career, due to her voice. Her sister Constance consoled her with, "Quit pressing your luck, baby. The critics can't knock those trust funds Mama set up for us." She made more than 300 movies but only three talkies. She kept her jewels, cash and other valuables in the vegetable bin of her refrigerator. Third person to have a Walk of Fame Star, 18 May 1927. After her popularity had waned in the 1930's, she told autograph seekers, "Get away, dears. I don't need you anymore and you don't need me." In 1956, she was voted one of the top five female stars of the pre-1925 era. Worth more than $1,000,000 at the time of her death.

Irving Thalberg (Irving Grant Thalberg)

b. 30 May 1899, d. 14 Sep 1936, = 47 yrs, 3 mos, 15 days. Produced more than 400 movies. Married 1 time.

NN: The Wonder Boy and Wunderkind. Born with the 'blue baby syndrome,' a congenital heart disease that limits the oxygen supply to the heart. Doctors said he would not live to see twenty, and certainly not thirty years. Coauthor of the movie production code. He was known as the foremost figure in motion picture history, even though he lived to be only 37 years old. Turned down a chance to produce Gone With the Wind with "Look, I have just made Mutiny on the Bounty and the Good Earth. And now you're asking me to burn Atlanta? No! Absolutely not!" and "No civil war picture ever made a nickel." With the exception of The Good Earth in 1937, he would not allow his name to be in the credits of his pictures. "If they don't want to come to the picture...you can't stop them." "Thalberg directed the film on paper, and then the director directed the film on film." A fellow producer. "Novelty is always welcome, but talking pictures are just a fad." 1929 COD: Pneumonia and heart failure. Buried in Glendale, California.

Sophie Tucker (Sophie Kalish)

b. 13 Jan 1887, d. 9 Feb 1966, 79 yrs, 27 days. Made 9 movies. Married 3 times.

BKF: Risque acts and sense of humor. NN: The Last of the Red Hot Mamas, The First Lady of Show Business. Cafe singer, vaudeville performer. Her theme song was Some of These Days. Wore pants before Greta Garbo was known for wearing them. "From birth to eighteen, a girl needs good parents. From eighteen to thirty-five, she needs good looks. From thirty-five to forty-five, she needs a good personality. Fifty-five on, she needs good cash." "I've been rich and I've been poor. Rich is better." COD: Lung ailment and kidney failure. Buried in Wethersfield, Connecticut.

Ben Turpin (Bernard Turpin)

b. 19 Sep 1869, d. 1 July 1940, 70 yrs, 9 mos, 12 days. Made 236 movies. Married 2 times.

BKF: Being the silent film star with the crossed eyes. He said his eyes weren't crossed until after an accident when he was a teenager. Did not make his first film until age 38. He is the first actor to get a pie in the face, in Mr. Flip, in 1909. He is the first movie star to be mentioned by name in a magazine, The Moving Picture World, a trade journal in 1911. It was probably because he was a contributing author to the magazine. Liked to introduce himself with, "I'm Ben Turpin; I make $3,000 a week." Being the first actor to insure a trademark feature, he had a $25,000 insurance policy with Lloyd's of London against his eyes uncrossing. Voluntarily retired in 1929 to care for his sick wife but occasionally appeared live for a $1,000 fee. He was one of the richest men in Hollywood due to his real estate investments. COD: Heart attack. Buried in Glendale, California.

Rudolf Valentino (Rodolpho Alfonso Raffaello Pierre Filibert Guglielmi de Valentina D'Antongoulla)

b. 6 May 1895, d. 23 Aug 1926, = 31 Yrs, 3 mos, 17 days. Made 39 movies. Married 2 times.

BKF: The Sheik, 1921, and being the first male sex symbol of the silent era. NN: The Great Lover, Valentino, The Sheik, The Sex God, The Latin Lover, The Idol, Rudy, The Pink Powder-puff. His name is variously spelled Rudolph, Rudolf or Rodolpho. Born in Italy, expelled from military school. Studied farming at an agricultural school. Was a pre-med student but quit to join the Italian Army. His father was a Captain in the Italian Cavalry. With a small inheritance of $4,000 he moved to the US at age 18. Was a tango dancer, busboy, gigolo, taxi driver, gardener and petty thief. He slept in Central Park when he was broke and between jobs. Had ear surgery to reduce their size. He spoke fluent English, French, Italian and Spanish. At the outbreak of WW1, he tried to enlist in the Italian Army through their New York Office but his chest circumference was too small and he couldn't pass the vision test. He was extremely near-sighted but was too vain to wear glasses. Arrested several times for fighting, vagrancy, petty theft and spent three days in jail in 1916 for being a gigolo. He also spent another three days in jail in 1916 on charges of blackmail. After he became a star, all of these arrest records mysteriously disappeared. He was the star of The Four Horseman of the Apocalypse, the first million dollar production in America and the highest-grossing silent film of that time. When a writer for the Chicago Tribune called him a 'pink powder-puff,' and accused him of the 'effeminization of the American male,' he challenged him to a duel, which never took place. Spent his first night married to Jean Acker locked out of his house because he waited until after they were married to confess to her that he had syphilis. This marriage was over in one day. The fact that, unknown to him at the time, the fact that she was in a lesbian triangle contributed to the problem. They separated but never divorced. The second time he was married, to actress Natacha Rambova, he spent his wedding night and the next six days in jail on bigamy charges. His valet started the celebrity relic-memento business by secretly selling his bathwater to women for $20 per vial. Discovered by New York actress Mae Murray, who later helped bring him to Hollywood. Made $100 per week in 1919. When he was in his twenties, an amusement park palm reader predicted he would die "very young." Started his career playing gangsters and villains. Wrote a book of poetry, Day Dreams, in 1932. He had two dogs named Maggie and Molly. His home was called Falcon's Lair, named after his wife's production company that never got off the ground. He had a six-sided swimming pool and the nation's first barbecue pit. His hobby was collecting rare books and working on old automobiles. He had an Irish wolfhound named Centaur Pendragon. After he became a star but before he became a superstar, he sold 50,00 autographed photos of himself for twenty-five cents apiece. Natasha was so controlling that a clause in his 1925 United Artists contract paid him $10,000 per week and a percentage of the gross, but with one important provision: she was prevented from coming on the set when he was working. When Metro refused to give him a modest increase in pay after making Camille, Paramount bought out his contract so he could make The Sheik, which made him a superstar.

Sheik condoms were introduced to the public in the 1930's, taking advantage of the his most recent popular movie and his reputation as a lover. His silhouette was on the packaging for years. This gave way to other brands called Trojan and Ramses. He said he hated The Sheik. He took a vacation and went back to Italy to rest for a while. When he returned to Hollywood, his friends asked him if he had been mobbed by fans. He said, "No, over there, I look like every other Italian fellow on the street." "To generalize on women is dangerous. To specialize in them is even worse." "We cannot know woman because she does not know herself." "A man should control his life. Mine is controlling me." I am beginning to look more and more like my miserable imitators." About Gene Acker, "She said she was my soul mate, but she proved to be my check-mate!" "Rudy looks best when he's naked." His wife Natasha Rambova. "Shortly before he died, he said, "I would like to disappear at the height of my powers, in an accident. I find nothing more stupid than to die of a disease." Last words: "Don't pull down the blinds. I want the sunlight to greet me." And then to Joseph M. Schenck, Chairman of the Board of United Artists, "Don't worry, Chief, I will be all right." And then to his doctor, he said, "Well, doctor, and do I now act like a pink powder-puff?" His doctor assured him, "No, sir. You have been very brave. Braver than most." COD: Peritonitis, appendicitis, uremic poisoning and septic endocarditis a few days after an ulcer operation. Two women attempted suicide at his hospital within hours of his death. His was the first celebrity death and it took three days for more than 100,000 mourners, mostly female, to pass by his open coffin at Campbell's Funeral Home in New York City. Movie studios shut down for the first time for an actor during his funeral. At least one dozen women committed suicide when he died. "Women are not in love with me, but with the picture on the screen. I am merely the canvas on which women paint their dreams." He had one funeral in New York and another in Hollywood. He is buried in a tomb between his screenwriter Joan Mathis and her husband in Hollywood, California. Epitaph: "RODOLFO GUGIELMI VALENTINO/ 1895 1926." Rudy Valee wrote a new song for him called "There's A New Star In Heaven

Tonight." Earned $5,000,000, died $200,000 in debt. His dog Kahar died a few days after he did. After he died, his brother was hired to take his place and even had cosmetic surgery to more resemble him. His will left his first wife Jean Acker nothing and his second wife Natacha Rambova only one dollar. For decades after his death, an unidentified woman left flowers on his grave on the anniversary of his death. "The biggest thing Rulolf Valentino ever did was die." His leading lady Alice Terry. After his death John Gilbert wrote, "He was a prince of gallantry, and beyond all his many other attributes of artistry, comeliness and charm, a gift of royal glamour to his being, which made him the hero lover of all time." In 1963, nearly four decades after he died, actress Jane Mansfield claimed that he had been receiving career advice from him via seances held at his former home. Actor John Travolta believes he is Valentino reincarnated. His likeness was on a US Postal Service 44-cent stamp designed by artist Al Hirschfield.

Conrad Veidt (Hans Walter Conrad Veidt)

b. 22 Jan 1893, d. 3 Apr 1943, = 50 yrs, 2 mos, 12 days. Made 119 movies. Married 3 times.

BKF: Playing Major Strasser in Casablanca. Served in the German Army as a Sergeant during WW1. While recovering from wounds, he was released from the Army so he could join a theater that entertained the troops. A German actor, he moved to the US to get away from the Nazis. In his role in The Man Who Laughs (1928) he played a circus performer whose face was cut into a permanent grin. This was the inspiration for the Batman character The Joker, taken from his 1928 movie The Man Who Laughs. He donated a substantial portion of his income to the anti-German war effort. Superstitious about the number 17. Early in his career he lived at 817 Camden Drive in Beverly Hills. Decades later, his wife bought for them the house at 617 Camden Drive, not knowing that he had lived on the same street earlier. Described himself as a man "with the sterling qualities of sincerity, kindness, and never-failing courtesy." He was the highest-paid actor in Casablanca, earning $5,000 per week ($225,000 total) to play Major Strasser to Bogart's $3,500 per week. COD: Heart attack while on a Los Angeles Golf course (the 8th hole) with his doctor, who pronounced him dead on the golf course. First star of Casablanca to die, he never knew it was going to be one of the greatest movies of all time. Cremated, ashes buried in North London.

Erich Von Stroheim (Erich Oswald Hans Carl Maria von Stroheim)

b. 22 Sep 1885, d. 12 May 1957, = 71 yrs, 7 mos, 20 days. Made 74 films. Married 3 times.

BKF: Directing Greed, a 10-hour epic that is considered to be a classic and the first feature-length movie filmed entirely on location. It was cut to six hours, then to four hours, then to two and one-hours and then lost forever when it was accidentally thrown in the garbage by a janitor. NN: The Man You Love to Hate, for the Nazi roles he liked to play. Son of Jewish hat maker. Emigrated to the US in 1905 and passed himself off as Austrian Nobleman Count Erich Oswald Hans Carl Maria von Strohiem und Nordenwell. His friends called him Von, which was the totally made-up part of his name. Played a chauffeur in Sunset Boulevard, 1950. He didn't know how to drive so his driving scenes were filmed with him sitting in the driver's seat with the car being pulled by ropes. Lived the last years of his life in France. His business manager was Elmer Cox, the father of Bewitched actor Dick Sargent. Last words: During a rambling diatribe against Hollywood: "This isn't the worst. The worst is that Hollywood stole 25 years of my life." COD: Prostate cancer.

Raoul Walsh (Albert Edward Walsh)

b. 11 Mar 1887, d. 31 Dec 1980, = 93 yrs, 9 mos, 20 days. Directed 138 movies, acted in 42 movies. Married 3 times.

BKF: Playing John Wilkes Booth in The Birth of a Nation, 1915. Played in Regeneration in 1915, the earliest known gangster film. Served as an officer in the US Army during WW1. One of the founding members of The Academy of Motion Picture Arts and Sciences. He was blinded in the right eye while filming In Old Arizona in 1929 when a jackrabbit shattered the window of his car. He was replaced by Warner Baxter, who won the Best Actor Oscar for the role. He was the first director to get a star on the Hollywood Walk of Fame, on 14 November, 1930. "To Raoul Walsh, a tender love scene is burning down a whorehouse." Jack Pickford. COD: Natural Causes. Buried in Simi Valley, California. Autobiography: Each Man In His Own Time.

Jack Warner (Jacob Lebzelter Walter, Jr.)

b. 2 Aug 1892, d. 9 Sep 1978, = 86, 1 mo, 7 days. Made 39 movies. Married 2 times.

BKF: President of Warner Bros. Studios for 45 years. WW2 Lt. Colonel in the US Army. Almost killed in an automobile accident in Cannes, France that left him in a coma for several days. He was thrown from the car, which burst into flames. He was put on Hitler's death list in 1939 because of his movie Confessions of a Nazi Spy. His friend Bugsy Siegel offered to put out a hit on Nazis Joseph Goebbels and Herman Goering for him. 1955 Cecil B. DeMille winner. To Albert Einstein: "I have a theory of relatives, too. Don't hire them." "What is a writer but a schmuck with an Underwood (typewriter)?" "Bette Davis is an explosive little broad with a sharp left." "Al Jolson said of Jack Warner, "For the life of me I can't see what Jack Warner can do with all of these awards. It can't say yes." "An empty taxi stopped, and Jack Warner got out." Many. "If I'm right fifty-one percent of the time, I'm ahead of the game." James Cagney's nickname for him was "The Shvontz." COD: Heart inflammation following a stroke. Buried in East Los Angeles, California. Worth $15,000,000 when he died.

Ethel Waters (Same)

b. 31 Oct 1896, d. 1 Sep 1977, = 80 yrs, 10 mos, 1 day. Made 29 movies. Never married.

BKF: Being the most influential Blues singer of the 1920's and 1930's. Born to a 12-year-old mother, who had been raped. Second black actress to be nominated for a Best Supporting Actress Oscar, after Hattie McDaniel in 1939, for Pinky in 1949. She was also the first black actress to be nominated for an Emmy, for a dramatic appearance on the Route 66 television show. She was also the first black actress to have her own television show, The Ethel Waters Show, which premiered on 4 June 1939, long before Nat King Cole had his show in 1956. Honorary Captain in the California State Militia. Lost tens of thousands of dollars in cash and jewelry in a robbery in 1950. October 15, 1953 was officially Ethel Waters Day in New York City. April 30, 1972 was Ethel Waters Day in Pennsylvania. Toured with Billy Graham in the 1960's. She is the great-aunt of singer Crystal Waters. COD: Uterine cancer and kidney failure. Buried in Glendale, California. Her 1933 hit Stormy Weather was inducted into the Grammy Hall of Fame in 2003. Autobiographies: His Eye Is On the Sparrow, 1951 and To Me, It's Wonderful, 1972.

Clifton Webb (Webb Parmelee Hollenbeck)

b. 19 Nov 1889, d. 13 Oct 1966, = 76 yrs, 10 mos, 24 days. Made 27 movies. Never married, avowed homosexual.

BKF: Playing the radio columnist Waldo Lydecker in 1944's Laura, starring Gene Tierney, and especially for playing Frank Gilbreth in Cheaper By the Dozen, 1950. Professional ballroom dancer, whose partner eventually dropped him for Rudolph Valentino. Performed in two dozen operettas on Broadway. Vaudeville performer. Credited with introducing the white mess jacket to the US. He was always on Hollywood's Best Dressed List. He was always the most prepared with his lines of any actor. Consequently, he always had a hard time whenever a word or line was changed while filming at the last minute. He is the actor that Mr. Peabody on The Bullwinkle Show is modeled after. Lived with his mother until she died at age 91, to which Noel Coward said, "It must be terrible to be orphaned at age 71." "I love Hollywood. I love anything about it, especially the opportunity to make more and more films, and the chance to make more and more money. I LOVE money and furthermore, I NEED it. Furthermore, I will do anything to get it." COD: Heart attack. Interred in Hollywood Forever Cemetery, Beverly Hills, California.

Mae West (Mary Jane West)

b. 17 Aug 1893, d. 22 Nov 1980, = 87 yrs, 3 mos, 5 days. Made 12 movies. Married 1 time. NN: Peaches, The Screen's Bad Girl.

BKF: Being the first actress to make movies that were exclusively about sexual affairs and her double entendres and quotes that pushed the boundaries of the censorship standards of the day. She invented the Shimmy dance in 1913. She was a writer, producer and stage performer before coming to Hollywood at age 40 in 1933. She used the name Jane Mast early in her career. In 1927 she was arrested for performing in a play called Sex and charged with "corrupting the morals of youth, even though there were no minors anywhere around. Given the choice of a fine or jail, she chose the 10 days in jail to make a point about free speech. She said, "The police investigating me really enjoyed it." When she was released two days early, one day for good behavior and one day for time served, she said, "That's the first time I ever got anything for being good." "A lot of my fans were there (in jail) with me. And I was treated like a society figure--the warden took me out every night." Moved from New York to Hollywood when she got a contract for $5,000 for two months' work in 1931. She did not arrive in Hollywood until she was forty years old. Her contracts stipulated that no one but her could wear white in her sets, that she would always have two versions of her costumes--one tight for standing and one looser for sitting. She said, "I want my clothes loose enough to prove I'm a lady but tight enough to show 'em I'm a woman." Her contract also stated she would never have to kiss her leading man on screen. Despite her reputation, her films had no nudity, no profanity and very little violence. She never smoked and rarely drank. She was five feet tall and weighed 126 pounds. Her measurements were 37 1/2" - 29 1/2" - 37 1/2". She wore 10" heels and false nipples. Her motto was, "So many men, so little time." Even though she and W.C Fields are usually thought of as a team, they actually made only one movie together, My Little Chickadee. Her contract stated that she wouldn't have to work with him if he showed up drunk, which happened only once. However, she and W. C Fields were so good at improv and adlibbing that the stage crew laughed so loud that they ruined the sound recording. The movie had to be dubbed to edit out the off-screen laughter. She was paid $40,000 to make the film, which was about one-tenth her salary on stage five years earlier. She single-handedly saved Paramount from bankruptcy with She Done Him Wrong in 1933. It was also the only film she ever made that earned a Best Picture Oscar nomination. In 1934, the Kansas Restaurant Association placed ads thanking her for "stemming the dieting craze stimulated by the sylph-like figures of Dietrich, Crawford and Harlow and for restoring well-rounded curves to healthy U.S. women." Her name was used to describe a tank, a flotation device, a parachute (that had failed to open properly, thus looking like a huge brassiere), and a cruller. She was unable to stomach visiting hospitals during WW2, so she did free standing room only shows for wounded soldiers at the National Theater. Broke her ankle in a slip and fall in a hotel in 1949. The hotel promptly put up a sign that said, "Mae West Slipped Here." When she did an interview for Charles Collingwood's Person to Person television show in 1959, it was never aired because they could not find one bit that could be cleared by the censors. She lived only three blocks from her studio for the entire 48 years she lived in Hollywood. Her phone number was listed in the Los Angeles telephone directory right up the time of her death and she would usually answer the phone herself. She did not like the color of the building across the street from her apartment so she bought the building and had it repainted. She donated her old limousines to convents because, as she said, "It depresses me to see nuns riding around in busses--or old Fords." Inspired a perfume by Elsa Schiaparelli called Shocking. "Is that a gun in your pocket or are you just glad to see me?" is correctly attributed to her but she never actually said it in a movie until she made Sextette in 1978, which was her last movie. "All discarded lovers should be given a second chance, but with someone else." "Hiring someone to write your autobiography is like asking someone to take a bath for you." "I always say, keep a diary and some day it'll keep you." "Look your best--who said love is blind." "Everything's in the mind. That's where it all starts. Knowing what you want is the first step toward getting it." "When you've got the personality, you don't need the nudity." "Your real security is yourself. You know you can do it and they can't ever take that away from you." "Marriage is a great institution, but I'm not ready for an institution." "Women with pasts interest men because they hope history will repeat itself." "You can say what you like about long dresses, but they cover a multitude of shins." "There are no withholding taxes in the wages of sin." "To err is human--but it feels divine." "Too much of a good thing can be wonderful." "A hard man is good to find." "A man has one hundred dollars. You leave him with two dollars. That's subtraction, baby." "I'm the girl who lost her reputation and never missed it." When gossip columnist Hedda Hopper asked her how she knew so much about men, she said, "Baby, I went to night school." "Sex must be in the face, not the body. If you have to show your body, then you haven't got it, dear." When asked by a reporter if sex was dirty, she said, "If you do it right, it is." "No gold-digging for me...I like diamonds! We may be off the gold standard someday." "One figure can sometimes add up to a lot." "I feel like a million tonight--but one at a time." "I never worry about diets. The only carrots that interest me are the number you get in a diamond." "I was once so poor I didn't know where my next husband was coming from." I'm the girl who works at Paramount all day and Fox all night." "It is better to be looked than overlooked." "I only like two kinds of men--domestic and imported." "Whenever I'm good I'm very good, but when I'm bad I'm better." "Whenever I'm caught between two evils, I always take the one I've never tried before." "I believe in censorship. I made a fortune out of it." "I speak two languages--English and Body." "I used to be Snow White but I drifted." "Brains are an asset, if you hide them." "Curve: the loveliest distance between two points." "Don't keep a man guessing too long--he's sure to find the answer somewhere else." "The censors wouldn't even let me sit on a guy's lap, and I've been on more laps than a table napkin." Anything worth doing is worth doing slowly." "An orgasm a day keeps the doctor away." "Men are my hobby, if I ever got married I'd have to give them up." "It's hard to be funny when you have to be clean." "I've always had a weakness for foreign affairs." After she was allowed to rewrite her lines in 1932's Night After Night, co-star George Raft said, "She stole everything but the cameras." "She's the kind of girl who climbed the ladder of success wrong by wrong." Anon. A critic on She Done Him Wrong: "The most flagrant and utterly abandoned morsel of sin ever attempted on the screen, and I must confess that I enjoyed it enormously." Appeared on an episode of Mr. Ed in 1964. When Perry Como told her he was a perfect gentleman, she replied, "Which are you: perfect or a gentleman?" When the Beatles asked her in 1967 if they could use her likeness on the cover of their Lonely Hearts Club Band album, she refused saying, "Why would I ever belong to a lonely hearts club?" They appealed to her in a personal handwritten letter and she gave her approval. She wrote a novel called (what else?) The Constant Sinner. She spent 48 years in Hollywood but made only 12 movies. She had a 69-year career, including her stage work in New York. She never said, "Come up and see me sometime." Instead, the actual quote is: "Why don't you come up sometime and see me?" In 1998, Playboy Magazine named her #44 of the 100 Sexiest Stars of the 20th Century. She is the most quoted woman of the 20th Century. "COD: Complications from a stroke. Buried in Brooklyn, NY. Autobiography: Goodness Had Nothing To Do With It, 1959, and Health, Sex and ESP, 1975.

Pearl White (Pearl Fay White)

b. 4 Mar 1889, d. 4 Aug 1938, = 49 yrs, 5 mos. Made 228 movies. Married 2 times.

BKF: Starring in 20 2-reel serials in The Perils of Pauline, 1915. NN: Queen of the Serials. Stage actress at age 6. Bareback horse rider for the circus at age 13. In 1914-1915 she was a bigger star than Mary Pickford. The movie viewing public had absolutely no idea that actors used stunt doubles until the stuntman performing a jump for her missed his landing and died of a fractured skull in 1922. Worth $2,000,000 by 1924, the year she voluntarily retired. She wanted to make a comeback in talkies but after a screen test was told that her voice prohibited it. She made all of her movies on the east coast. On why she never remarried after her divorce: "Mine was not a divorce of convenience, but one of necessity, and I have no idea of making it a necessity again." She is the first movie star to write her autobiography, Just Me, in 1919. COD: Cirrhosis of the liver. Buried in Paris, France.

Dame May Whitty (Mary Louise Webster)

b. 19 Jun 1856, d. 29 May 1948, = 82 yrs, 11 mos, 10 mos. Made 37 movies. Married 1 time.

BKF: Playing Lady Beldon in Mrs. Miniver in 1942. First actress to be made a Dame Commander of the Order of the British Empire (DBE), in 1918. "I've got everything Betty Grable has--only I've had it longer." COD: Cancer.

Monty Woolley (Edgar Montillion Wooley)

b. 17 Aug 1888, d. 6 May 1963, = 74 yrs, 8 mos, 19 days. Made 36 movies. Never married.

BKF: 738 stage performances in The Man Who Came to Dinner and the 1942 movie of the same title. NN: The Beard. Born in Manhattan's

Bristol Hotel, which his father owned. Earned a B.A. from Yale and a Ph.D. from Harvard, later taught for 12 years as a Professor of Drama at Yale. WW1: 1st Lieutenant in the US Army assigned to the General Staff in Paris. Grew his iconic beard to emulate his hero George Bernard Shaw, who he met in 1927. He said his beard was worth $8,000. Lived in apartments, hotels, dined and drove alone. "I live loneliness." Got the lead in The Man Who Came to Dinner in 1941 even though First Lady Eleanor Roosevelt called director Hal Wallis and told him that only Orson Welles could play the part. COD: Heart and kidney failure. Buried in Saratoga County, New York.

Adolph Zukor (Same)

b. 7 Jan 1873, d. 10 Jun 1976, = 103 yrs, 5 mos, 3 days. Worked on 738 films. Married 1 time.

NN: The Father of the Feature Film. Fur Trader, operated Nickelodeons. "The public is never wrong." "If I had known I was going to live this long, I'd have taken better care of myself." COD: Natural causes during an afternoon nap.

APPENDIX 1 - LONGEVITY, YOUNGEST TO OLDEST

YR	MO	DAYS	
27	04	24	Bobby Harron
30	02	02	Virginia Rappe
31	03	17	Rudolph Valentino
31	09	03	Wallace Reid
35	00	05	Renee Adoree
36	04	16	Jack Pickford
36	05	30	John Gilbert
37	03	14	Mable Normand
39	03	07	Jeanne Eagles
42	08	21	Agnes Ayers
44	00	03	Thomas Ince
46	03	05	Fatty Arbuckle
46	11	26	Alice Brady
47	03	15	Irving Thalberg
47	04	25	Lon Chaney, Sr.
49	00	05	Pearl White
50	01	29	Leslie Howard
50	02	12	Conrad Veidt
50	11	18	Buck Jones
51	05	05	John Bunny
52	11	26	Florence Lawrence
54	02	02	Gertrude Lawrence

55	09	11	Will Rogers
56	02	02	Richard Dix
56	06	19	Douglas Fairbanks, Sr.
57	11	12	Alan Hale, Sr.
57	11	22	Humphrey Bogart
58	10	03	Warner Oland
59	03	17	Frank Morgan
59	04	16	Hattie McDaniel
60	03	15	John Barrymore
60	08	11	Shemp Howard
60	09	06	Tom Mix
61	01	15	Fred Allen
61	11	08	Warner Baxter
63	04	21	Elmo Lincoln
63	05	14	Charles Laughton
63	06	28	Norma Talmadge
64	00	14	Wallace Beery
64	04	27	Al Jolson
64	08	19	Marion Davies
65	05	10	Emil Jannings
65	06	20	Oliver Hardy
65	07	00	Fanny Brice
65	08	19	Marie Dressler
66	01	10	Alla Nazimova
66	02	08	Edward Arnold
66	03	04	Nita Naldi
66	10	26	W. C. Fields
67	00	02	Walter Huston
67	02	18	Jack Holt
67	03	10	Ronald Colman
68	03	08	Joe Frisco
68	11	00	Ruth Chatterton

69	01	01	Gracie Allen
69	05	04	ZaSu Pitts
69	08	05	Harry Carey, Sr.
69	08	09	Theda Bara
69	10	21	Jean Hersholt
70	00	17	Hoot Gibson
70	03	28	Buster Keaton
70	09	12	Ben Turpin
70	10	16	Rod LaRocque
71	05	18	Cedric Hardwicke
71	07	20	Erich Von Stroheim
72	00	19	Eddie Cantor
72	03	21	Bert Lahr
72	06	00	Bill Robinson
72	07	07	Alan Mowbray
72	08	07	Carl Laemmle
72	10	04	Barry Fitzgerald
72	10	18	Victor McLaglen
72	11	05	Ralph Morgan
73	03	03	John Boles
73	03	10	Noel Coward
73	03	17	Louis B. Mayer
73	06	01	D. W. Griffith
73	08	11	Adolphe Menjou
73	09	27	Bela Lugosi
73	10	30	Rex Ingram
74	00	22	Sydney Greenstreet
74	02	18	Guy Kibbee
74	04	04	Maria Ouspenskaya
74	04	09	Fay Bainter
74	06	19	Chico Marx
74	08	07	Stan Laurel

74	08	19	Monty Woolley
75	01	08	Basil Rathbone
75	10	05	Harpo Marx
76	01	07	Monte Blue
76	06	18	Lionel Barrymore
76	06	21	Juanita Hansen
76	06	22	Bud Abbott
76	06	27	Richard Arlen
76	06	30	John Ford
76	10	08	Charles Bickford
76	10	24	Clifton Webb
76	11	01	William Farnum
77	03	00	Cecil B. De Mille
77	06	20	Claude Rains
77	07	14	Fredric March
77	09	14	Paul Robeson
77	09	26	George Arliss
77	10	15	Moe Howard
77	10	16	Harold Lloyd
78	09	05	Zeppo Marx
79	00	05	William Frawley
79	00	27	Sophie Tucker
79	01	14	Edward G. Robinson
79	10	03	Ethel Barrymore
80	01	18	Walter Brennan
80	02	20	Paul Lukas
80	08	30	Hedda Hopper
80	09	19	Mack Sennett
80	10	01	Ethel Waters
80	10	12	Jack Benny
81	02	04	Moms Mabley
81	02	10	Boris Karloff

81	06	17	William S. Hart
81	07	05	Carmel Myers
81	08	16	Alfred Hitchcock
81	09	27	Jack Haley
81	11	08	Joe E. Brown
81	11	11	Edmund Gwynn
82	04	14	Margaret Dumont
82	10	30	Gladys Cooper
82	11	10	Dame May Whitty
83	03	19	Maurice Chevalier
83	07	13	Francis X. Bushman
83	09	02	Gabby Hayes
83	11	04	Pat O'Brien
84	02	11	Charles Coburn
84	05	13	Sessue Hawakaya
85	01	17	Marjorie Main
85	01	26	Mary Fuller
85	04	29	C. Aubrey Smith
85	09	07	Billie Burke
85	10	11	Clara Blandick
86	01	07	Jack Warner
86	02	08	George M. Cohan
86	04	16	George O'Brien
86	05	30	Gale Sondergaard
86	08	13	James Cagney
86	09	19	Tim McCoy
86	10	17	Groucho Marx
86	10	29	Henry Hathaway
86	10	29	Raymond Massey
86	11	19	Jimmy Durante
87	00	02	Walter Pidgeon
87	01	21	Mary Pickford

87	03	05	Mae West
88	01	12	Fred Astaire
88	05	06	Colleen Moore
88	08	09	Charlie Chaplin
88	09	29	Ruth Gordon
88	11	28	Jane Darwell
89	01	07	Randolph Scott
90	02	19	Blanche Sweet
90	05	25	Yakima Canutt
90	06	29	Pola Negri
90	07	30	Gilbert Anderson
90	10	01	Marian Anderson
91	04	03	Louella Parsons
91	07	05	William Powell
91	08	08	Beulah Bondi
91	08	15	Irene Dunne
93	09	20	Raoul Walsh
94	00	08	Gloria Swanson
94	03	16	Frank Capra
94	05	14	Samuel Goldwyn
94	07	12	Beatrice Lillie
99	04	13	Lillian Gish
100	01	18	George Burns
103	05	03	Adolph Zukor
107	07	06	George Abbott

About the Author

Ken Warren is the world's biggest-selling author of poker books and now he has turned his attention to the incredibly interesting subject of trivia about famous movie actors and actresses. He uses his teaching background to research and collect in this book thousands of bits of trivia that is generally unknown to the public. It's an engaging, absorbing read that you can't put down.